The Law of Business Organizations

Martin Schulz • Oliver Wasmeier

The Law of Business Organizations

A Concise Overview of German Corporate Law

Springer

Prof. Dr. Martin Schulz, LL.M. (Yale)
GGS German Graduate School
of Management and Law
Bildungscampus 2
74072 Heilbronn
Germany
martin.schulz@ggs.de

Oliver Wasmeier
Karl-F. Böhringerstr. 12
79595 Rümmingen
Germany
oliver-wasmeier@gmx.de

ISBN 978-3-642-17792-7 e-ISBN 978-3-642-17793-4
DOI 10.1007/978-3-642-17793-4
Springer Heidelberg Dordrecht London New York

Library of Congress Control Number: 2011942141

Printed on acid-free paper

Springer is part of Springer Science+Business Media (www.springer.com)

Preface

This book provides a concise overview of the relevant legal framework governing German business organizations. Thus, our book is neither meant to be fully comprehensive in scope, nor can it substitute the advice and guidance of qualified attorneys and tax advisors in individual cases. Rather, this book is intended to provide the reader with a basic introduction into some key aspects of German business law in general, and of German corporate law in particular. Our goal is to help business practitioners and international students to familiarize themselves with the general framework and the characteristic features of German corporate law.

The first chapter provides an introduction into the economic background and general aspects of conducting business in Germany. To this purpose we present some characteristic features of the German legal system, outline the legal framework, and give an overview of typical forms of business organizations. The next two chapters focus, in particular, on the German stock corporation (*Aktiengesellschaft, AG*) and the German limited liability company (*Gesellschaft mit beschränkter Haftung, GmbH*) as the most popular and widespread German corporate forms. Using these corporate forms as an example, we then look at some persistent corporate law issues such as capitalization requirements, managerial duties, shareholders' liability and employees' participation rights. Furthermore, we illustrate the process of designing a GmbH's articles of associations to the benefit of the shareholders and we provide a brief introduction into the regulations governing capital market transactions in Germany. After addressing some key aspects of corporate acquisitions in the fourth chapter, we discuss some typical problems faced by companies engaged in cross-border activities, including the relevant EU framework, in the fifth chapter. The supplementary materials include some recommendations for further reading, selected bilingual excerpts of important statutes, as well as examples of some important corporate documents.

Our special gratitude is devoted to Ms. *Elisabeth Littell Frech*, LL.M., M.A. of Frech Language Services, Frankfurt am Main, and Mrs. *Martha Morris Frech*, M.A., for their great help and support in revising our manuscript and in helping us in our effort to make German law comprehensive for a foreign reader. We would also like to very much thank Mrs. *Sabine Küper* and Dr. *Marcus Mackensen*, both attorneys-at-law and Knowledge Management lawyers with Freshfields Bruckhaus Deringer LLP, for their helpful comments regarding our overview of Mergers and

Acquisitions in Germany, as well as Mrs. *Camilla Froehlich*, Mr. *Soeren Lenerz* and Mr. *Christoph Vollmer* for their help in preparing the appendices. Last but not least, we would like to thank the *German Graduate School of Management and Law (GGS)*, Heilbronn, for the generous support of this project.

Heilbronn and Frankfurt am Main — Martin Schulz
Freiburg im Breisgau — Oliver Wasmeier

Contents

About the Authors

Prof. Dr. Martin Schulz, LL.M. (Yale) is Professor of German and International Private and Corporate Law at the German Graduate School of Management and Law (GGS) in Heilbronn. He also works as an attorney-at-law and a Knowledge Management lawyer in the Frankfurt office of the international law firm Freshfields Bruckhaus Deringer LLP. His research activities and areas of expertise focus on German and International Corporate Law as well as Knowledge Management for lawyers.

GGS German Graduate School of Management and Law, Bildungscampus 2, 74072 Heilbronn, Germany
e-mail: martin.schulz@ggs.de

Ref. iur. Oliver Wasmeier works as a legal clerk at the lower district court of Freiburg im Breisgau. He has worked in the Frankfurt office of the international law firm Freshfields Bruckhaus Deringer LLP and was a research fellow at the Institute of Information and Business Law at the Karlsruhe Institute of Technology (KIT). His research activities and areas of expertise focus on German and International Corporate Law in which field he is writing his doctoral thesis.

Karl-F. Böhringerstr. 12, 79595 Rümmingen, Germany
e-mail: oliver-wasmeier@gmx.de

Introduction

1

Abstract

In the following first chapter, we will provide an introduction to the legal and economic environment to be aware of when considering doing business in Germany. Beginning with a short summary of the economic framework conditions of the German market, we will explain some basic features of the German legal system, including the structure of the legislative and judicial system, and will describe some of the most important legal frameworks. Thereupon, we will outline some of the key aspects of German business law to be considered when deciding upon establishing a business enterprise in Germany. We will continue our presentation by introducing the main options for foreign entrepreneurs to this purpose, by outlining the requirements for establishing a branch office for an existing foreign company as well as by a brief presentation of the most important non-corporate and hybrid forms of German business organizations available. Finally, we will provide a brief introduction into the German legal framework governing insolvency and restructuring of companies as a matter of utmost practical importance for any business operation.

Contents

M. Schulz, O. Wasmeier, *The Law of Business Organizations*,
DOI 10.1007/978-3-642-17793-4_1, © Springer-Verlag Berlin Heidelberg 2012

1.1 Conducting Business in Germany

1.1.1 Case Study

Case Study

A-Corporation (*A*) is incorporated in the state of Delaware, USA, with its headquarters in Wilmington. **A** manufactures components for automobile brakes. **A** conducts business throughout the US and is considering a future expansion of its business into Europe. John B. (***B***), the CEO of **A**, is interested in Germany in particular. He has visited the International Automobile Fair in Frankfurt/M. and has gained the impression that Germany would be well suited for the sale and distribution of **A**'s products. **B** was especially impressed by the number of visitors to the Frankfurt Fair interested in automobiles. Seeing them as potential buyers (of cars and their components, such as **A**'s products), **B** calls Peter C. (***C***), head of A's legal department, to ask him to prepare a memorandum on the framework for doing business in Germany.

B asks **C** to address the following issues and questions:

- Elaborate on the general economic background and business climate in Germany.
- What advantages does Germany have to offer to a foreign investor?
- What are the key features of German business law?

1.1.2 Economic Background

Germany is one of the world's leading industrial nations and, e.g. in terms of total economic output, Germany is also one of the leading economies within Europe. In 2009, Germany exported goods amounting to EUR 803.2 billion and imported goods amounting to EUR 667.1 billion. Germany has a highly developed free market system; its economy is closely linked to the other Member States in the European Union. Trademarks of Germany's economic system are its highly developed infrastructure, its qualified workforce and its international, export-oriented focus.

Many German companies generate a great deal of their profits through exports and many jobs are dependent on foreign trade. From 2003 until 2008, Germany was the world export champion ('*Exportweltmeister*') since no other country exported more goods to other countries during this time period.[1] In 2009, China surpassed

[1] Source: German Federal Statistical Office (Statistisches Bundesamt), Export, Import, Globalisierung, 2010, p. 37.

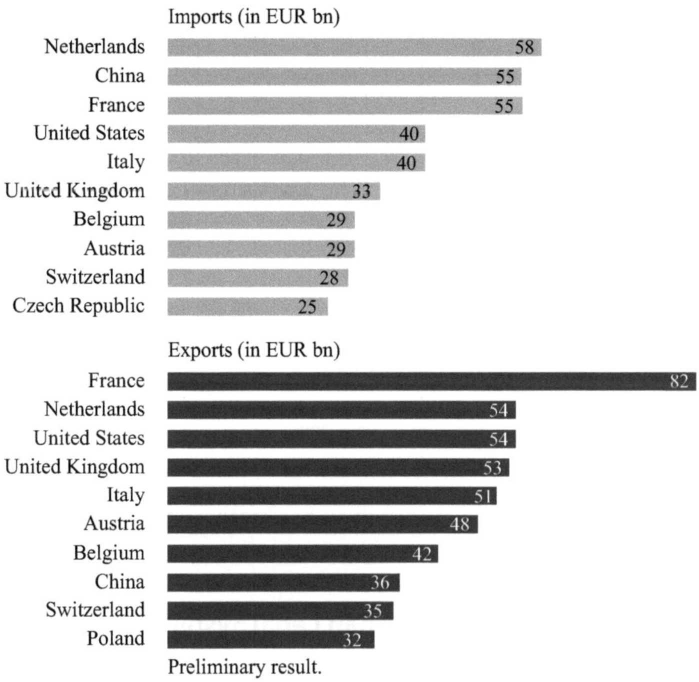

Fig. 1.1 Germany's major trading partners in 2009. (Source: Statistisches Bundesamt, Wiesbaden 2010)

Germany, however, Germany was second, still ahead of the US. Also, with regard to the import of goods, Germany remains one of the leading countries worldwide; in 2009 only the US and China imported goods with a higher aggregate value.[2] For this reason, Germany has traditionally been attractive to foreign investors looking for business opportunities in Germany. Germany's most important trading partners are EU Member States like France and the Netherlands.[3] Almost three out of four goods 'Made in Germany' are delivered to European countries. In 2009, 63% of goods were delivered to EU Member States. However, in 2009 the second important market for German products was Asia with a share of about 14%, ahead of the US market with a share of about 10% (Figs. 1.1 and 1.2).

In an advanced economy such as that of Germany, business organizations are important economic and social institutions. The success of these business organizations obviously depends on the legal framework surrounding them. Since Germany is a member of the European Union, cross-border commercial activities in the European market and the resulting legal issues become more and more important for investors in the German market.

[2] Source: World Trade Organization (http://www.wto.org./english/res_e/statis_e/its_e.htm).

[3] Source: German Federal Statistical Office (Statistisches Bundesamt), Wiesbaden 2010.

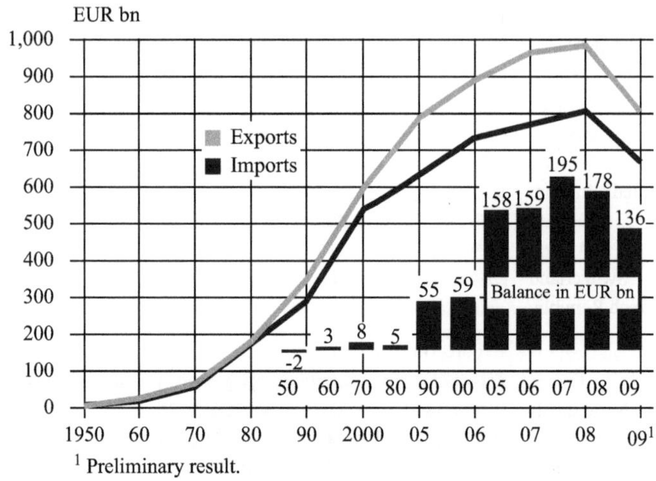

Fig. 1.2 Development of German foreign trade from 1950 to 2009. (Source: Statistisches Bundesamt, Wiesbaden 2010)

1.1.3 Core Features of the German Legal System

As its name suggests, the Federal Republic of Germany is organized as a federal system consisting of 16 federal states (*Bundesländer*), each of which is responsible for the government of its own state, including law-making powers in many areas, provided that they are not preempted by Federal law.

Furthermore, Germany is a Member State of the European Union (EU). This is the association of a large number of European states and, as such, the impact of European law on many areas of national law has become more and more important. This is particularly true for those areas of EU law which are either directly or indirectly applicable, such as EU Regulations or the Directives. It is also true for the case law of the European Court of Justice (ECJ) which often plays a decisive role in legal disputes when the national courts of EU Member States have to interpret the scope of applicability of the Union Treaties.

1.1.3.1 Hierarchy of Norms and Constitutional Framework

In Germany, the highest written national norm is the Federal Constitution. The Constitution or so-called 'Basic Law' (*Grundgesetz, GG*), which was promulgated by the Parliamentary Council on 23 May 1949, defines and regulates the political and legal system of the Federal Republic of Germany (Fig. 1.3).

Germany is a republic and a democracy; it is a federal state based on the rule of law and social justice. The *Grundgesetz* contains a catalogue of fundamental rights and values to be protected against any form of infringement, such as the dignity of man, freedom of religious belief, freedom of speech, freedom of arts and sciences, freedom of assembly, freedom of association, the right to freely choose one's profession, the principle of equality before the law and a constitutional guarantee

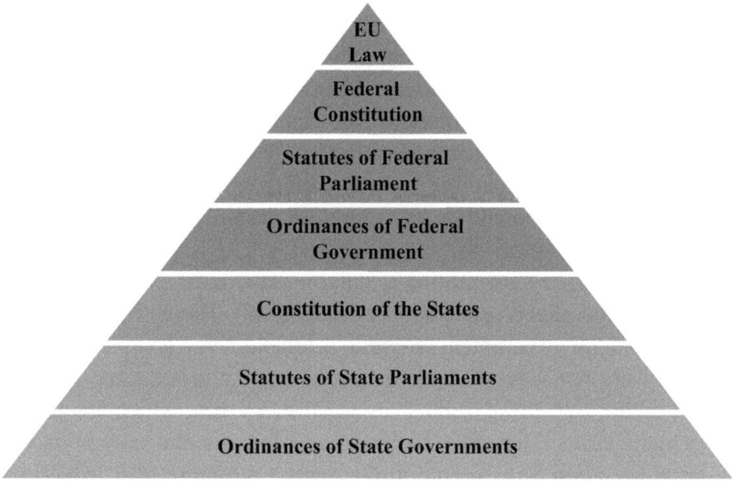

Fig. 1.3 Hierarchy of norms

of private property. These fundamental rights are binding as to legislation, judicial decisions and the executive branch as law with immediate effect. Depending on the nature of the fundamental rights, they are not only applicable to individuals but also to legal persons such as corporations.

The *Grundgesetz* also includes the law on voting rights, citizenship, political parties and the regulation of the functioning of the various organs of state such as the Federal Parliament (*Bundestag*) and the Federal Council (*Bundesrat*), the Federal President (*Bundespräsident*), the Federal Government (*Bundesregierung*) and the Federal Chancellor (*Bundeskanzler*). However, the *Grundgesetz* does not prescribe any specific form of economic order (such as a free market economy) but is considered neutral from an economic policy perspective.

The fundamental rights and values codified in the *Grundgesetz* are primarily designed as providing protection for the individual against any infringement of her/his guarantees by the government, regardless whether such infringement results from a legislative act, any form of executive power or from the judiciary. However, the *Grundgesetz* may also have an impact on the legal relationships between private individuals or business entities. This so-called third party effect (*Drittwirkung*) was developed by the *Bundesverfassungsgericht* (Federal Constitutional Court) in the famous *Lüth*-decision of 1958.[4] Dealing with the question whether a civil law injunction based on Sec. 826 of the German Civil Code (*Bürgerliches Gesetzbuch, BGB*) violated the complainant's fundamental right of free speech under Art. 5 of the *Grundgesetz,* the court held that the civil courts should interpret the provisions of the *BGB* in the light of the *Grundgesetz*, since the Constitution represents an objective set of values always to be taken into account when deciding legal issues. Based on this concept of third party effect of fundamental constitutional rights, the

[4] BVerfGE 7,198, 15 January 1958, 1 BvR 400/51—*Lüth*.

Bundesverfassungsgericht, as the guardian of the Constitution, has invalidated various legal provisions on the grounds that they were incompatible with the Constitution (e.g. with respect to discrimination against gender, age etc). More generally, the Constitution always plays an important role when statutes need to be interpreted. If a statutory provision is amenable to several different interpretations, then the interpretation which would make the law compatible with the Constitution is always to be preferred. Constitutional law has, therefore, traditionally played an important role in civil law and business law.

Next in rank from the Constitution is statutory law in the form of statutes passed by the Federal parliament (*Gesetz im formellen Sinne*). Thereafter come ordinances passed by the Federal government (*Bundesrechtliche Verordungen und Satzungen*). Although they are not a product of the parliamentary process but passed by administrative authorities, these ordinances are abstract rules which are generally applicable to many cases. Therefore, they are regarded as statutes in a material sense (*Gesetz im materiellen Sinne*). Due to Germany's structure as a federal republic, consisting of 16 federal states (*Bundesländer)*, the same hierarchy of norms can be found at each state level, starting with the respective state constitution and followed by statutes (*Gesetze der Länder*) and ordinances (*Landesrechtliche Verordungen und Satzungen*) of the respective state. As a general rule, federal law always takes precedent over state law (see Art. 31 GG). This means that if the law of a particular German state collides with a law made by the Federal Government, then the federal law will prevail. Subordinate legislation at federal level will take precedence even over the constitution of a state, insofar as the Federation has the competence to pass a law on the matter in question.

1.1.3.2 Predominance of Federal Law

As indicated, and similar to the US, Germany has a federal system with the law-making powers divided between the federal government (*Bund*) and the individual German states (*Länder*). However, (unlike the US) in most areas of civil, commercial and business law, the law-making power lies with the federal government. As Germany belongs to the family of so-called civil law systems, the legal landscape has traditionally been dominated by comprehensive codes and statutes promulgated by the legislature in all major areas of the law. Most areas of civil, commercial and business law are, therefore, covered by federal statutes issued by Germany's Federal Parliament. As one obvious advantage of such predominance of federal law, market participants will find a uniform legal framework for business throughout Germany (in contrast to the diverse legal landscape e.g., in the US). We will, therefore, look at the relevant statutory regulations and also discuss the question whether, in some cases, the statutory regime for a specific company form has been altered by the courts with judge-made rules or may be altered by the shareholders by contractual provisions.

1.1.3.3 Distinction Between Public and Private Law

Derived from its historical origins in Roman law, the German legal system still remains characterized by the distinction between private and public law, both areas

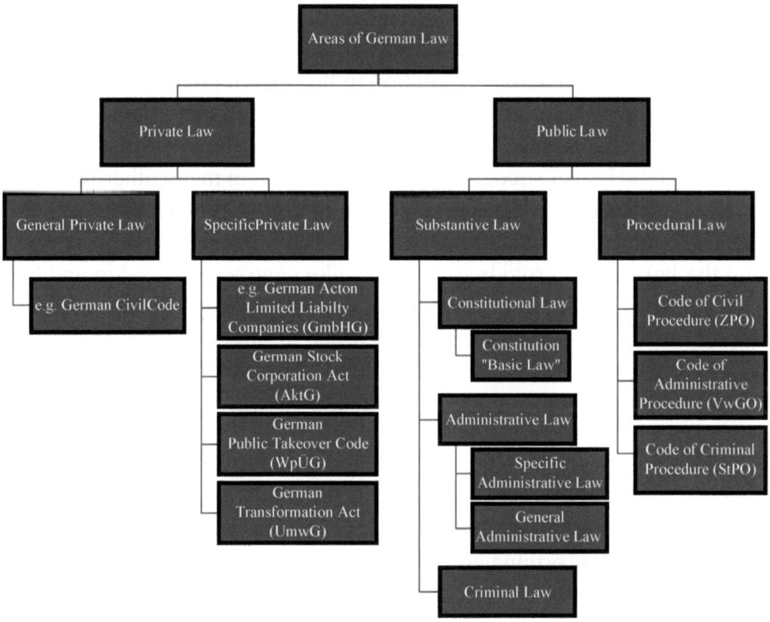

Fig. 1.4 Areas of German law

of law covering different legal issues and being dealt with by courts with different jurisdictions. Public law is usually defined as the embodiment of those rules conferring powers and imposing obligations exclusively on holders of public office. This means in particular the federal government, the German federal states and supranational organizations such as the European Union. On the other hand, private law is directed at all legal subjects (Fig. 1.4).

Public Law

Public law covers areas such as constitutional law, administrative law, tax law and social security law. Public law also includes the general principles of administrative law, as well as its various specialized fields, such as police law, the law of communal administration, public construction law and the law relating to foreigners and asylum. Data protection law, public service law, media law, traffic law, environmental law, the law of taxation and procedural law are also included. Furthermore, criminal law is also considered as a part of public law, since only the state has the authority to inflict punishment.

Private Law—General and Specific Regulation

Private law generally governs one's private legal affairs such as entering into contracts, acquiring and transferring property, receiving compensation for injuries, or establishing a business. German private law is regulated in numerous individual statutes dealing with general issues of private law such as contracts, property or compensation for damages and specific issues of private law like intellectual property, labor law or the law of business associations.

The most important statutory regulation in the area of private law is the German Civil Code (*Bürgerliches Gesetzbuch, BGB*) comprising more than 2,300 sections and covering, among others, the law of contracts, the law of torts, property law, family law and the law of succession. In Germany (as in many other jurisdictions), private law is based on the fundamental assumption of private autonomy, i.e., the idea that legal subjects should, in principle, be free to arrange their private legal affairs and the law should provide institutions like contract, ownership and business forms to facilitate this freedom. However, the history of private law is also a history of defining the limits of such freedom in order to protect certain interest groups which (in the eyes of the courts and the legislature seem to) need specific legal protection, e.g. consumers, employees or creditors.

German Civil Code (*BGB*)

The German Civil Code came into force on 1 January 1900 and can be seen as a result of the unification process and of the codification movement of the 1900s. The codification movement originated in the age of enlightenment and also produced other famous European codifications of Civil Law, such as the French Civil Code of 1804 (the so-called '*Code Napoleón*') or the Austrian General Civil Code (*Allgemeines Bürgerliches Gesetzbuch*) of 1811.

From the time of its enactment until today, the BGB has been amended numerous times in order to adapt the legal framework to the ever-changing political, social and economic environment. Typical amendments are the introduction of specific regulations protecting certain interest groups like consumers, employees and tenants. With ongoing European integration, further changes have become necessary to implement rules under mandatory European law, including a particularly important reform in 2002 (the Act on the Modernization of the Law of Obligations, *Schuldrechtsmodernisierungsgesetz*). However, in many respects the BGB still reflects some of its historical legal concepts, in particular, some classic ideas of '*laissez faire*'—liberalism, such as the notions of private autonomy and freedom of contract. Although private autonomy and freedom of contract are still regarded as the cornerstones of German private law, the original ideas of the authors of the BGB based on the rather idealistic (and somewhat artificial) concept of a contract formed by two legal subjects with equal bargaining power freely negotiating the terms of their agreement with each other. This concept had been subject to criticism even at the time of its origin, as it completely ignores social realities, and, in particular, the widespread inequality of bargaining powers between contracting parties, such as employees and employers, tenants and landlords or consumers and manufacturers. Thus, the history of the German Civil Code can be seen as a history of expanding protection of the 'weaker party' and, as of today, the BGB reflects an interesting amalgam of different—and in part conflicting—value sets and concepts.

Among other things, the BGB regulates general issues of contract law, as well as specific types of contracts, such as purchase, lease, service, manufacturing, suretyship, civil law partnership, negotiable instruments, transfer of title and real property and damages or claims for restitution in cases of unjust enrichment.

As it has been often criticized for its rather sophisticated and technical language, the BGB does offer the advantage of having quite a clear and systematic structure. The *BGB* consists of five books and begins with a book of general provisions (*Allgemeiner Teil*). This deals with fundamental concepts and issues of private law, such as the definition of general legal capacity, the definition of legal subjects and objects, the specific requirements for legal transactions (in particular for contracts), the law of agency (*Stellvertretung*) and provisions relating to limitation periods (*Verjährung*). These fundamental definitions and concepts apply to all the following sections of the *BGB*. The second book covers the law of obligations (*Schuldrecht*) and is subdivided into a general and a specific part. The general part contains rules on the performance of contracts, remedies for non-performance, rules on the transfer of rights and duties and rules on transactions involving several creditors or debtors. The specific part deals with certain specific types of contracts, such as purchase agreements (*Kaufvertrag*), leasehold contracts (*Mietvertrag*), contracts for services and for specific services (*Dienst- und Werkvertrag*) and loan agreements (*Darlehensvertrag*). The specific part also includes rules on the compensation for delicts for unjust enrichment. The third book of the BGB deals with the law of property (*Sachenrecht*) comprising the legal relationships between persons and things, e.g. the right of ownership, titles of possession and other rights *in rem*, such as mortgages. The fourth book contains family law and deals with the law of engagement, marriage, divorce and the law of custody of children, and the fifth book contains the law of succession (*Erbrecht*).

The German Civil Code distinguishes between consumers (*Verbraucher*), meaning any natural person who enters into legal transactions for a purpose outside her/his trade or profession[5], and entrepreneurs (*Unternehmer*), defined as a natural or juristic person or a partnership with legal personality who or which acts in exercise of her, his or its trade when entering into a legal transaction.[6] Consumers are often protected by specific legal provisions, e.g. with regard to specific information rights or specific rights to withdraw from contractual obligations. One prominent example is the law on standard terms of contract (*Allgemeine Geschäftsbedingungen* or *AGB*).[7] Such AGB are of considerable practical significance, as numerous businesses associations use these standardized legal tools when dealing with their customers. In order to address the risks associated with using standard terms for the contract party being subjected to them (i.e. unfair surprise by disadvantageous contract terms), German law provides for specific requirements regarding the inclusion of AGB into a contract, as well as several control mechanisms regarding their content. In principle, the provisions on standard terms apply to consumers and entrepreneurs alike. However, the level of protection provided for consumers and entrepreneurs varies considerably, since entrepreneurs and business associations are considered to have

[5] See Sec. 13 BGB.

[6] See Sec. 14 BGB.

[7] Or, as they are also-called, general terms of business/conditions of business.

sufficient legal knowledge to negotiate effectively and enter into agreements, i.e. they do not require the same level of protection as consumers. Therefore, only specific provisions of the law on AGB will apply to them, for example, the invalidation of terms which unreasonably discriminate against the contractual partner contrary to the requirements of good faith and fair dealing (Sec. 307 BGB).

German Commercial Code (*HGB*)

With regard to other important areas of private law, such as commercial law, the German Commercial Code (*Handelsgesetzbuch, HGB*) contains specific rules for so-called 'merchants' (*Kaufleute*), i.e. anyone who carries out a commercial activity (as defined by Sec. 1 HGB) regardless of the field of commercial activity (e.g. production, trade, services) and for commercial transactions related to them.[8] The HGB contains special rules providing for the specific needs of commercial life.[9] For example, a different treatment of commercial transactions is justified, since businesspeople often expect and rely on speedy transactions.

In addition, since merchants are expected to have some basic commercial and legal understanding for business operations (in contrast to consumers), they supposedly do not require the same extent of legal protection as ordinary citizens. The HGB, therefore, contains various deviations from the general rules of the German Civil Code, e.g. regarding the level of the duty of care owed by merchants or the requirements for binding contracts with regard to form. The Commercial Code is limited to the buying and selling of goods, but also comprises other areas of business life, such as transport, banking and insurance industries, manufacturing and craftsmanship.

Sources of Corporate Law

Unlike other European jurisdictions, such as e.g. the UK, Germany has no single act or codification regulating all companies and business associations, but has several statutes for various types of business associations (with or without corporate form).

The statutes most relevant to business organizations without corporate form in Germany (such as the civil law partnership or the commercial partnership) are the German Civil Code and the Commercial Code. Apart from the legal areas already mentioned above, the German Civil Code also regulates so-called civil law partnerships (*BGB-Gesellschaft* or *GbR*). The HGB includes rules for specific business forms, such as the general commercial partnership (*offene Handelsgesellschaft* or *oHG*), the limited commercial partnership (*Kommanditgesellschaft* or *KG*) and the silent partnership (*Stille Gesellschaft*).

[8] An exception is made for private practitioners as defined under Sec. 18 German Income Tax Act (*Einkommenssteuergesetz, EStG*), to whom the Commercial Code is not applicable, regardless of the size and success of their enterprise, e.g. attorneys-at-law, architects or medical doctors.

[9] The legal distinction between merchants and non-merchants as set forth in the HGB is not identical to the legal distinction between entrepreneurs and consumers within the meaning of the BGB; while a merchant will nearly always also be considered as an entrepreneur under the BGB, such entrepreneur may—due to the size or nature of her/his business—well not qualify as a merchant according to Secs. 1 *et seq.* HGB.

Corporations, on the other hand, are regulated in specific statutes. The Stock Corporation Act (*Aktiengesetz* or *AktG*) governs the German stock corporation (*Aktiengesellschaft* or *AG*), as well as the commercial partnership limited by shares (*Kommanditgesellschaft auf Aktien* or *KGaA*), the latter being a stock corporation with fully liable general partners. In addition, the Stock Corporation Act regulates affiliated companies and determines the level of liability among parent companies and their subsidiaries.

The Limited Liability Company Act (*GmbH-Gesetz* or *GmbHG*) sets out the rules for the German Limited Liability Company (*Gesellschaft mit beschränkter Haftung* or *GmbH*), which is the most popular German corporate form, especially for small and medium-sized businesses.

Moreover, the Transformation Act (*Umwandlungsgesetz* or *UmwG*), set into force in 1994, sets out provisions for reorganizations of legal entities, namely by way of mergers (*Verschmelzungen*), divisions (*Spaltungen*), comprehensive transfer of assets (*Vermögensübernahmen*)[10] and changes of corporate form (*Formwechseln*).

Negotiable Instruments

In addition to the BGB and the HGB and some other important statutes in the area of company law (which will later be discussed in more detail), there are several other statutes which are relevant for conducting business, some of which should be briefly mentioned. One such area is the law governing negotiable instruments.

The legal rules regarding negotiable instruments and securities (*Wertpapierrecht*) are contained in various statutes, including the German Civil Code, Commercial Code, the Bills of Exchange Act (*Wechselgesetz*), the Checks Act (*Scheckgesetz*), the Stock Corporation Act (*Aktiengesetz*), and the Securities Deposit Act (*Depotgesetz*).

Competition and Antitrust Law

Competition law is governed by the Unfair Competition Act (*Gesetz gegen den unlauteren Wettbewerb*) and deals with various forms of competition which are considered to be unfair. This regulation aims to protect a functioning market economy. It also intends to protect individuals and business associations against unfair practices by competitors and to protect consumers against the risk of being misled and overcharged. Any person whose trade practice is classified as unfair competition (*unlautere Wettbewerbshandlung*) can be prevented from doing so by way of injunction and may also be liable for damages. Antitrust law (*Kartellrecht*) is also directed primarily at the protection of a functioning market economy; its main goal is the prevention of cartels and unfair restrictions of competition. In Germany, it is regulated in the Act against Restrictive Trade Practices (*Gesetz gegen Wettbewerbsbeschränkungen*) together with provisions of European Union law governing cartels and mergers.

---

[10] The rules on restructuring by way of a 'comprehensive transfer of assets' as defined in the act are intended to provide specific rules for privatizations of state industries. In other areas of practice they are of little relevance.

Intellectual Property Law

The law on intellectual property is regulated in different statutes. Patent law, which provides special protection for technical inventions, is regulated in the Patent Act (*Patentgesetz*). A patent secures a right for its owners to be protected against the exploitation of the invention by other persons. The patent lasts for twenty years in Germany and requires the payment of fees. There are numerous international treaties which attempt to extend the protection of patents beyond national boundaries. To obtain Europe-wide protection for a patent, an application must be made to the European Patent Office in Munich.

If an invention does not qualify for a patent, its owner can obtain a lesser degree of protection by registering the invention as a so-called utility model (*Gebrauchsmuster*). After a utility model has been registered, only the owner may produce it for commercial purposes and put it into circulation, use it or market it. Industrial designs and models (*gewerbliche Muster und Modelle*) are protected by the Design Act (*Geschmacksmustergesetz*) if they are new and original.

Another very important statute dealing with intellectual property is the German Act on the Protection of Trademarks (*Markengesetz*). A trademark is a symbol of distinction that identifies the particular products of a trader to the general public. A trader may register a trademark at the *Deutsche Patentamt* in Munich. She/he then enjoys the exclusive right to use the trademark in connection with the goods for which it was registered.

Finally, German copyright law is contained in the German Copyright Act (*Urheberrechtsgesetz* or *UrhG*). Traditionally, German copyright law puts a special emphasis on the relationship between a work and its author, regarding a work eligible of legal protection if it constitutes a personal intellectual creation (*persönliche geistige Schöpfung*). This has several consequences: First, in contrast to patent law, legal protection under the UrhG does not require a registration but applies automatically (*ipso iure*) to such works that meet these requirements. Second, German courts have set out considerably different standards for works of fine arts on the one hand and works of applied arts on the other. According to the so-called doctrine of '*kleine Münze*' ('small coin'), a work of fine art may be considered eligible of copyright protection even though it only shows a minimum of creativity, originality and individuality, while the threshold for applied arts is considerably higher. Third, from this point of view, there is neither a 'corporate copyright' nor a complete transfer of the author's legal position. Although it is possible to license some or even all rights of use of a work to third parties, the author retains certain inalienable rights, especially morale rights (*Urheberpersönlichkeitsrechte*).

Labor Law

Another important area of private law is labor law. There is no uniform German labor act, but rather, labor law is governed by numerous different statutes. One characteristic feature of German labor law is the fact that broad areas are not regulated by statutes at all. Therefore, court decisions and judge-made law play a prominent role. In contrast to other legal regimes, German labor law is characterized by its scope of protection for employees (*Schutzprinzip*) as one of its guiding principles.

Despite of being a part of private law, German labor law also contains some elements of public law (e.g. regulation regarding safety measures in the workplace and maximum hours of work). German labor law is usually subdivided in the so-called individual labor law (*Individualarbeitsrecht*), which deals with the relationship between employer and employees, and the law of industrial relations (*Kollektivarbeitsrecht*). The law on industrial relations regulates unions and employers' associations as specific types of association relevant in the employment sphere. *Kollektivarbeitsrecht* also includes the law on industrial disputes (*Arbeitskampfrecht*), on collective agreements between the various associations, i.e. agreements arising from industry-wide collective bargaining (*Tarifverträge*) and on employee's rights of representation (*Betriebsverfassungsrecht*) as codified in the Employees' Representation Act (*Betriebsverfassungsgesetz*) and the Co-Determination in Industry Act (*Mitbestimmungsgesetz*).[11]

Relevance of Conflict of Laws

Given the increasing importance of EU law and the growing globalization of economic relations, the question of which law applies to a commercial relationship or dispute becomes more and more decisive. Growing international relations, competition and increasing market globalization often raise the question of the applicable law. Differences among the legal systems and the fact that a unification, harmonization or assimilation of law (*Rechtsvereinheitlichung*) often remains quite incomplete within the EU result in the decision on the applicable law in cross-border cases to a specific legal system to be decisive.

The question of the applicable law is answered by the rules of 'conflict of laws'. These rules determine which national legal regime is to be applied in cases with multi-jurisdictional elements. However, the name '*Internationales Privatrecht*', (private international law), as this area of the law is referred to in Germany, may appear something of a paradox, since it is, to a great extent, neither private (it also covers various areas of public law), nor is it truly international. On the contrary, conflict of law rules are often not internationally harmonized, but instead are a constituent part of national law.

Legal Sources

German conflict-of-laws rules are embodied in various legal sources, including codified norms, as well as judicial decisions, national statutes and supra-national legislation, multilateral conventions and bilateral treaties.

In Germany, the traditional and most comprehensive set of rules regarding conflict-of-laws is provided for in Art. 3–46 of the Introductory Act to the German Civil Code (*Einführungsgesetz zum Bürgerlichen Gesetzbuch, EGBGB*). Apart from some general provisions on determining the applicable law in cross-border cases (Art. 3–6 EGBGB), the EGBGB also contains conflict-of-laws principles regarding the rights of natural persons (e.g. legal capacity), the name, the form of legal transactions (Art. 7–12 EGBGB), as well as conflict-of-laws principles regarding family

[11] For more detail on the German system of employee participation see *infra*, Sect. 2.5.

law matters (e.g. marriage and matrimonial property issues, divorce, descent and adoption, see Art. 13–24 EGBGB), conflict-of-laws principles regarding succession (Art. 25–26 EGBGB) and non-contractual obligations (such as compensation for unjust enrichment and torts, see Art. 38–42 EGBGB) and finally, conflict-of-laws principles regarding matters of property (Art. 43–46 EGBGB).

Conflict-of-laws issues play a decisive role in cross-border contractual transactions. E.g., pursuant to Art. 3 para. 1 of the Council Regulation on the Law Applicable to Contractual Obligations (Rome I-Regulation)[12] a contract is governed by the law chosen by the parties. The choice of law must be expressed or implied with sufficient certainty by the provisions of the contract or the circumstances of the case. The parties may make the choice of law for the entire contract or for a part thereof. Thus, with the exception of some consumer and employment contracts, German conflict-of-laws generally endorses the principle of free choice of law for contractual relationships. As one can easily imagine, this option can be crucial for such issues as the scope of liabilities, damages, warranty periods etc., which are typical parts of most contractual relationships.

The legal framework for cross-border transactions has been subject to considerable harmonization efforts on the European level. The most important European legal instruments are the Council Regulation on Jurisdiction and the Recognition and Enforcement of Judgments in Civil and Commercial Matters (Brussels I-Regulation)[13], the Council Regulation on the Law Applicable to Contractual Obligations, the Council Regulation on the Law Applicable to Non-Contractual Obligations (Rome II-Regulation)[14] and the Council Regulation on Insolvency Proceedings (Insolvency-Regulation).[15] As, pursuant to Art. 288 of the Treaty on the Functioning of the European Union (TFEU)[16], EU Council Regulations shall have general application in all EU Member States (i.e. not requiring to be transposed into national laws by means of implementing measures), the above-mentioned legal instruments shall take priority over any national provision on the same subject matter.

Conflict-of-laws rules may originate in international treaties and conventions, a prominent example is the Treaty of Friendship, Commerce and Navigation[17] between Germany and the US, which governs a broad range of cross-border issues including the mutual recognition of lawfully incorporated companies. An example for a multilateral convention is the Vienna Convention on Contracts for the Interna-

[12] Regulation (EC) No 593/2008 of the European Parliament and of the Council of 17 June 2008, OJ L 177/6 as of 4 July 2008. When the Rome I Regulation entered into force on 17 December 2009, it replaced the Rome Convention of 1980 and its national implementing legislation in the EU Member States.

[13] Council Regulation (EC) No 44/2001 of 22 December 2000, OJ L 12/1 as of 16 January 2001.

[14] Regulation (EC) No 864/2007 of the European Parliament and of the Council of 11 July 2007, OJ L 199/40 as of 31 July 2007.

[15] Council Regulation (EC) No 1346/2000 of 29 May 2000, OJ L 160/1 as of 30 June 2000.

[16] OJ C 115/47 as of 9 May 2008.

[17] Treaty of Friendship, Commerce and Navigation between the Federal Republic of Germany and the United States of America (*Freundschafts-, Handels- und Schifffahrtsvertrag zwischen der Bundesrepublik Deutschland und den Vereinigten Staaten von Amerika*) as of 29 October 1954.

tional Sale of Goods of 1980 (CISG)[18], which entered into force in Germany on 1 January 1991. Depending on its scope of applicability, the CISG may automatically govern a cross-border sales contract if it has not been excluded by the parties to the contract.

Finally, even though Germany is a civil law country strongly relying on codified rules, conflict-of-laws principles have sometimes been developed solely in case law. One important example of judge-made rules of conflict of laws is the area of international company law, which will be discussed later on in detail.[19]

General Principles

In conflict-of-laws rules, the so-called connecting factors (*Anknüpfungspunkte*) such as nationality, domicile, location of property, statutory or real seat of a company, intention of the parties or place of tort (*Deliktsort*) serve to establish a connection (*Anknüpfung*) between specific elements of a cross-border case and the legal rules of a national legal system. As a result of this connection, conflict-of-laws provisions determine the international scope of applicability of a specific rule, i.e. the extra-territorial scope of the substantive law.

If the law of a foreign state is applicable according to German conflict-of-laws rules, the applicability of foreign law generally refers to all aspects of a particular dispute, including the foreign state's conflict-of-laws rules. This principle is called 'global remission' (*Gesamtverweisung*). However, if the foreign conflict-of-laws rules provide substantive rules for the subject matter different from those of German law, the foreign law may remit the dispute for decision according to German law (*Rückverweisung*) or it may refer the dispute to the law of a third state (*Weiterverweisung*). Such a situation, a so-called '*renvoi*', may, subject to the relevant conflict-of-laws rules concerned, either affect the case as a whole, or only certain aspects of it (*gespaltene Rück- oder Weiterverweisung*).[20] According to Art. 4 para. 1 EGBGB the German courts are required to recognize a *renvoi*.

Conflict-of-laws is based on the idea that a case should be decided on the merits of the law with the closest connection to the case and, therefore, rests on the assumption of the equality of legal systems around the world. In contrast to this ideal, German law (as almost all other legal systems) provides for a so-called public policy exception as a safeguard against foreign law: if the law of a foreign state (which is applicable according to German conflict-of-laws rules) violates German public policy (*ordre public*), the foreign law either shall not be applied, it shall be applied

[18] United Nations Convention on Contracts for the International Sale of Goods as of 11 April 1980.

[19] See *infra*, Sect. 5.1.

[20] For example, pursuant to Art. 25 EGBGB the law of succession is governed by the law of the country of which the deceased was a *national* at the time of her/his death, regardless of what kind of property may be part of the descendant's estate. In contrast, the conflict-of-laws rules of France and most US states distinguish between personal property and real property, the first being subject to the *domicile* at the time of death, the latter being governed by the *lex rei sitae*, i.e. the law of the state where the real property is located. A situation of a *gespaltene Rück- und Weiterverweisung* would arise if a German court, e.g., ought to decide a heritage dispute concerning the estate of a US American citizen, resident in Hamburg, Germany and owning a summer cottage in Cannes, France.

in a different way or it shall be substituted by German substantive law. Such public policy control of foreign law applies, in particular, if an application of foreign law would violate the fundamental rights as defined in the German Constitution.

Court System and Mechanisms of Dispute Resolution

In Germany, the legal framework on the structure and functioning of the court system is set out in the Constitution (in particular, in Art. 20 para. 3 and Art. 92 GG), establishing the rule of law (*Rechtsstaatsprinzip*) as a fundamental principle and providing for the independence of the judiciary. In addition, the Judicature Act (*Gerichtsverfassungsgesetz, GVG*) regulates different types of jurisdiction depending on the subject matter of the dispute. The German courts are essentially divided into five groups which correspond to the main areas of the law: there are the so-called regular courts (*ordentliche Gerichtsbarkeit*) dealing with private law and criminal law matters, the Labor Courts, the General Administrative Courts, the Social Courts and finally, the Financial Courts competent of deciding disputes arising from taxation issues, contributions and fees. In addition to these courts, there is the German Federal Constitutional Court (*Bundesverfassungsgericht*), which serves as a safeguard of the *Grundgesetz*. The *Bundesverfassungsgericht* may declare null and void any statute, decision or other expression of governmental authority if it violates fundamental principles of the Constitution (in particular, any of the fundamental rights). In contrast to the court system in many other countries, in Germany there is no supreme court with general jurisdiction over all aspects of the law equivalent to the Supreme Court (formerly the House of Lords) in Britain, the US Supreme Court or the Swiss *Bundesgericht*.

Further details for particular branches of the German court system are regulated by various procedural acts. The most important of these are the Code of Civil Procedure (*Zivilprozessordnung, ZPO*), the Code of Criminal Procedure (*Strafprozessordnung, StPO*), the Rules of the Administrative Courts (*Verwaltungsgerichtsordnung, VwGO*), the Labor Court Law (*Arbeitsgerichtsgesetz, ArbGG*), the Tax Court Code (*Finanzgerichtsordnung, FGO*), the Social Court Act (*Sozialgerichtsgesetz, SozGG*) and the Federal Constitutional Court Act (*Bundesverfassungsgerichtsgesetz, BVerfGG*).

The court of first instance will always be the *Amtsgericht* (Municipal Court) or the *Landgericht* (District Court). The *Amtsgerichte* have subject matter jurisdiction (*sachliche Zuständigkeit*) over disputes with an amount in controversy (*Gegenstandswert*) of up to EUR 5,000 (Sec. 23 no. 1 GVG) and for matters particularly assigned to them, e.g. lessor and tenant disputes and domestic proceedings (Sec. 23 no. 2 GVG). At the *Amtsgericht* level, civil law disputes are decided by a single judge.

A *Landgericht*, one step higher, is either a district or regional court with subject matter jurisdiction over all disputes with an amount in controversy exceeding EUR 5,000 (unless the case is assigned by special statute specifically to the *Amtsgericht*). For claims exceeding EUR 5,000, the *Landgericht* is the court of first instance. Furthermore, the *Landgericht* is automatically the court of first instance for claims arising out of violations of official duties irrespective of the amount in controversy (Sec. 71 para. 1 GVG). At the *Landgericht* level, the case is decided

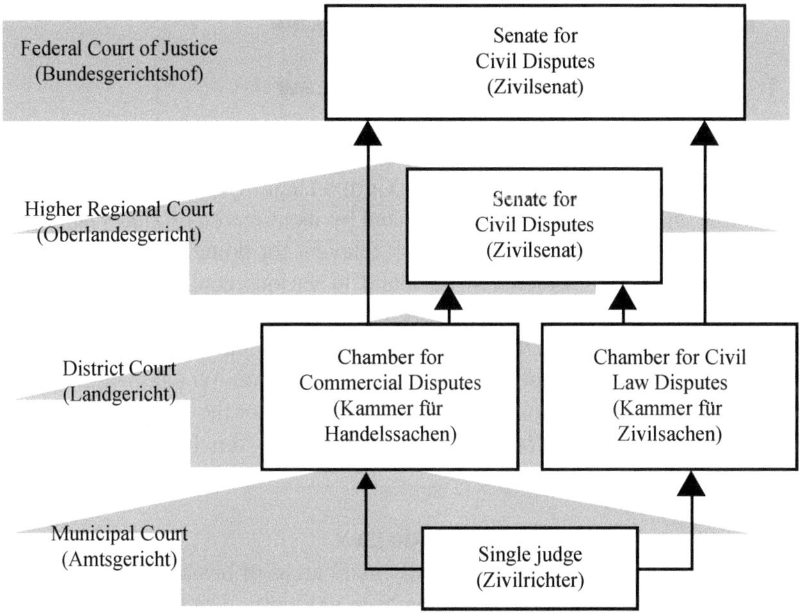

Fig. 1.5 Stages of appeal for civil law matters

either by a single judge (*Einzelrichter*) or, if the merits of the case include special areas of law (e.g. banking, finance or insurance issues), by a panel of three judges (*Kammer*). However, depending on the difficulties of the case in question, it can be transferred from a single judge to the panel or vice versa (Secs. 348, 348a ZPO). At the level of the *Landgericht* (and superior courts) party representation by a lawyer is mandatory.

Above the *Landgericht* is the Higher Regional Court (*Oberlandesgericht*) and finally there is the highest of the regular courts, the *Bundesgerichtshof* or *BGH* (Federal Court of Justice), which has its seat in Karlsruhe and Leipzig. The BGH is one of the supreme federal courts and its territorial jurisdiction covers the whole of Germany. The *Oberlandesgerichte* are the highest courts of a particular state; each is responsible for several *Landgerichte*, which in turn are responsible for several *Amtsgerichte* (Fig. 1.5).

In addition to this brief overview of the German court system, the growing significance of the decisions of the courts of the European Community should be noted. These courts are the Court of First Instance and the European Court of Justice (ECJ), both of which are seated in Luxembourg. The procedural framework is provided for in EU law, in particular, the procedure for preliminary rulings of the ECJ on those questions of Member States' law, which raise issues under EU law. According to this procedure for preliminary rulings, national courts of EU Member States can refer cases to the ECJ if the case raises a question of the scope of applicability of EU law. The decision by the ECJ is binding for the referring court (Art. 267 TFEU). By this procedure the ECJ can ensure uniform interpretation of EU legislation in all of the EU Member States.

1.2 Key Aspects of German Business Law

1.2.1 Codified Rules and Judge-made Law

1.2.1.1 German Law as a Civil Law System

From a comparative legal perspective, the German legal system belongs to the group of 'civil law' systems which is characterized by its numerous statutes and codified legal rules. Thus, the statutory framework relevant for doing business in Germany is mostly 'written law' which can be found in various codifications, such as the German Civil Code (*Bürgerliches Gesetzbuch, BGB*) or the German Commercial Code (*Handelsgesetzbuch, HGB*), the German Act on Limited Liability Companies (*GmbH-Gesetz, GmbHG*), the German Stock Corporation Act (*Aktiengesetz, AktG*), the Transformation Act (*Umwandlungsgesetz, UmwG*) or the Public Takeover Code (*Wertpapiererwerbs- und Übernahmegesetz, WpÜG*)—this list being far from exhaustive.

1.2.1.2 Importance of Judge-Made Law

However, in many areas of law, especially in all areas of business law, one also has to consider relevant case law, which has been gradually developed by the German courts when applying codified rules to business practice.

While there are considerable differences between common law jurisdictions (like the UK or the US) and civil law systems such as Germany, one should—at least from a functional point of view—not overrate them.

On the one hand, case law in Germany is not regarded as a formal source of law, since the function of the courts is seen in applying the law rather than creating it. This is a major distinction to common law jurisdictions, which are typically characterized by a predominance of judge-made law. Under the traditional rule of the binding precedent ('*stare decisis*') all courts of a jurisdiction are legally bound to follow the decisions of higher courts of the same jurisdiction insofar as the legal reasoning ('*ratio decidendi*') applies to the facts of the case. By contrast, in Germany, judicial decisions generally do not have a comparable binding legal effect, rendering a reliance on past decisions considerably more risky.[21]

On the other hand, even in a civil law system like Germany, court decisions, and in particular decisions of the highest courts of each judicial branch, are of great significance. Case law plays an important role in supplementing the law by expanding or narrowing the scope of its application. A complete statutory coverage of all legal issues is obviously impossible since the legislator cannot foresee all circumstances or future developments. Furthermore, statutes most often need to be interpreted, which gives judges a certain discretion when applying the law to the facts of the case. Finally, the legislator sometimes deliberately avoids specific regulation but

[21] First-instance decisions generally have no binding effect at all. However, the Federal Court of Justice held that a failure of a lawyer or notary public to familiarize herself/himself with and advise her/his or her clients according to last-instance decisions is considered negligence.

leaves the development of the law to the courts. Consequently, court decisions and judge-made law play an important role in Germany.[22]

1.2.1.3 Interpretation of Statutes

However, when interpreting statutes, the German courts tend to show more self-restraint compared to their counterparts in a common law system. German judges are not free in their application of statutes but need to abide by the following standards of interpretation developed by the courts and legal scholars:

1. According to the so-called 'literal approach' (*Auslegung nach dem Wortlaut*) a judge needs to analyze closely the wording and grammatical construction of the statute, including its punctuation. The literal approach is often characterized as the most important means of interpretation and may limit the application of the other methods of interpretation.
2. Under the so-called 'systematic' or contextual approach (*systematische Auslegung*) the judge is required to analyze the context of the statute in order to define its meaning. According to this approach, the provision is observed as being part of a bigger picture, i.e. the statute as a whole, and—in turn—the statute as a whole is analyzed as being part of an interconnected legal framework. Thus, the judge will analyze the statute as a whole, taking into consideration preceding and following sections and subsections of the statutory provision to be applied, as well as other statutes that are closely related to the subject matter.[23]
3. The so-called 'historical approach' (*historische Auslegung*), also known as the genetical approach (*genetische Auslegung*) aims at finding the meaning of a provision on the basis of its historical origins. It is meant to reveal the original intention of the legislator at the time of legislation, e.g. by means of explanatory guidelines or reports on draft statues. The historical approach can be of particular importance when statutes have been changed, e.g. certain provisions have been abandoned. In such cases the meaning of a provision can often be discovered by comparing the new provision with the original legal situation. On the other hand, the historical approach is arguably the 'weakest' interpretation method, since the current understanding of a statutory provision will usually have greater weight

[22] This becomes evident when regarding general clauses (*Generalklauseln*), i.e. provisions that are intentionally worded in a most general way. For example, Sec. 242 of the German Civil Code simply states that an obligor has a duty to perform ,according to the requirements of good faith, taking customary practice into consideration'. Despite—or one might better state because of—the concise wording of the provision courts have developed a substantive body of case law, which can be divided into four functions and more than ten different case groups, with one of the leading commentaries on the provision featuring more than 116 narrowly printed pages. The inherent principle of 'good faith' has thus become a general principle, influencing all areas of German law, not limited to civil law alone and can be seen as having—in parts—a similar effect to the concept of 'equity' in common law systems.

[23] For example, the position of a provision within the context of the statute alone may reveal that it is an exception to a general rule. General rules are meant to be the standard procedure for dealing with certain aspects and exceptions. In contrast, if the provision is implemented only for a specific situation, a narrow interpretation of the provision is required.

than the original intentions of the legislator, especially if the provision in question is particularly old.

4. The so-called 'teleological interpretation' (*teleologische Auslegung*) is based on the notion of legal rules as instruments to realize certain legal, social or economic goals and values. When utilizing the teleological approach, the judge will analyze the provision as to its underlying purpose and will adapt its application to the facts of the case accordingly. Teleological interpretation often plays a crucial role in the interpretation of statutory provisions either by justifying a choice between two possible alternatives of interpretation (found according to the other methods of interpretation), as well as by supporting less obvious interpretations by reference to the injustice entailed by an alternative, and prima facie more obvious interpretation.
5. Finally, judges are bound to interpret a statutory provision in such a way that its application is in line with the principles and provisions of higher-ranking law, in particular the German Constitution and EU law. Therefore, statutes always have to be interpreted in such a way that they are in conformity with the *Grundgesetz* (*verfassungskonforme Auslegung*) and with EU law (*gemeinschaftsrechtskonforme Auslegung*).

1.2.2 Increasing Importance of European Law

With the increasing importance of European Union institutions and EU law, it is not surprising that European sources of law have become more relevant in the national context.

1.2.2.1 European Legal Instruments

European law is typically divided into so-called primary EU law and secondary EU law. The sources of primary legislation are the Founding Treaties and the Accession Treaties, including the various attached annexes and protocols. The Treaties are agreed upon by the EU Member States. Primary legislation lays down the basic policies of the Union, establishes and defines its institutional structure, legislative procedures and the powers of the Union vis-à-vis the EU Member States. The most significant change in the recent past has been brought about by the Treaty of Lisbon, which entered into force on 1 December 2009. The Treaty of Lisbon amended the Treaty on the European Union (*Treaty of Maastricht*) and the Treaty Establishing the European Community (*Treaty of Rome*), the latter having been renamed in the process to Treaty on the Functioning of the European Union (TFEU).

The term 'secondary legislation' is used for the legal sources enacted by the EU institutions based on the powers conferred to them under the Treaties. Legislative instruments available to the EU institutions comprise EU Regulations, EU Directives, EU Decisions and Recommendations, which differ as to their binding force for the EU Member States.[24]

[24] See Art. 288 TFEU.

- *EU Regulations* have general application in all Member States. They are binding in their entirety and they are directly applicable in all EU Member States. EU Regulations are self-executing, i.e. they do not need to be transposed into national law by national implementation measures. EU Regulations automatically override national legislation dealing with the same subject matter. Nevertheless, it is common for national legislation to be passed dealing with consequential matters arising from the legal framework of a regulation.
- In contrast to EU Regulations, *EU Directives* are generally not self-executing but require that each Member State pass special implementing legislation. As such, EU Directives are binding only as to the result to be achieved. Thus, they typically leave a certain amount of leeway to the Member States as to the exact rules to be adopted. However, EU Directives may become directly applicable in specific circumstances, e.g. if a Member State fails to adopt implementing measures in a timely manner.
- *EU Decisions* are legal instruments aimed at dealing with certain, individual aspects of European law, typically having a specific addressee. Important examples are those decisions, whereby the European Commission formally concludes an inquiry in relation to a certain undertaking of a Member State in the areas of competition law or state aids. *EU Decisions* are binding only on the addressed Member State.
- *EU Recommendations* and *Opinions* have no binding force. They are, however, of considerable political importance and may be utilized in order to prepare future (binding) legislation for the Member States.

1.2.2.2 Supremacy of European Law

One reason for the great importance of EU law is the doctrine of supremacy of European law in relation to national legislation. This doctrine of supremacy is not stated in the founding Treaties but has been established by the ECJ. The ECJ stated in its famous decision *Costa v. ENEL*[25] that

> the law stemming from the treaty, an independent source of law, could not, because of its special and original nature, be overridden by domestic legal provisions, however framed, without being deprived of its character as community law and without the legal basis of the community itself being called into question.

While it is common consensus today that European legal acts take precedent over national acts of parliament and legislative measures inferior to them, the question as to what extent this doctrine of supremacy also applies to provisions of the national constitutions (e.g. the fundamental rights under the *Grundgesetz*) has not yet been finally settled.

The ECJ generally regards the conclusion of the founding Treaties as being a transfer of sovereignty from the Member States to the European institutions leading

[25] ECJ, case C-6/64 *Falminio Costa v ENEL* [1964] ECR 585, at p. 593.

to an absolute supremacy of European law. Accordingly, in its decision of the case *Internationale Handelgesellschaft*[26] the ECJ ruled that

> [r]ecourse to the legal rules or concepts of national law in order to judge the validity of measures adopted by the institutions of the Community would have an adverse effect on the uniformity and efficacy of Community law. The validity of such measures can only be judged in the light of Community law [...] The validity of a Community measure or its effect within a Member State cannot be affected by allegations that it runs counter to either fundamental rights as formulated by the constitution of that state or the principles of a national constitutional structure.

Similarly, the Constitution of Ireland states in Art. 29.4.5 that

> no provision of this Constitution invalidates laws enacted, acts done or measures adopted by the State which are necessitated by the obligations of membership of the European Union or of the Communities.

In contrast, the German Federal Constitutional Court emphasizes the position of the EU Member States as 'Master of the Treaties' and recognizes a general supremacy of EU law over the Grundgesetz only subject to the limitation, that the European laws and institutions providing for an effective protection of fundamental rights of German citizens largely equivalent to that of the German constitution.[27]

Supremacy of EU law is secured in three ways:

First, the European Commission is authorized to take infringement procedures against Member States found to be in breach of their duties under EU legislation (Art. 258 *et seq.* TFEU). Second, national courts have a duty to apply EU law and to test national measures as to their compatibility with European legislation. Third, if a national court comes to the conclusion that its decision of a case raises a specific question as to the application of a European legislative act, it is obliged under Art. 267 TFEU to refer this question to the ECJ for a preliminary ruling. Such referral to the ECJ is mandatory for questions regarding the interpretation of provisions of the EU Treaties, the validity and interpretation of acts of institutions of the EU and for the interpretation of statues of bodies established by an act of the Council. Where the case is clear, however, national courts may apply European law directly, without the need of prior reference (so-called '*acte claire*' doctrine). Preliminary rulings have become the principal vehicle for the development of European law.

1.2.2.3 Fundamental Freedoms

One of the key functions of the European Union is to establish an internal market. It is, therefore, a fundamental task of the EU institutions to abolish obstacles to intra-community trade, e.g. custom duties and charges, barriers to free movement of products or factors of production. Accordingly, Art. 26 TFEU states that "the internal market shall comprise an area without internal frontiers in which the free

[26] ECJ, case C-11/70 *Internationale Handelsgesellschaft v. Einfuhr- und Vorratsstelle für Getreide und Futtermittel* [1970] ECR 1125.

[27] BVerfGE 73, 339, 22 October 1986, 2 BvR 197/83—*Solange II.*

movement of goods, persons, services and capital is ensured in accordance with the provisions of the Treaties."

Apart from EU legislation, the principal legal tools to achieve this goal are the so-called 'Fundamental Freedoms': the free movement of workers (Art. 45 *et seq.* TFEU), the free movement of goods (Art. 28 *et seq.* TFEU), the freedom of establishment (Art. 49 *et seq.* TFEU), the freedom to provide services (Art. 56 *et seq.* TFEU) and the free movement of capital (Art. 63 *et seq.* TFEU).

As business transactions increasingly have a multi-national dimension, the Fundamental Freedoms (as interpreted by the ECJ) have become important safeguards for EU foreign investors doing business in Germany. While a comprehensive analysis of the EU Freedoms and their implications for business transactions in Europe is beyond the scope of this book, we will provide further detail on some of the most important aspects regarding the Freedom of Establishment later-on.

1.2.3 (Re-)current Issues in Corporate Law

When discussing the key aspects of German business law, one should also outline some recurrent features characteristic for Germany's legal system. Generally, while dealing with German corporate law, we will look at the classic interest groups involved in most corporate law issues, i.e., the shareholders of a company, its managers, employees and creditors.

For example, in contrast to the common law systems in which great emphasis is placed on shareholders' interests in a corporation, in Germany one should more correctly refer to 'stakeholder interests' since this broader term would include other interest groups also having interests (or 'stakes') in a corporation, in particular employees. The specific German rules on the co-determination of employees prescribe that all German companies with a workforce exceeding a certain number of employees must provide for the participation of employees' representatives in the company's supervisory board.[28] In this way, employees and their representatives have a certain amount of influence on these companies since the management board is, to some degree, accountable to the supervisory board (a number of its members being employees' representatives). Although other jurisdictions in the EU also provide for employees' co-determination, the German system is unique. The recurrent issues in German corporate law, therefore, not surprisingly, include the ongoing debate on the scope and limits of employees' participation, as well as the debate on the scope and limits of shareholders' rights and managers' duties and liability. It also includes the controversial discussion on the need of a statutory minimum share capital as a means for the protection of creditors. Although far from being a new topic, mandatory capital requirements have become a controversial subject in the legislative proceedings for the European Private Company (SPE) as well.[29]

[28] See *infra*, Sect. 2.5.3.

[29] See *infra*, Sect. 5.3.

1.3 The Legal Framework for Business Organizations in Germany

1.3.1 Case Study

Case Study

Having read **C's** memorandum, **B** is now convinced that it is worthwhile to pursue his plans. He gives **C** another call and schedules an appointment with him to discuss in more detail the options available to **A** for doing business in Germany.

B wants to know which forms of business organization are available and asks **C** to prepare a comparative analysis highlighting the advantages and disadvantages of each type of business.

1.3.2 Options for Conducting Business in Germany

A foreign investor or enterprise considering options for conducting business in Germany will typically choose between establishing a branch office (i.e. a dependent business unit) of the corporation in her/his own jurisdiction, or establishing a subsidiary of her/his home corporation in Germany (by establishing or acquiring a German company). In contrast to a subsidiary, a branch office is not a separate legal entity (but is considered a permanent establishment for taxation purposes). On the other hand, when considering using a subsidiary as a separate legal entity for doing business in Germany, an investor will have the choice between various unincorporated or incorporated business organizations. Thus, after looking at the requirements for establishing a branch office in Germany, we will briefly outline different German business forms available. In the following chapters we will then look at the legal framework governing the limited liability company (*GmbH*) and the stock corporation (*AG*) in more detail.

1.3.2.1 Establishing a Branch Office

A branch or branch office (*Zweigniederlassung*) is defined as a dependent operational unit of a foreign enterprise. A branch office has no separate legal personality distinct from its head office and is thus subject to the law governing the head office. Nevertheless, the branch has to be entered in the Commercial Register (*Handelsregister*) of the local District Court and the statutory requirements of Secs. 13 *et seq.* HGB therefore have to be met. Although setting up a branch might sometimes be preferable for tax purposes, and has been quite popular in Germany in the case of limited liability companies formed in accordance with the laws of England and Wales, it is quite a complicated and time-consuming procedure, since many documents must be filed with the competent German Commercial Register.

The registration must be filed by the directors authorized to represent the company. It has to be filed in German (Sec. 184 GVG) with the court in the district where the branch operates (Sec. 13d HGB).

The following check list for information and documents required for the registration of a branch of an private company limited by shares formed in accordance with the Companies Act of England and Wales (Ltd.) will introduce you to this procedure:

Check List for the Registration of a Branch
[Example: UK private company limited by shares (Ltd.)]
Information and documents necessary to register a branch of a Limited in Germany (see Secs. 13d, 13g HGB)

1. **Information concerning the company and its foreign head office**
   - Name, registered office and object of the company
   - Commercial Register with which the company is registered and subsequent registration number
   - Date of formation and data on the duration of the company
   - Amendments to the Articles of Association and date thereof
   - Amount of issued share capital
   - Number of shares and par value per share
   - Details of any contributions in kind
   - Name, address and date of birth of each shareholder
   - Name, address and date of birth of each managing director, including power of representation
   - Company's legal form
   - Publication requirements for official notices by the company
2. **Information concerning the branch**
   - Name of the branch (admissible under German law)
   - Location of branch
   - Address and object of the branch
   - Name (address and date of birth not compulsory) of the persons who are authorized to represent the company with respect to the business of the branch as permanent representatives in and outside of court
   - Names (address and date of birth are not compulsory) of persons who are granted '*Prokura*' (holder of an unlimited power of attorney) and their power of representation
3. **Documents which need to be attached to the application form**
   - Certificate concerning the adequate formation of the company, (as a general rule) Certificate of Incorporation with copies of the Articles of Association and the Memorandum of Association
   - List of shareholders
   - Certificate concerning the appointment of the managing directors and their powers of representation (issued by the company secretary)
   - Signature sheet containing the signatures of the managing directors
   - Signature sheet containing the signatures of the permanent representatives and the '*Prokurist*' of the branch, if applicable
   - Licenses with respect to the object of the company (where required)

Given the complicated procedure of establishing a branch as outlined above, many investors prefer instead to establish a new German company as a subsidiary. The following section gives an overview of different possible forms of business organizations.

1.3.2.2 Overview of Various Forms of Business Organizations

German business law provides for various types of business organization such as corporations, partnerships and associations. The most important types of corporations are the GmbH and the AG.[30] There are three types of partnership, the *BGB-Gesellschaft* (civil law partnership), the *oHG* (general commercial partnership) and the *KG* (limited commercial partnership). Although corporations, and in particular the GmbH, are quite popular, there may also be reasons to choose a partnership as the legal vehicle for conducting business, e.g. partners have a greater flexibility in management issues and in regards to the dissolution of the partnership. Moreover, in a partnership there are fewer publication requirements and a higher level of confidentiality. For these reasons partnerships are often selected as the business vehicle for small entities or family-owned enterprises.

Sole Proprietorship (*einzelkaufmännisches Unternehmen*)

This business form is typically used by small enterprises. Since it is the easiest way to start and run a business, it is one of the most prevalent forms of small business organizations for entrepreneurs in Germany. A sole proprietorship is an unincorporated business, owned by a single person and operated in her/his name or under a trade name. The sole proprietorship is not a legal entity. Thus, it cannot have any rights and obligations of its own, nor can it sue or be sued in court. Instead, it is the owner (*Einzelkaufmann*) who holds all the rights and who is fully liable for all business debts and obligations. Depending on its size and range of activities, the sole proprietorship has to be registered with the Commercial Register. If the sole proprietor is not legally obliged to register, she/he may still choose to do so voluntarily. However, in both cases (mandatory and voluntary registration), the sole proprietor—being a 'merchant' according to the definition of German commercial law—has to comply with many of the HGB's regulations.

Civil Law Partnership (*GbR*)

In contrast to the AG and GmbH, the civil law partnership (*Gesellschaft bürgerlichen Rechts, GbR* or *BGB-Gesellschaft*) is an association of two or more persons without corporate organization. The GbR does not have the status of a corporation as a separate legal entity. The GbR is established by setting up a partnership agreement between at least two partners wishing to pursue any legal purpose. However, if the partners intend to pursue a commercial business, this partnership will be treated as a general commercial partnership (oHG) or as a limited commercial partnership (KG).

[30] Both the AG and the GmbH will be explained in detail *infra* in Sects. 2 and 3 respectively; the SE will be introduced in Sect. 5.2. The following presentation therefore is limited to a brief overview of the most important non-corporate and hybrid forms of business organizations available under German law.

The GbR is managed and represented jointly by all partners, unless the partnership agreement provides otherwise. The assets of the partnership belong to its partners jointly. All partners are jointly and severally liable for the firm's debts and obligations. Such liability may be limited to the partnership assets only by agreement with the third party creditor or by restrictions set out in the partnership agreement and made known to the third party creditor. Because of its flexibility, the GbR is used for a great variety of business purposes.

Beginning in 2001, the *Bundesgerichtshof* fundamentally changed the traditional statutory regime for the GbR in several landmark decisions by treating this company form in a way similar to that of a general commercial partnership.

- In its decision of 29 January 2001,[31] the BGH acknowledged the capacity of a GbR to sue and be sued in private proceedings. Furthermore, the court applied the liability rules for partners of German commercial partnerships (oHG, KG) to partners of a private law partnership. The extension of these liability rules means that, for claims against that partnership, creditors may hold partners of a private law partnership personally liable.
- With its decision of 24 February 2002,[32] the BGH further extended the liability of the civil law partnership by ruling that damages caused by the managing directors have to be compensated by the civil law partnership. The court emphasized that partners of a private law partnership are personally and jointly liable for the liabilities of that partnership.
- In another landmark decision of 7 April 2003,[33] the BGH held that a new partner of a private law partnership may be held liable for obligations that arose even before she/he joined the private law partnership. With this decision, the Court thus further expanded the personal liability of partners of a private law partnership by analogizing them to partners of a commercial law partnership.

In essence, the *Bundesgerichtshof* has treated the private law partnership as a legal entity quite similar to the general commercial partnership (described below) and, in effect, thus transformed the GbR into a legal entity that now largely approximates the general commercial partnership.

General Commercial Partnership (*oHG*)

The general commercial partnership (*offene Handelsgesellschaft, oHG*) is a partnership established by two or more persons for the purpose of operating a commercial business within the meaning of the Commercial Code (*vollkaufmännisches Handelsgewerbe*) under a company name, provided that all partners are fully liable for the partnership's debts and obligations. It is formed by agreement between the partners, which may be concluded even by conduct. After that, the oHG must be registered in the Commercial Register.

In contrast to the GbR, the oHG has a company name under which it may acquire rights of its own, incur obligations and sue or be sued in court (see Sec. 124 HGB).

---

[31] See BGHZ 146, 341, 29 January 2001, II ZR 331/00.

[32] See BGHZ 154, 88, 24 February 2003, II ZR 385/99.

[33] See BGHZ 154, 370, 7 April 2003, II ZR 56/02.

Although the oHG has a status similar to that of a corporation regarding its dealings with third parties, significant differences to corporations do remain. For instance, the assets of the oHG belong to all partners jointly and the partners are jointly and severally liable for the oHG's debts and obligations. Each partner is individually entitled to manage and represent the partnership, unless the partnership agreement provides otherwise by consent of all partners.

The oHG is a business form typically used by a small number of partners who personally rely on each other and wish to commit all their assets to a joint undertaking. However, the overall importance of the oHG has significantly decreased and other company forms (not demanding the personal liability of its members) have become more popular. As of 1 January 2010 in Germany 27,422 oHGs were registered.[34]

Limited Commercial Partnership (*KG*)

The limited commercial partnership (*Kommanditgesellschaft*, *KG*) is a general partnership similar to the oHG, in that it is also a partnership established for the purpose of operating a commercial business. In contrast to the oHG, however, the KG has two kinds of partners. There are one or more general partners (*persönlich haftende Gesellschafter* or *Komplementäre*) with unlimited personal liability (identical to a partner in an oHG). These partners with personal liability manage and represent the limited commercial partnership. On the other hand, there are one or more 'limited partners' (*Kommanditisten*) whose personal liability is limited to the amount of a fixed capital contribution to be paid to the partnership. The amount of this capital contribution is registered in the Commercial Register (*Handelsregister*) and, to the extent it has been paid into the limited commercial partnership and has not been repaid, the limited partner is discharged from personal liability. The limited partners are excluded from the management and representation of the partnership, unless the partnership agreement provides otherwise.

The KG is frequently used for family-owned enterprises. Quite often it has also been used to bring together capital from investors for particular ventures. The KG is particularly popular in a form in which the sole general partner is a corporation, typically, a GmbH. As of 1 January 2010 there were 236,554 limited commercial partnerships registered in Germany.[35]

Hybrid Commercial Limited Partnership (*GmbH & Co. KG)*

A frequently used combination of the limited commercial partnership and the corporation is that of a KG, in which the only general partner is a GmbH (so-called *GmbH & Co. KG,* Fig. 1.6).

By allowing the KG to have corporations such as the GmbH as a partner with full personal liability (so-called *Komplementär*), personal liability can be avoided in a legally permissible way since, in principle, only the GmbH (and not its shareholders) will be liable vis-à-vis the creditors of the KG.

[34] See Kornblum 2010, p. 740.

[35] See Kornblum 2010, p. 740.

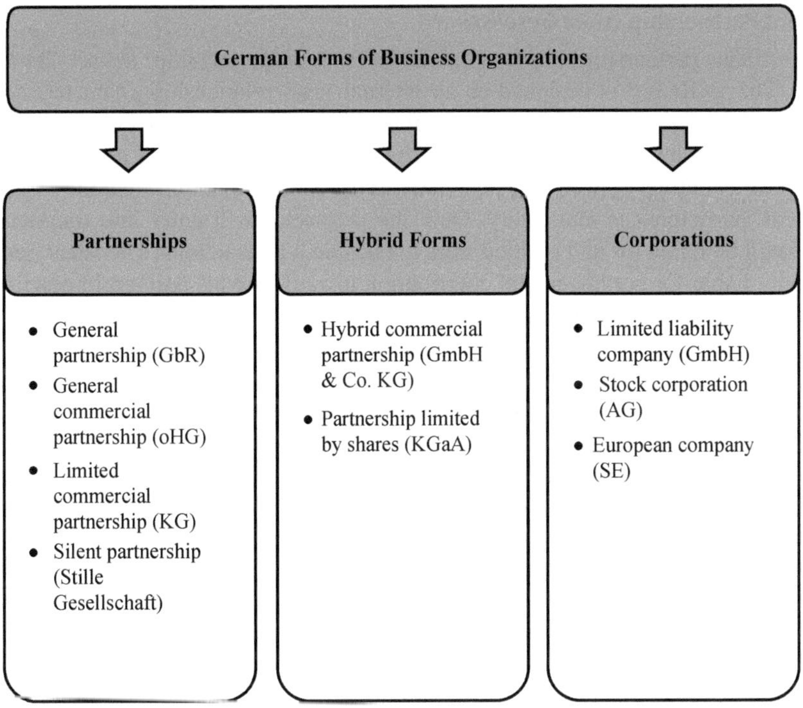

Fig. 1.6 Forms of business organizations in Germany

The attractiveness of the GmbH & Co. KG results from the fact that it combines the advantages of a partnership (tax benefits) with those of a corporation (limitation of liability), which may outweigh the disadvantages resulting from a somewhat complex corporate structure.

Partnership Limited by Shares (*KGaA*)

The partnership limited by shares (*Kommanditgesellschaft auf Aktien, KGaA*) is another hybrid business form combining elements of a limited commercial partnership with those of a stock corporation. Partnership law is applicable for those partners with personal liability whereas the KGaA and the partners with limited liability (*Kommanditaktionäre*) are subject to the German Stock Corporation Act (Sec. 278 paras. 2 and 3 AktG). Due to its relative complexity the KGaA is not common in German legal practice: As of 1 June 2010 only 225 partnerships limited by shares were in existence.[36]

[36] See Bayer and Hoffmann 2010, p. R286.

Silent Partnership (*stille Gesellschaft*)

The silent partnership (*stille Gesellschaft*) is a partnership as set forth in Sec. 705 BGB but is designed as an internal legal relationship characterized by someone participating in the commercial trade of another person with a capital contribution which will then be transferred to the assets of the business partner. For this purpose a contract between the proprietor of the commercial trade and the so-called 'silent' participant is mandatory. Only the proprietor will enter into transactions and will be liable for and entitled from the business transactions. The silent partner is only liable for her/his capital contribution towards her/his partner. In practice, a silent partnership may be chosen for tax reasons or because of confidentiality interests of the investor (e.g. in a family business).

Registered Co-operative (*eingetragene Genossenschaft*)

The registered co-operative (*eingetragene Genossenschaft, eG*) is an association with an unlimited number of members whose purpose is to promote the goals of its members—this can be a commercial goal as well as for a social or cultural purpose. This type of business association originated in the nineteenth century and was a popular vehicle especially for craftsmen and farmers. But even today, the eG is quite common in some business sectors (e.g. retail and banking), and there are approximately 7,000 registered co-operatives with nearly 20 million members.[37]

The eG is defined as a separate legal entity and can acquire rights and assume liabilities; it may acquire ownership and other real property rights, and it can sue and can be sued.

1.4 A Brief Introduction into German Insolvency Law

The regulatory framework for insolvencies in Germany has been subject to various changes. In 1999, the German legislature passed a new Insolvency Code (*Insolvenzordnung, InsO*) which replaced the rules of the former Bankruptcy Code (*Konkursordnung*) of 1877 and the Settlement Act (*Vergleichsordnung*). The former legal framework had been criticized for not achieving the main goal of insolvency law, namely, a fair and equal satisfaction of the creditors. In many insolvency cases, creditors received only very small distributions on their claims, or the courts did not even commence insolvency proceedings for lack of sufficient assets within the company.[38] The reform of Germany's Limited Liability Company Law in 2008 by the Act on the Modernization of the Limited Liability Company Law and the Prevention of Abusive Acts (*Gesetz zur Modernisierung des GmbH-Rechts und zur Bekämpfung von Missbräuchen, MoMiG*), which will be discussed in more detail later on[39], also included amendments to insolvency rules, e.g., regarding the scope of duties of a managing director in case of insolvency of a GmbH.

[37] See Klunzinger 2009, p. 310.

[38] For more details on this reform see Braun 2005, pp. 59 *et seq.*

[39] See *infra*, Sect. 3.1.

1.4.1 Objectives of German Insolvency Law

As indicated above, the main purpose of German insolvency law is to ensure a fair satisfaction of the creditors of an insolvent company. Under the original Bankruptcy Code which regulated insolvency cases until 1999, equal satisfaction of the creditors was to be achieved solely by liquidation of the debtor's assets and distribution of the proceeds. Under the Insolvency Code such liquidation is still the most important aspect of the insolvency procedure. However, the new statutory framework has brought a shift in perspective. Apart from liquidation of the debtor's assets, the current insolvency law also allows for debtor and creditors to reach an arrangement by means of a so-called insolvency plan procedure in order to enable the company to reorganize and to continue its business.

1.4.2 Reasons for Opening Insolvency Proceedings

Pursuant to Sec. 16 InsO, opening an insolvency proceeding requires the existence of specific reasons (*Insolvenzgründe*). The InsO stipulates three such reasons, i.e., (1) illiquidity of the debtor, (2) over-indebtedness and (3) so-called imminent illiquidity.

1.4.2.1 Illiquidity

Illiquidity (*Zahlungsunfähigkeit*) refers to a situation of cash-flow insolvency, where the debtor is unable to pay her/his debts on the date of maturity. Illiquidity, therefore, requires a mature debt, as well as the inability to discharge the debt. Whether or not a company is considered illiquid has to be determined for a period of time encompassing three weeks, rather than a particular date.

Exceptions are made for such liquidity shortages which are only temporary or which are limited in their volume:

- First, temporary liquidity shortages may constitute an 'illiquidity' under Sec. 17 InsO only where the debtor's funds available for the next three weeks do not cover the debts becoming due in the same period.
- Second, 'illiquidity' does not apply where the inability to discharge mature debts relates to not more than 10% of total matured debts and there is no substantial likelihood that the uncovered amount will increase beyond this threshold in the near future.

Once occurred, illiquidity can be avoided, e.g., by executing a formal stand-still agreement (which technically eliminates maturity) or by reaching an informal agreement with certain lenders about a temporary forbearance of their claims (which does not).

1.4.2.2 Over-indebtedness

The insolvency reason of over-indebtedness (*Überschuldung*) requires a negative net asset position (balance-sheet insolvency).[40] A negative net asset position is

[40] As part of the Financial Market Stabilization Act (*Finanzmarktstabilisierungsgesetz*) which entered into force on 18 October 2008 as a reaction to the financial crisis, the definition of over-

given, where the balance of total assets minus the liabilities of the debtor is negative. The assets have to be valued at a fair market value, i.e., the net value likely to be achieved if the assets were to be sold at the time of calculation in a regular course of business (estimated sale price minus sale costs). On the negative side of the net asset status (*Überschuldungsstatus*), all claims by third party creditors have to be taken into account, e.g., loans, provisions for contingent liabilities or loss compensation obligations vis-à-vis subsidiaries. An exception applies to such liabilities that have been subordinated and thus are ranked behind the claims of all other debtors by way of a subordination agreement (*Rangrücktrittsvereinbarung*) or a debtor's warrant (*Besserungsschein*).

1.4.2.3 Imminent Illiquidity

Finally, insolvency proceedings may be filed in case of imminent illiquidity (*drohende Zahlungsunfähigkeit*). A situation of imminent illiquidity is given, when a liquidity forecast shows that a company will become illiquid within the current or subsequent fiscal year. The insolvency reason of imminent illiquidity was introduced by the legislature in 2002 and had no equivalent in the Bankruptcy Code in force until this date. By introducing the concept of 'imminent illiquidity,' the legislature aimed at more insolvency proceedings to be opened in a timely manner to increase creditor protection, as well as to improve the chances of successful restructuring. For this purpose companies are given the option of filing insolvency proceedings voluntarily at a time prior to actual incapability to pay their debts, i.e., when more assets and liquidity are available, as a foundation for rehabilitation or reorganization efforts. Therefore, the insolvency reason of imminent liquidity (a) constitutes a right, not an obligation to file insolvency proceedings and (b) does so only in favor of the company, not for its creditors.

1.4.3 Insolvency Proceedings—Steps and Options

1.4.3.1 Petition to Open Insolvency Proceedings

Insolvency proceedings shall only be opened upon written petition. Such petition for insolvency proceedings (*Insolvenzantrag*) may generally be filed either by the insolvent company itself or by its creditors.[41] The petition is to be filed with the Municipal Court (*Amtsgericht*) competent for the debtor's place of residence

indebtedness was temporarily narrowed. According to the amendment, a negative net asset position only constituted a situation of over-indebtedness in the absence of a substantial likelihood for a continuation of the business. This permitted managers not to file insolvency proceedings if the company was more likely than not to remain in the business in the medium-term. The amendment was limited in time and expired on 31 December 2010. Since 1 January 2011 the old definition of over-indebtedness applies again.

[41] In the case of imminent illiquidity, only the company is entitled to file a petition.

(if the debtor is a consumer[42]) or the debtor's place of business (in case the debtor is a businessperson, sole proprietor or company).

In the case of illiquidity or over-indebtedness, the company is obliged to file the petition.[43] If the company becomes insolvent, the managing director of the company is personally responsible for filing the petition for insolvency proceedings without undue delay (*ohne schuldhaftes Zögern*), but not later than three weeks following the date the insolvency becomes identifiable to the director.[44]

A managing director failing to meet this requirement risks personal liability under civil law and under criminal law:

- First, pursuant to Secs. 15a para. 1 InsO and 823 para. 2 BGB, the managing director will be held personally liable for such damages caused to the company and its creditors by a delayed filing for insolvency proceedings. In case of more than one managing director, all directors are held jointly and severally liable.[45]
- Second, pursuant to Secs. 64 GmbHG, 92 para. 2 AktG, the managing director is obliged to reimburse the company for any payments made to the shareholders or to third parties after the company has become illiquid or after its over-indebtedness has been established.
- Third, deliberately delaying a necessary filing for insolvency is a criminal offense under Sec. 15 para. 4 InsO, which is punishable with imprisonment of up to three years. Depending on the facts of the case, other criminal charges (e.g. bankruptcy) may apply as well. Any conviction on these grounds will lead to the offender's being generally disqualified from taking the office of a managing director of any other corporation for a period of five years, see Sec. 6 para. 2 no. 3 GmbHG.

1.4.3.2 Preliminary Proceedings

Insolvency proceedings will not be opened because of the petition alone, but, in addition, require a formal decision to open insolvency proceedings by the local court. Until such decision is made, the court will order preliminary measures to prevent detrimental changes to the company's assets. Usually it appoints a preliminary administrator (*vorläufiger Insolvenzverwalter*). Such a preliminary administrator may—depending on the scope of the court order—either have the right to comprehensively take over the company's management or be limited to supervision of the existing management and to take only clearly defined actions.

[42] Different from other insolvency regimes, the German Insolvency Code applies both to natural persons not running a business, as well as to businessmen, merchants and companies.

[43] In the case of imminent illiquidity the company is entitled, not obliged, to file a petition.

[44] As the filing has to be made without undue delay, the director may, depending on the individual circumstances, be required to file for insolvency proceedings before the lapse of the three-week period. This may be the case where within the three weeks timeframe reorganization or restructuring measures cannot be taken or are more likely than not to remain unsuccessful.

[45] Since it may be difficult for creditors to retrospectively establish details regarding the financial situation of the company in order to prove that on a given date the company was illiquid, the burden of proof lies with the directors.

1.4.3.3 Regular Insolvency Proceedings

If the court holds that an insolvency reason does exist and the remaining assets of the company are sufficient to cover the costs of the proceedings (court fees, expenses, and remuneration of the insolvency administrators), it will formally initiate insolvency proceedings by appointing a (regular) insolvency administrator.[46] The insolvency administrator acts as the sole representative of the insolvency estate and as such has the sole right to manage the company and to dispose of its assets during the proceedings.

Any claims against the insolvent company may only be pursued under the rules of the insolvency proceedings. Creditors have to file their claims with the administrator. Their claims will fall into one of three categories:

- preferential claims (*Masseverbindlichkeiten*);
- regular claims (*Insolvenzverbindlichkeiten*); or
- subordinated claims (*nachrangige Verbindlichkeiten*).

Creditors whose claims arise only after the opening of the insolvency proceedings (*Massegläubiger*) enjoy preferential treatment insofar as they have to be fully satisfied by the proceeds of an enforcement of the assets by the insolvency administrator before any regular insolvency creditor (*Insolvenzgläubiger*) receives any payment from such proceeds. Creditors of subordinated claims (e.g. a claim for repayment arising from a shareholder's loan) will be satisfied even after the insolvency creditors and will typically leave empty-handed. In contrast, a preferred ranking usually assures that the creditor will be paid in full. Within each category, the insolvency administrator is obliged to treat all creditors equally.

Secured creditors who have a security interest over assets in the insolvency estate may, depending on the type and scope of their security right, be entitled to a separation right (*Aussonderungsrecht*) or may demand separate disposition of the asset concerned (*Absonderungsrecht*). Creditors who have a separation right (e.g., owners of an asset under a retention-of-title agreement) do not fall in one of the above-mentioned categories but have an in-rem claim for return of the asset, which is enforceable individually, independently from the insolvency proceedings. Creditors who may demand separate disposition (e.g. creditors whose claims are secured by a land charge) are privileged in that they may demand that the asset be disposed of separately and that the proceeds from this particular disposition are preferentially used to satisfy their claims.

With regard to pending contracts, i.e. contracts, which have not yet been executed by either party in full, the insolvency administrator has the right to choose between performance and immediate termination. Damages suffered by the counterparty from choosing termination constitute non-preferential insolvency claims. Moreover, the insolvency administrator has the right to set aside certain transactions (*Anfechtungsrecht*) which have been made by the company prior to filing for insolvency or the opening of the insolvency proceedings on grounds that the transaction has reduced the value of the insolvency estate.

[46] If, however, the court rejects the opening on grounds of the remaining assets being insufficient to cover the costs of proceedings, the company will be dissolved.

Despite the strong legal position of the insolvency administrator, the fundamental decisions are to be made by the creditors. To this purpose, creditors either establish a creditors' committee and/or come together in the so-called creditors' assembly. The creditors' assembly decides whether the insolvent company's business shall be temporarily continued or closed and has the right to replace the court-appointed insolvency administrator. Furthermore, for transactions of particular importance, the insolvency administrator has to obtain consent of the creditors' committee or—in case no such committee has been elected—the creditors' assembly.

1.4.3.4 Reorganization Proceedings

One of the core features of the Insolvency Code of 1999 is the introduction of reorganization as an alternative to the standard insolvency proceedings. This alternative option was inspired by US bankruptcy law, in particular, by the so-called 'Chapter 11' plan proceedings. Briefly summarized, the new reorganization regime allows for the submission of an insolvency plan (*Insolvenzplan*) and voting on such a plan by various groups of creditors. The main idea of this reorganization regime is to enhance party-autonomy: specific solutions necessary to deal with an insolvent company may best be developed by the parties affected, i.e., the company and its creditors. Thus, the rules of the insolvency plan may deviate from large parts of the statutory provisions of the InsO. Moreover, the insolvency plan may provide for a liquidation of the company, as well as for a reorganization. Although reorganization can be seen as an alternative option, its legislative implementation in Germany is widely considered to be too complex and bureaucratic. Therefore, the importance of the insolvency plan proceedings in practice has up until now remained limited.

Currently, however, German legislature is acting to counter these shortcomings. At the time of this writing, the German government has recently submitted a draft for an Act Serving the Further Facilitation of the Reorganization of Enterprises (*Gesetz zur weiteren Erleichterung der Sanierung von Unternehmen, ESUG*) to the Federal Parliament (*Bundestag*). The draft comprises a set of measures to facilitate restructuring and to this purpose, *inter alia*, aims at improving the reorganization plan proceedings. Therefore, once the Act will be enacted, it will for the first time be possible, take account of participation interests, i.e. shareholders' rights, in the insolvency plan. By integrating the shareholders into the plan proceedings, it will, among others, be possible to provide for debt-equity-swaps in the plan proceedings.

References

Bayer W, Hoffmann T (2010) Statistiken zur AG—eine kritische Bestandsaufnahme. Die Aktiengesellschaft, pp R283–R286

Braun S (2005) German insolvency act: special provisions of consumer insolvency proceedings and the discharge of residual debts. GLJ 7:59–70

Klunzinger E (2009) Grundzüge des Gesellschaftsrechts, 15th edn. Vahlen, Munich

Kornblum U (2010) Bundesweite Rechtstatsachen zum Unternehmens- und Gesellschaftsrecht. GmbH-Rundschau, pp 739–748

Stock Corporation (*AG*) 2

Abstract

The following chapter provides an introduction into the legal framework for the German stock corporation, the *Aktiengesellschaft* (*AG*). After outlining its characteristics and some of the reasons for entrepreneurs to choose this corporate form, the institutional design of the AG will be explained in detail. We will have a closer look at the corporate bodies (*Organe*) of the AG, covering their composition, their respective functions and competencies, and explaining their relationship to each other. Then, we will outline the capital regime of the German stock corporation, as one of the most distinctive features of the AG. Furthermore, we will briefly describe how an entrepreneur would establish an AG under German law and how it is dissolved. We will continue our presentation by discussing the German system of employee participation, including collective wage bargaining, works councils and board-level co-determination. In the final section, we will outline some of the most important rules to be aware of when considering 'going public', i.e. listing an AG on a stock exchange.

Contents

M. Schulz, O. Wasmeier, *The Law of Business Organizations*,
DOI 10.1007/978-3-642-17793-4_2,

2.1 Introduction

2.1.1 Case Study

Case Study

Having read **C**'s memorandum, **B** is convinced that a future expansion of **A**'s business into the German market will require the establishment of at least one corporation under German law. As **B** is aware that the setting-up of a competitive business unit in Germany will require access to additional financial resources, he considers establishing a stock corporation, possibly as a holding company in a corporate group structure. He therefore asks **C** to prepare a presentation on the statutory framework of the German stock corporation (*Aktiengesellschaft, AG*) with a special focus on issues of financing. Furthermore, being unfamiliar with the German two-tier board system and the scope of stockholders' rights under German stock corporation law, **B** is particularly interested in the role and competencies of the statutory bodies in the *AG*. In this regard **B** has also heard that under German law employees have extensive participation rights and asks **C** also to briefly touch upon this issue in his presentation.

2.1.2 Characteristics of the AG

Like the German limited liability company (*Gesellschaft mit beschränkter Haftung, GmbH*)[1] the AG is a juristic person. As such, it is a legal entity being distinct from its founders and stockholders.[2] The AG has the capacity to hold rights, e.g. the title of ownership, by itself and may sue or be sued under its corporate name. In principle

[1] The GmbH will be dealt with in detail in the next chapter, see *infra*, Sect. 3.

[2] See Sec. 1 para. 1 AktG. In German stock corporation law, the shareholders of an AG are called '*Aktionäre*'; to reflect this we will use the English term 'stockholders'.

(and subject to some exceptions to be discussed later)[3] neither the stockholders of the AG (*Aktionäre*) nor the members of its management board are personally liable for obligations of the AG. The AG is considered to be a merchant according to the definition under the German Commercial Code (*Handelsgesetzbuch, HGB*), i.e. the special rules of the HGB also apply to any AG irrespective of its specific business purpose.

Under German corporate law, an AG has three mandatory bodies (*Organe*): the stockholders' meeting (*Hauptversammlung*)[4], the supervisory board (*Aufsichtsrat*)[5], and the management board (*Vorstand*)[6], each with its own, non-alterable sphere of competence.

The most important characteristic of the stock corporation is that its registered stock capital is typically divided into a high number of stocks (*Aktien*) which can be easily transferred and listed on a stock exchange.

2.1.3 Advantages of the AG

Choosing an AG as the legal vehicle for one's business has many advantages. Compared to a GmbH, the AG provides stockholders with greatly improved options to raise equity capital. The company's stock can be split into a high number of stocks with a low nominal value. In contrast to shares in a GmbH, it is quite simple for investors to transfer the stocks of an AG, since stocks in an AG can be listed on an organized market (stock exchange) and offered to the public. By this access to a public market, an AG may raise substantial amounts of capital from a large number of investors, addressing larger institutionalized investors, as well as smaller private investors. In addition, for further fundraising, German law provides for additional financial instruments such as debentures and bonds.

From the point of view of an investor, an investment in stocks of an AG can be interesting, as even a relatively small investment enables the investor to participate in the productive property of the company. If the AG is listed on an organized stock exchange, the investor can thus directly benefit from the company's growth, while her/his risk is limited to the initial contribution. Furthermore, with an investment in an AG the identity of the stockholders can be kept secret, since, even if a stock register is kept, the corporation will not disclose the identity of its stockholders to the public.

In summary, a stock corporation typically grants access to larger financial resources, either 'directly' in terms of equity capital and additional financial instruments, as well as 'indirectly' in terms of greater borrowing power due to a better debt-equity ratio. This enables the company to invest, for example, in large-scale production facilities or expensive research and development projects, which may in

[3] See *infra*, Sect. 3.5.

[4] See Secs. 118 *et seq.* AktG.

[5] See Secs. 95 *et seq.* AktG.

[6] See Secs. 76 *et seq.* AktG.

turn lead to competition advantages, cost reduction and improved business performance. Therefore, the company form of an AG is ideally suited for larger undertakings.

2.1.4 Disadvantages of the AG

On the other hand, an entrepreneur considering an AG as the suitable form for her/his business activities should also be aware of some disadvantages.

For example, the rules for incorporating and managing an AG and for controlling its management board are stricter and more complex compared to those applicable to the GmbH. In general, the formation process, as well as the decision-making process will take much longer in the case of an AG and are more expensive. Furthermore, with an amount of EUR 50,000.00 the minimum capital required to establish an AG is twice as high as compared to the required minimum capital for the GmbH.

Moreover, raising additional funds by selling stocks of the AG bears the risk of diluting (or even loosing) ownership and control over the AG's activities. Profits have to be shared among a greater number of stockholders, and a considerable amount of the profits have to be used for the administration of the stockholders' meeting and the on-going information of the stockholders and the public—since public disclosure of financial affairs is mandatory.

Last but not least, if choosing an AG as the legal vehicle for conducting business, an entrepreneur will have to conform to many more statutory regulations, from classic corporate laws (e.g. capital maintenance rules) to more exotic but equally important legal requirements (e.g. under the corporate governance code, or specific risk management requirements). In German law the vast majority of rules set out in the Stock Corporation Act (*Aktiengesetz, AktG*) is mandatory and (in contrast to the more flexible legal framework for the German GmbH) cannot be modified by the stockholders (so-called *Prinzip der Satzungsstrenge*).[7] A deviation from the statutory framework for the AG is only possible if the matter is not exclusively regulated or if the statutory framework explicitly allows a modification by the parties.[8]

---

[7] In comparison, e.g. Swiss law does not know this principle. As a consequence, although the statutory provisions of Swiss law are very similar to those in Germany, the Swiss AG is considered to be a more flexible tool for economic activity. It is not limited to larger enterprises but is also appropriate for small and medium sized enterprises and has become the customary legal form for economic activity in Switzerland. In contrast, the GmbH traditionally has played only a very minor role in Switzerland; this has begun to change lately due to abandoning size limitations in the 2008 Swiss GmbH Act.

[8] See Sec. 23 para. 5 AktG. This is rarely the case. e.g. according to Sec. 179 para. 2 sentence 1 AktG an amendment of the articles generally requires the approval of three-quarters of the stockholders' meeting. Sentence 2 of the provision, however, allows for this quota to be modified.

2.2 Internal Organization

2.2.1 Governance Structure and Bodies of the AG

The AG has three mandatory corporate bodies: the stockholders' meeting, the supervisory board and the management board. These bodies have the following competencies and functions:

Firstly, the stockholders as the owners of the AG are responsible for appointing the supervisory board and for passing resolutions on the most fundamental issues regarding the corporation, whereas the management board has the task of strategic alignment and operational management of the AG (principle of separation of ownership and control). Consequently, in contrast to the shareholders' meeting of the GmbH, the stockholders' meeting of an AG has comparably little influence on the day-to-day management of the company. In turn, the power and responsibilities of the management board are much broader than those of the managing directors (*Geschäftsführer*) of the GmbH.

Secondly, with regard to the management of the AG the German stock corporation law provides for a strict separation of executive and supervisory functions, each of which need to be carried out in separate institutional bodies. This mandatory two-tier board system is a characteristic of German corporate law shared only by a handful of other European continental jurisdictions[9], whereas other legal systems provide for only one board of directors, including both executive and non-executive managers at the same time.[10] A frequent criticism of the German model is that the mandatory two-tier structure is rather bureaucratic and hinders time-efficient decision-making. Furthermore, the German model has been criticized as it can enable some manipulations by the management board, since the latter typically provides most of the information upon which the supervisory board's decisions are based.[11] The possibility to 'escape' the mandatory two-tier structure in favor of a one-tier management board system is apparently one of the reasons for German entrepreneurs to choose the business form of the European Company (*SE*), which will be explained in more detail later on.[12]

---

[9] See e.g. Sec. 111 Danish Companies Act (*lov om aktie- og anpartsselskaber*); Art. 2:158 Dutch Civil Code (*Burgerlijk Wetboek*); Secs. 70 *et seq.*, 86 *et seq.* Austrian Stock Corporation Act (*Aktiengesetz*).

[10] See e.g. Sec. 1 subsec. A no. 3 UK Combined Code; Art. 707, 716, 716a Swiss Code of Obligations (*Obligationenrecht*); in France the two-tier board system is only applicable if provided for in the company's articles of association, see Art. L225–7 French Commercial Code (*Code de Commerce*).

[11] In more technical terms: separate legal bodies for executive and non-executive managers may well amplify the asymmetric distribution of information between both, worsening the inherent principal-agent-problem. Of course, one-tier board structures are no guarantee for proper information sharing either, and in turn may well lead to a stronger factual influence on the non-executive board members, thus impairing their supervisory power.

[12] See *infra*, Sect. 5.2.

2.2.2 Management Board (*Vorstand*)

2.2.2.1 Composition and Appointment

The management board of the AG may consist of one or more persons. In case of larger companies (i.e. the corporation's stock capital exceeds 3 million Euros), the management board must consist of at least two persons, unless the articles provide otherwise. It goes without saying, that due to the size and complexity of stock corporations, management boards in practice typically comprise a much higher number of members.

A member of the supervisory board is not allowed to be a member of the management board at the same time. In case of vacancies, however, individual members of the supervisory board may act as a stand-in for a period of time to be fixed in advance, but not exceeding one year. During this term of office as a deputy to the management board, they are temporarily barred from exercising their functions as supervisory board members.[13]

The supervisory board appoints the members of the management board for a period not exceeding five years. The appointment may be renewed or the term of office extended as long as the term of each such extension or renewal does not exceed five years.[14] If the management board (as it usually does) consists of more than one person, the supervisory board may appoint one of the members as chairman of the board (*Vorstandsvorsitzender*).

As part of its supervisory function the supervisory board also has the authority to revoke appointments of individual members of the management board (or the appointment as chairman of the board) for 'good cause'.[15] Such good cause in particular includes a gross breach of duties or the inability to manage the corporation properly. Furthermore the appointment may be revoked after a vote of lack of confidence by the stockholders' meeting. In this case, however, the supervisory board may abstain from a revocation if the vote of lack of confidence took place for manifestly arbitrary reasons.[16]

2.2.2.2 Functions and Responsibilities of the Management Board

The management board is the executive board of the AG, responsible for its operative management,[17] as well as the representation of the AG in and out of court.[18]

---

[13] See Sec. 105 AktG.

[14] See Sec. 84 AktG.

[15] See Sec. 84 (3) AktG.

[16] This authority is not to be taken for granted, since the supervisory board therewith decides against the explicit will of the corporation's owners. It is but one example of the institutional principle of separating ownership and control in public liability companies.

[17] See Sec. 76 AktG.

[18] See Sec. 78 AktG.

Management of the AG

The management board is exclusively responsible for the management (*Geschäftsführung*) of the AG. 'Management' is meant in its broadest sense and includes any legal or factual actions or measures carried out in order to realize the purpose of the company.

With regard to the management of the corporation, the AktG vests the management board with a comprehensive and exclusive sphere of competence, which includes extensive discretionary powers (see Sec. 93 para. 1 sentence 2, so-called 'business judgment rule'). In particular, the management board is, in general, not bound by any instructions of either the supervisory board or the stockholders' meeting, nor can the management board be compelled to take specific actions or enter into agreements against its own will.

However, in some cases the exclusive competence of the management board with regard to management decisions may be restricted in several ways:

Firstly, in practice, the articles of association (*Satzung*) of the AG or the internal rules of procedures (*Geschäftsordnung*) passed by the supervisory board typically provide for unusual, extraordinary business matters to require a prior approval of the supervisory board (e.g. entering into transactions beyond a certain financial limit). Any actions taken by the management board without such prior approval are on the one hand principally valid vis-à-vis third parties but will, on the other hand, constitute a breach of the duty of care owed by the management board to the AG and may lead to claims for damages by the AG and to the revocation of appointment of the management board members for good cause. The management board can, however, turn to the stockholders' meeting to pass a resolution on whether or not a certain transaction may be carried out[19], the resolution requiring a qualified majority, i.e. 75% of all votes cast. The incentive of the management board to do so can be derived from Sec. 93 para. 4 AktG, according to which, members of the management board cannot be held liable by the corporation for managerial decisions mandated by a resolution of the stockholders' meeting.

Secondly, according to the case law of the *Bundesgerichtshof* (German Federal Court of Justice) the management board also has to observe certain so-called unwritten competencies of the stockholders' meeting when exercising its managerial power.

- In its landmark decision *Holzmüller*,[20] the court held that with regard to certain restructuring measures, the management board was not only entitled but also obliged to obtain approval of the stockholders' meeting prior to carrying out the respective transaction. In this case, the management board of a stock corporation decided to carve out about 80% of the most valuable assets of the corporation and transfer them to a subsidiary. The court held that an obligation to obtain the approval of the stockholders' meeting, even though not provided for in the statutory law, applied automatically in respect of such measures which constitute a

[19] See Sec. 119 para. 2 AktG.

[20] BGHZ 83, 122, 25 February 1982, II ZR 174/80—*Holzmüller*.

'material interference'. Furthermore, they have a 'substantial impact' on rights of the stockholders. Thus, the management could 'not reasonably assume that it was entitled to take decisions in the matter on its own responsibility'.

- In the *Gelatine* decisions[21] the Federal Court of Justice specified the *Holzmüller* doctrine, laying down further quantitative and qualitative prerequisites. The court did not lay down a specific catalogue of measures which oblige the management board to request the approval of the stockholders' meeting. However, the court clarified that an approval requirement only applies, where (1) the transaction in question touches upon the core of the business of the corporation and (2) approximately reaches the 80% threshold. Although an exact threshold cannot be concluded from the decision, the judgment considerably improved the position of managers as to legal certainty, since the court explicitly disapproved of an extensive interpretation of *Holzmüller* and clearly stated that unwritten requirements for approval of the stockholders' meeting were strict exceptions.
- Finally, in its decision in the case of *Macrotron*[22] the Federal Court of Justice acknowledged an inherent power of the stockholders' meeting with regard to the decision of whether or not to delist a listed stock corporation. In this case, however, the court did not base its reasoning on the *Holzmüller* doctrine but referred to the constitution, more precisely: the basic right protecting private property (Art. 14 GG).

Finally, the managerial powers of the management board will also be limited where the company is part of a corporate group structure. In this case, the management board will be subject to directions of the controlling enterprise.

Representation of the AG

The power of the management board to represent the company in and out of court (*Vertretungsbefugnis*) is comprehensive in scope and cannot be restricted in relation to third parties.[23] The scope cannot be limited by way of an amendment to the articles of association, nor do obligations to procure the consent of another corporate body have effect vis-à-vis third parties.[24]

In certain exceptional cases, however, statutory law restricts the otherwise comprehensive power of representation of the management board. This applies in particular to certain agreements which entail a potential risk of embezzlement[25] or

[21] BGH, 26 April 2004, II ZR 154/02, NZG 2004, 575—*Gelatine I*; BGH, 26 April 2004, II ZR 155/02, NJW 2004, 1860—*Gelatine II*.

[22] BGH, 25 November 2002, II ZR 133/01, ZIP 2003, 387.

[23] See Sec. 82 para. 1 AktG.

[24] A violation of such obligations may, naturally, constitute a breach of duty and may entail the risk of personal liability vis-à-vis the company.

[25] See Sec. 112 AktG: In transactions between the corporation and members of the management board only the supervisory board may represent the corporation.

which may affect the property and pecuniary rights of stockholders.[26] A violation of these restrictions will render the transaction null and void.

Unless otherwise provided for in the articles, the members of the management board (*Vorstandsmitglieder*) represent the corporation jointly in actively committing the company although each member has authority to receive commitments from third parties individually. In practice, however, it is common for the articles to contain a provision allowing any two members of the management board to jointly enter into commitments on behalf of the corporation in order to simplify operative procedures.

The power of representation of the management board also includes the authority to grant limited or unlimited power of attorney to employees of the company.

Reporting Obligations of the Management Board

The management board is obliged to deliver regular, conscientious and accurate reports to the supervisory board on the intended business strategy and on other fundamental matters regarding the present and future strategic alignment of the corporation, in particular on such matters as the planning of financial investments and human resources, expected turnover and profitability of the corporation, as well as on important corporate transactions.[27]

Furthermore, event driven ad-hoc reports shall be made to the chairman of the supervisory board (*Aufsichtsratsvorsitzender*), where significant developments occur, including developments concerning the business of an affiliated company, which may have a material impact on the stock corporation.[28]

Although the management board has to fulfill these reporting obligations proactively, the supervisory board also has the right to request, at any time, special reports by the management board on matters of relevance to the corporation, its relations to affiliated companies, as well as such business developments in affiliated companies, which may have any material impact on the AG.[29]

In addition, further information and reporting requirements of the management board may be provided for in the rules of procedure for the management board (*Geschäftsordnung für den Vorstand*).

2.2.3 Supervisory Board (*Aufsichtsrat*)

2.2.3.1 Composition and Appointment

The supervisory board shall consist of at least three members. The maximum number of members depends on the amount of stock capital, the articles of association

[26] See Sec. 293 AktG: Validity of enterprise agreements with affiliated companies is contingent to prior approval of the general meeting.

[27] See Sec. 90 para. 1 sentence 1 AktG.

[28] See Sec. 90 para. 1 sentence 3 AktG.

[29] See Sec. 90 para. 3 AktG.

and the applicable co-determination regime regarding the AG's employees. Only natural persons can be members of the supervisory board.

As a special feature of German corporate law, depending on the number of employees, the supervisory board of an AG is subject to mandatory co-determination (*unternehmerische Mitbestimmung*) by employees' representatives. In these cases, the supervisory board must consist of both stockholders' representatives, as well as employees' representatives. The stockholders' representatives on the supervisory board are appointed and removed by resolution of the stockholders' meeting. The employees' representatives, on the other hand, are elected in a special procedure provided for in the applicable German co-determination laws.[30]

The stockholders' representatives are elected for a term, not exceeding five years, by the stockholders' meeting[31]. The resolution requires a majority of more than 50%. However, the articles of association may provide special appointment rights to a particular stockholder (*Entsendungsrecht*). In this case, the respective stockholder will have the right to appoint a number of stockholders' representatives specified in the articles, not exceeding one third of all such representatives, independently outside the stockholders' meeting.

In the event of a member of the board's resigning during her/his term, the stockholders' meeting may either appoint a substitute until the regular completion of the term or elect a new, regular member for a full term. For the interim period between resignation and appointment, the management board can apply for the court to appoint a temporary stand-in.

Appointments of stockholders' representatives can be terminated without cause by the stockholders' assembly. The resolution requires a qualified majority; however, in the articles of association, this threshold may be reduced. Moreover, the supervisory board itself has the right to apply to the court, in order to remove one of its members from office.

2.2.3.2 Functions and Responsibilities of the Supervisory Board

The supervisory board is entrusted with the appointment, supervision and control of the management board. It appoints the members of the management board, as well as the chairman of the management board (*Vorstandsvorsitzender*) and may also dismiss them for good cause.[32] It receives reports from the management board on a regular basis, but also may at any time request a specific report on the on the company's affairs, its legal and business relationships with affiliated companies and on important transactions.[33]

The supervisory board may not issue binding instructions to the management board with regard to the operative management of the AG. However, the supervisory board may pass special rules of procedures for the management board

[30] For further detail see *infra*, Sect. 2.5.3.

[31] Appointment is limited to one third of the members of the supervisory board, AktG, Sec. 101 para. 2.

[32] See Sec. 84 AktG.

[33] See Secs. 90, 111 AktG.

(*Geschäftsordnung für den Vorstand*). Such rules of procedure typically provide for a catalogue of managerial decisions which require the prior approval of the supervisory board.[34]

In order to avoid potential conflicts of interest, German law provides that the supervisory board must represent the AG in transactions with members of the management board, and in particular, regarding employment contracts.[35] The supervisory board also represents the corporation in retaining an auditor for the annual financial statement, which it must review.[36]

In practice, certain tasks of supervision are often prepared by a special committee (*Aufsichtsratsausschuss*, e.g. an auditing committee or a HR-committee). However, the supervisory board as a whole remains responsible for any breach of duty of care by such a committee so that every member of the supervisory board has to constantly supervise the committee's work.

2.2.4 Advisory Board (*Beirat*)

As in the case of the GmbH, additional bodies such as advisory boards or administrative boards may be created, provided that the general allocation of responsibilities between the management board and supervisory board remains untouched. Many AGs will use a *Beirat* in order to gain access to specific regional or industrial expertise.

2.2.5 Stockholders' Meeting (*Hauptversammlung*)

2.2.5.1 Sphere of Competence of the Stockholders' Meeting

The stockholders' meeting (*Hauptversammlung*) is the forum in which the stockholders exercise their rights with respect to the AG and as such it is the principal corporate body of the German stock corporation. Its task is to pass resolutions on matters concerning the AG falling within its sphere of competence. In contrast to the GmbH, however, this sphere of competence is limited in scope. The stockholders' meeting has the right to pass a resolution only if and insofar as statutory law (as interpreted by the courts) specifically provides for such a right with regard to the subject matter in question. Thus, in particular the influence of the stockholders' meeting on management decisions is limited compared to the influence of the shareholders on the managing directors of a German GmbH[37].

---

[34] See Sec. 111 para. 4 AktG.

[35] See Sec. 112 AktG.

[36] See Sec. 111 para. 2 AktG.

[37] According to Sec. 119 para. 2 AktG the stockholders' meeting may, as a rule, pass a resolution concerning matters of the operative management of the corporation only if the management board explicitly requests it to do so.

Following the principle of separation of ownership and control, German statutory law limits the sphere of competence of the stockholders' meeting to certain fundamental issues of essential importance, including, among others:

- Amendments to the articles of association;[38]
- Capital reductions[39] and capital increases;[40]
- Dissolution and liquidation of the corporation;[41]
- Election[42] and removal[43] of members of the supervisory board;
- Discharge of the members of the management board and the supervisory board[44]
- Appropriation of distributable profits;[45]
- Appointment of the auditor for the annual financial statement;[46]
- Corporate restructuring measures as provided for by the German Transformation Act (*Umwandlungsgesetz, UmwG*), in particular mergers[47], changes of corporate form[48], hive-down[49], spin-off[50], corporate division;[51]
- Squeeze-out of minority stockholders.[52]

In addition to subject matters specifically allotted to the stockholders' meeting by statutory law, the *Bundesgerichtshof* has defined further, so-called inherent powers of the stockholders' meeting. This unwritten sphere of competence covers a delisting of the corporation,[53] as well as restructuring measures, which touch upon the core of the business and concern about 80% of the corporation's assets.[54]

An annual general meeting of the stockholders must take place within the first eight months of every fiscal year.

2.2.5.2 Decision-Making Procedure

Decisions by the stockholders can only be validly made in a meeting prepared and conducted strictly according to the mandatory rules of the German Stock Corporation Act (*AktG*). Any failure to adhere to these requirements will make any resolution passed in the meeting challengeable in court, which will bar the resolution from

[38] See Secs. 119 para. 1 no. 5, 179 para. 1 AktG.

[39] See Secs. 119 para. 1 no. 6, 222 para. 1, 237 para. 1 AktG.

[40] See Secs. 119 para. 1 no. 6, 182 para. 1, 192 para. 1 AktG.

[41] See Secs. 119 para. 1 no. 8, 262 para. 1 no. 2 AktG.

[42] See Secs. 119 para. 1 no. 1, 101 para. 1 AktG.

[43] See Sec. 103 para. 1 AktG.

[44] See Secs. 119 para. 1 no. 3, 120 para. 1 AktG.

[45] See Secs. 119 para. 1 no. 2, 174 para. 1 AktG.

[46] See Sec. 119 para. 1 no. 4 AktG.

[47] See Secs. 13, 65, 76 UmwG.

[48] See Sec. 193 para. 1 UmwG.

[49] See Secs. 125, 65 para. 1 UmwG.

[50] See Secs. 125, 65 para. 1 UmwG.

[51] See Secs. 125, 65 para. 1 UmwG.

[52] See Sec. 327a para. 1 AktG.

[53] See BGH, 25 November 2002, II ZR 133/01, ZIP 2003, 387—*Macrotron*.

[54] So-called '*Holzmüller* doctrine', see see *supra*, Sect. 2.2.2.2.1.

coming into effect. The management board of the AG is responsible for preparing and heading the stockholders' meeting.

Preparation of the Stockholders' Meeting

All stockholders entitled to participate in the stockholders' meeting have to be invited in an orderly fashion. The invitation has to be published online in the Federal Gazette (*elektronischer Bundesanzeiger*) at least one month prior to the meeting.[55] If the company has issued registered stocks only, it may instead mail the invitation to its stockholders. Simultaneously with the invitation, the management board has to publish the agenda of the stockholders' meeting.[56] The agenda has to be comprehensive in the sense that it has to cover all issues on which a stockholder resolution is intended; a resolution adopted on an issue not stated on the agenda is invalid.[57] For every stockholder resolution on the agenda the management board has to provide a specific proposal. The proposal must be worded in a way that allows the stockholders to either approve or reject the proposal. The management board must also include countermotions and nominations made by stockholders if they are received in a timely manner.[58] Once published, the agenda can be validly amended only within ten days after its publication. The management board is obliged to make an amendment if a minority of stockholders representing at least 5% or an absolute amount of over EUR 500,000 communicates a corresponding request.[59]

Voting Procedure

In general, a stockholder can exercise her/his voting rights only in the stockholders' meeting, which means that she/he will, as a rule, have to attend the stockholders' meeting in person or be validly represented by proxy. In the latter case, the powers of attorney of the representative have to be in writing if the articles of association do not provide otherwise; however, the AG has to provide for an electronic authorization procedure.[60]

Until recently, attendance at the stockholders' meeting—either in person or by proxy—was the only possibility for stockholders to validly cast their votes. This often presented an obstacle for many minority stockholders, who were not resident in the place where the AG had its registered office. Therefore, the European legislature in 2007 passed a directive intended to facilitate the exercise of voting rights in a cross-border context.[61] Since the German legislature implemented the

---

[55] See Secs. 123 para. 1, 25 AktG; additionally, the articles of association may determine a national newspaper in which the invitation may be published.

[56] See Sec. 121 para. 3 AktG.

[57] See Sec. 124 para. 4 AktG.

[58] See Secs. 126, 127 AktG.

[59] See Secs. 124, 122 para. 2 AktG.

[60] See Sec. 134 para. 3 AktG; in case of institutional representatives (e.g. banks), the requirements are slightly reduced, see Sec. 135 AktG.

[61] Directive 2007/36/EC of the European Parliament and of the Council of 11 July 2007 on the exercise of certain rights of stockholders in listed companies, OJ L 184/17 as of 14 July 2007.

Directive in 2009, the German Stock Corporation Act now allows for the articles of association to provide for procedures enabling stockholders to exercise their rights via electronic communication[62] and, in particular, to cast their votes via electronic communication and/or postal letter.[63]

Generally, passing a stockholders' resolution requires a simple majority, i.e. 50% of all votes cast plus one vote (*einfache Stimmrechtsmehrheit*). However, for certain subject matters a higher threshold may be required, either by statutory provisions or by the articles of association. Apart from the simple majority, the majority threshold most frequently required under the German Stock Corporation Act is that of a so-called qualified majority of the capital participating in the passing of the stockholders' resolution (*qualifizierte Kapitalmehrheit*).[64] To pass a resolution for which such a majority is required, it is necessary that the majority voting in favor of the proposal comprises (1) 75% of all stocks participating in the voting (i.e. yes or no votes; abstentions and invalid votes will not be taken into consideration), as well as (2) 50% of all votes cast. A majority that meets condition (1) typically also fulfills (2); exceptions may arise where the company has issued stocks with multiple or limited voting rights.[65]

2.2.5.3 Minority Rights of Stockholders

Apart from pecuniary rights (e.g. the right to receive a share of earned profits[66] and liquidation proceeds[67]) a stock grants its owner a number of rights regarding her/his participation in the corporation (so-called participation rights). The scope of rights granted to a stockholder, i.e. her/his options of action, depend on the quota which her/his stock represents (possibly in concert with other stockholders). Some minority rights apply to any stockholder provided she/he holds at least one stock (so-called individual minority rights), while other minority rights require a certain quota of votes to come into effect (so-called collective minority rights).

Individual Minority Rights of Stockholders

The most important individual participation right is, of course, the right to cast a vote in the stockholders' meeting[68], which in turn implies the right to attend the meeting.[69] In order to enable stockholders to make the best possible use of their voting right, German law puts a strong emphasis on stockholders being provided with

[62] See Sec. 118 para. 1 sentence 2 AktG.

[63] See Sec. 118 para. 2 AktG.

[64] This majority is—*inter alia*—required for: amendments of the articles of association (Sec. 179 para. 2 AktG); ordinary capital increase (Sec. 182 para. 1 AktG); restriction of subscription rights on a capital increase (Sec. 186 para. 3 AktG).

[65] Please note, however, that stocks granting multiple voting rights have been abolished for companies listed on a stock exchange.

[66] See Sec. 58 para. 4 AktG.

[67] See Sec. 271 AktG.

[68] See Secs. 12, 134 AktG.

[69] See Sec. 118 AktG.

the necessary information to do so. Thus, in the stockholders' meeting any stockholder has the right to request information about corporate issues, if and insofar as such information is necessary to permit a proper assessment of an item set out in the agenda.[70] The management board may refuse to answer only in exceptional cases, in particular, if such an answer would entail a substantial risk of material damage to the corporation.[71]

If a stockholder is of the opinion that the management board has violated her/his rights with regard to the stockholders' meeting, she/he has the right to register an objection in the minutes and may, within one month after the meeting, file an action to challenge the respective resolution(s). Even if the court rejects the action and deems the resolution valid, such action may come at great expense for the company. A substantial number of resolutions have to be registered in the Commercial Register to come into effect.[72] Typically, however, a registration will be postponed until the challenge of the resolution has been decided.

In some cases, this extensive protection rule has lead to abusive practices. So-called predatory stockholders (*räuberische Aktionäre*) abused their right to request information to provoke mistakes and then sought an annulment of the resolutions of the stockholders' meeting, hoping that the company would try to pay them off. Typically such stockholders acquired only a negligible amount of stocks immediately before the stockholders' meeting for this specific purpose.[73]

To combat such abusive practices the German legislature has introduced a special release procedure (*Freigabeverfahren*) for important stockholder resolutions.[74] The release procedure allows, subject to a balancing of the parties' interests, a stockholders' resolution to be registered even though appeal proceedings are still pending. In particular, a *de minimis* threshold applies, according to which the plaintiff is required to have held stocks with a total nominal value of at least EUR 1,000.– at the date when the stockholders' meeting was called.[75]

---

[70] See Sec. 131 para. 1 AktG; this includes relations of the corporation to affiliated companies.

[71] See Sec. 131 para. 3 sentence 1 AktG.

[72] This includes resolutions addressing, *inter alia*, vital and time-critical topics such as capital increases, capital reductions or conclusions of enterprise agreements.

[73] For example, in a particular famous case the plaintiff filed an action to set aside a stockholders' resolution pertaining to a capital reduction of the defendant, a real estate investment company. The plaintiff claimed a violation of his membership rights; at the time of the action, the plaintiff held a total of 47 stocks (0.0253%) of the company. However, as the proceedings have proved, the real reason of the action was to 'persuade' the company to enter into an amicable settlement which provided for further 3,500 stocks to be awarded to the plaintiff in return for his withdrawing the action. In its judgment of 23 January 2009 the competent Higher Regional Court (*Oberlandesgericht*) in Frankfurt dismissed the action to set aside the resolution and instead ordered the plaintiff to pay damages to the company on grounds of his behavior being *contra bonos mores* (Sec. 826 BGB).

[74] See Sec. 246a AktG.

[75] See Sec. 246a para. 2 no. 2 AktG.

Table 2.1 Minority rights of stockholders in a German stock corporation

Quota	Minority right
1% or EUR 100,000 of the stock capital	Right to apply for a special audit[a]
	Right to assert claims for damages or loss compensation against (1) members of the management board or (2) members of the supervisory board or (3) third parties based on undue use of their influence on the company[b]
5% or EUR 500,000 of the stock capital	Right to demand the calling of a stockholders' meeting and right to demand that items be placed on the agenda of a stockholders' meeting[c]
	Right to take action against a resolution of the stockholders' meeting on the appropriation of balance sheet profits in certain cases
5% of the stock capital + 1 stock	Right to prevent integration into another corporation[d]
10% or EUR 1,000,000 of the stock capital	Right to request an individual (instead of general) exoneration of members of the management board or supervisory board[e]
10% of stock capital represented at stockholders' meeting	Option to prevent a waiver or settlement of a claim for damages
	(1) against members of the managing board based on breach of their duty of care;[f]
	(2) against members of the supervisory board based on breach of their duty of care; and[g]
	(3) against third parties based on undue use of their influence on the company[h]
25% of the stock capital represented at the stockholders' meeting plus 1 stock	Option to prevent the adoption of rules of procedure for the general meeting[i]
	Option to prevent
	(1) the amendment of the articles of association;[j]
	(2) the conclusion of an enterprise agreement, e.g. a profit and loss transfer agreement;[k]
	(3) any measures to transform the AG under the German Act on Transformation of Companies, i.e. mergers, spin-offs, split-offs, conversions etc.[l]
25% of votes cast + 1 stock	Option to prevent the removal of elected members of the supervisory board by the stockholders' meeting[m]
50% of votes cast + 1 stock	Right to pass any stockholder resolution requiring a simple majority, e.g. to enforce a claim for damages against members of the management board.[n]

[a] See Sec. 142 para. 2 and 4 AktG
[b] See Sec. 148 para. 1 AktG
[c] See Sec. 122 para. 1 and 2 AktG
[d] See Sec. 320 para. 1 AktG
[e] See Sec. 120 para. 1 AktG
[f] See Sec. 93 para. 4 AktG
[g] See Secs. 116, 93 para. 4 AktG
[h] See Secs. 117 para. 4, 93 para. 4 AktG
[i] See Sec. 129 para. 1 AktG
[j] See Sec. 179 para. 2 AktG
[k] See Sec. 293 para. 1 and 2 AktG
[l] See Secs. 65 para. 1, 73, 125 UmwG
[m] See Sec. 103 para. 1 AktG
[n] See Sec. 147 para. 1 AktG

Collective Minority Rights of Stockholders

Collective minority rights are 'rights' in the sense that they confer a legal position which grants an option on action to the minority stockholder(s), and 'collective' in the sense that they do not arise from holding a single stock but require a certain participation threshold. A stockholder who wishes to exercise such a 'collective' right must, therefore, fulfill the respective participation quota by her- or himself, i.e. hold enough stocks, or act in concert with other stockholders to fulfill the quota. Some collective minority rights are listed in Table 2.1.[76]

2.3 The Capital of the AG

2.3.1 Equity and Capital Structure

Corporate growth requires capital and this is true in particular for the AG, as it is the typical business vehicle for large enterprises. With regard to the origin of financial funds, two sources of capital can be distinguished: internal and external financing.

2.3.1.1 Internal Financing

The company may use its profits as a source of capital for new investments instead of distributing the profits to the stockholder. This so-called *internal financing* of the company may include various measures, *inter alia* amortization, the building of reserves (e.g. pension reserves), the retention of earnings or the sale of tangible corporate assets. Internal financing has several advantages, such as being a quick way to raise funds while avoiding control procedures required by banks, and saving interest rates. However, internal financing is typically limited in volume.[77] Furthermore, an emphasis on internal financing may lead to conflicts with certain interest groups, e.g. a decision on the retention of profits may collide with the interest of the stockholders to receive dividends. In any case, internal financing often lacks sufficient flexibility both in time and volume to match market circumstances and, last but not least, may also have negative tax effects.[78]

2.3.1.2 External Financing

As an alternative to internal financing, the AG may obtain 'fresh money', i.e. raise funds from sources outside of the company (so-called *external financing*). With regard to external financing one may distinguish between debt financing, equity financing and mezzanine financing:

[76] For a comprehensive table see Wirth et al. 2010, pp. 161 *et seq*.

[77] Of course, external financing is limited as well—both in theory and in practice. It is, however, safe to assume that there is more money available outside the company than within it.

[78] While, e.g., interest on debt capital constitutes business expenditures and may be deducted from taxable income (see Secs. 4, 4a Income Taxation Act, *EStG*), the income resulting from a sale of tangible assets may be subject to taxation itself.

Debt financing basically means borrowing money. In return for granting a loan, the creditor receives the promise that the principal and interest on the debt will be repaid. The interest rate to be paid typically includes the so-called 'market rate of interest' plus a risk premium depending—*inter alia*—on the following factors: the borrower (start-up vs. well-established company), certain collaterals used to secure the debt (secured vs. unsecured debt), the maturity of the loan (short-term vs. long-term) and the volume of the loan (low volume vs. high volume). Apart from specific loan agreements (such as bilateral or syndicated loans), common types of debt financing are bonds, mortgages and promissory notes.

When making use of *equity financing*, the company tries to raise capital from its stockholders.[79] This can be achieved either by additional share capital contributions of its existing stockholders or by admitting new, additional stockholders to the company, which will then have to pay their share capital contributions.

The so-called *mezzanine financing* refers to specific financial instruments which are a hybrid of debt and equity financing.[80] Mezzanine financing comprises subordinated debts or preferred equity instruments which represent a claim on a company's assets only senior to that of the common shares. Because mezzanine capital is subordinated to debt provided by senior lenders it is treated like equity on the company's balance sheet, making it easier to obtain further debt financing. On the other hand, mezzanine debt holders will ask for higher rates of return (approximately 14–30% above the ordinary interest rate) in order to be compensated for the additional risk. Because of these higher costs mezzanine instruments are used primarily for temporarily filling in financial gaps, especially when financing M&A transactions.

2.3.1.3 Determining the Right Capital Structure

In planning and designing the capital structure of a company, i.e. the combination of various tools of internal and external financing and, in particular, those of equity instruments and debt and mezzanine instruments, many aspects are to be considered.[81] Debt financing, for example, can be a powerful and flexible tool to finance the company's assets. Debt obligations are limited to the loan repayment period, after which the lender has no further claims. Furthermore, by repaying the debt on time the company may improve its credit rating, thereby enhancing its chances for future fundraising. Furthermore, since interest on debt can be deducted from taxable income, debt financing my also create some tax benefits. The primary advantage of debt financing, however, is that it allows the shareholders to fully retain their

[79] In finance the term 'equity' refers to the subjective value of an ownership interest in property, i.e. the amount of money someone is willing to pay for a property minus any attached liability.

[80] The financial term "mezzanine" derives from the architectural term 'mezzanine' (from ital. 'mezzo' for 'half') for an intermediate floor between two main floors of a building.

[81] Economic research suggests that given an ideal market, the source of financing employed by a company will have no influence on its corporate value (so-called *Modigliani-Miller* theorem). Reality, however, is not a perfect market but suffers heavily from information asymmetries, agency costs, bankruptcy costs and—of course—taxes.

ownership, as well as their right to earnings from the company. In contrast, admitting new shareholders (by selling shares of the existing shareholders' equity in the company or by creating new shares by way of a capital increase) as a typical form of equity financing will generally dilute the influence of the existing stockholders in the stockholders' meeting and will also dilute their right to the net profits.

On the other hand, a disadvantage of debt financing is that it typically requires payments to the lender in regular intervals, these payments being completely independent of the project's degree of success. Such payments will have an adverse effect on the company's working capital, i.e. its net assets, and may restrict the financial freedom of the company to a considerable extent.[82] Extensive repayment obligations of the company may lead to liquidity squeezes and finally to cash-flow insolvency (*Zahlungsunfähigkeit*, see Sec. 17 Insolvency Code, *InsO*). Lenders and investors might consider a large amount of debt financing to be a risk factor, which would make further fundraising more difficult. Compared to these disadvantages of debt financing, equity financing is less risky, because equity constitutes an obligation to pay dividends to the stockholders only to the extent that the company returns a net profit. Thus, equity investors typically have a strong interest in the success of the company, i.e. its growth, its profitability and an increase of its value. Finally, a sufficient amount of equity capital is essential for raising further debt equity.

2.3.2 Share Capital of the Stock Corporation

The registered share capital of a stock corporation is divided into stocks (*Aktien*).[83] Stocks can be subscribed either by the founders at the time of formation or subsequently by the stockholders in the case of a capital increase. Furthermore, stocks can be acquired via transfer or transmission from existing shareholders, typically on an organized secondary market, i.e. a stock exchange.

2.3.2.1 Types of Stock

Under the German Stock Corporation Act, there are various classes and forms of stock.

Distinction as to Denomination

As to their denomination, stocks may be issued as either par value shares or non-par value shares.[84] The company may choose freely between the two classes, but may not simultaneously adopt both types of denomination.

[82] Additional disadvantages may arise from requirements to pledge assets of the company to the lender or to provide personal guarantees of the owners of the company for repayment. Furthermore, debt instruments often contain restrictions on the company's activities, preventing the entrepreneurs from pursuing non-core business activities or alternative financial options.

[83] See Sec. 1 para. 2 AktG.

[84] See Sec. 8 para. 1 AktG.

- Par value stocks (*Nennbetragsaktien*) have an individual nominal value (par value) denominated in EUR, which is printed on the share and stated in the articles. The minimum par value is EUR 1.00.[85] The fraction of the share capital attributable to a par value share is determined by the ratio of its nominal value to the registered share capital.[86]
- Non-par value stocks (*Stückaktien*) have no specific individual nominal value. All non-par value shares participate equally in the registered share capital.[87] Therefore, the exact amount attributable to each share is determined by the total number of stocks outstanding in relation to the share capital[88], which is stated in the articles of association and must have a total nominal amount denominated in EUR.[89]

Issuing shares without a par value should not be confused with issuing shares at a price below their value (so-called *Unter-Pari-Emission*). According to Sec. 9 para. 1 AktG an AG is not allowed to issue shares under conditions in which the contribution of the subscriber made for the subscribed share is less than the EUR amount attributable to each subscribed share, i.e. their par value or the amount of share capital attributable to the individual no-par value share.

In contrast, issuing shares for a price exceeding their value is permissible and quite common in practice. In these cases, the resulting premium (*Agio*) between the contribution of the subscriber and the value of the shares has to be allocated to the capital reserves.

Distinction as to Membership Rights (Classes of Stocks)

With regard to the membership rights conferred to the stockholder, one can distinguish between three different classes of stocks (*Aktiengattungen*): ordinary stocks, preferred stocks and stocks with limited voting rights.

Ordinary Stocks

Ordinary Stocks (*Stammaktien*) confer the full set of membership rights and obligations available under the AktG to the stockholder, including the right to participate in (*Teilnahmerecht*), as well as to vote in (*Stimmrecht*) the stockholders' meeting, the right to receive the distributable profits (*Gewinnbeteiligungsrecht*) and the right to subscribe for new stocks in case of a capital increase (*Bezugsrecht*).

Preferred Stocks

Preferred stocks (*stimmrechtslose Vorzugsaktien*) confer no general voting rights to the stockholder but, in return, have priority over common stock in the payment of dividends.[90] Dividend payments on ordinary stocks may only be made after a

[85] See Sec. 8 para. 2 sentence 1 AktG.

[86] See Sec. 8 para. 4 AktG.

[87] See Sec. 8 para. 3 sentence 2 AktG.

[88] See Sec. 8 para. 4 AktG.

[89] See Sec. 6 AktG.

[90] See Sec. 139 para. 1 AktG.

preference dividend (*Vorzugsdividende*) has been paid on all preferred stocks outstanding. Preferred stocks may amount to 50% of the registered stock capital.[91] As a general rule, preferred stocks do not include voting rights in the stockholders' meeting. However, with regard to specific subject matters, in particular, their approval is mandatorily required for any changes of the articles of association which could adversely affect the privileged status of the preferred stockholders (*Vorzugs aktionäre*).[92]

Stocks with Limited Voting Rights

Stocks with limited voting rights (*Aktien mit beschränktem Stimmrecht*) serve as a tool for dealing with majority power. The articles of association may stipulate a restriction of the voting rights regardless of the number of stocks owned by the respective stockholder. However, the practical significance of such a restriction is limited: firstly, the limitations described above are only admissible for unlisted stock corporations.[93] Secondly, limitations of voting rights apply only to such resolutions of the stockholders' meeting, which require a simple majority (50% of the votes cast) and, consequently, do not prevent the exercise of majority power regarding the more fundamental resolutions (including a change of the articles of association, e.g. the abolishment of the voting rights limitation itself, which requires a higher majority).

Distinction as to the Form of the Stocks

A third distinction can be made as to the form of the stocks issued by the AG (*Aktienart*). According to the AktG, the founders may choose to issue either bearer stocks (*Inhaberaktien*) or registered stocks (*Namensaktien*).[94] According to a recent survey approximately 40% (approx. 5,700) of all stock corporations registered in Germany (16,932) have issued registered stocks.[95]

Bearer Stocks

Bearer Stocks are anonymous securities, which indicate that whoever holds the physical stock certificate is entitled to the underlying stocks. The issuing AG neither registers the owner of the stock nor does it track subsequent transfers of ownership on a secondary market. Dividends are paid upon presentation of a coupon to the firm. In general, a transfer of ownership requires the physical delivery of the stocks.[96] As a practical matter, however, since most stocks are kept in collective security custody (*Sammelverwahrung*), such physical delivery will typically be replaced by a transfer of accounts.

Since bearer stocks are not registered, they are ideally suited for investors who wish to keep their anonymity. On the other hand, bearer stocks may bear the risk of

[91] See Sec. 139 para. 2 AktG.

[92] See Sec. 141 AktG.

[93] See Sec. 134 para. 1 AktG.

[94] See Sec. 10 para. 1 AktG.

[95] Bayer and Hoffmann 2011, p. 6.

[96] See Sec. 929 sentence 1 BGB.

complete loss of the title in case of loss, theft or destruction of the physical stock certificates.

Registered Stocks

If registered stocks are issued, the company has to keep a stock register (*Aktienbuch*) in which the name, the address and the date of birth of each stockholder are entered.[97] The stock register is updated continuously. Each stockholder is entitled to check the information on her- or himself in the stock register.

From the point of view of the company, registered stocks have several advantages. First, the stock register provides the AG with the information necessary to track changes in stock ownership and to contact its stockholders, e.g. in order to invite them to stockholders' meetings. Second, registered stocks may also be useful with respect to plans for a future potential listing abroad. For example, it is quite common for listed US stock corporations to issue registered stocks. Therefore, a German stock corporation planning to be listed on the New York Stock Exchange may also prefer to issue registered stocks in order to comply more easily with the US listing standards. Third, registered stocks may also be advantageous in a takeover situation, since the stock register provides some information about the target company, e.g. regarding its shareholder structure. Furthermore, in a takeover scenario it is even more important to issue so-called restricted registered stocks (*vinkulierte Namensaktien*), which may only be validly transferred with the explicit approval of the management board. *Vinkulierte Namensaktien* may therefore be used proactively to inhibit acquisitions of stocks by possible (hostile) bidders.

2.3.3 Capital Increases

If the AG wishes to increase its registered capital subsequent to its formation, it has to follow strict (and in most cases mandatory) rules, which aim at protecting creditors and shareholders. Interests of creditors may be involved, if, e.g. the AG issues new stocks below par value. In general, stockholders have to be protected against any involuntary changes or dilutions of their effective stock ownership.

The *AktG* provides for four such sets of rules on capital increases: so-called ordinary capital increases against contributions (*Kapitalerhöhung gegen Einlagen*), contingent capital increases (*bedingte Kapitalerhöhung*), capital increases from authorized capital (*Kapitalerhöhung aus genehmigtem Kapital*), and capital increases from company resources (*Kapitalerhöhung aus Gesellschaftsmitteln*).

2.3.3.1 Ordinary Capital Increase Against Contributions

In an ordinary capital increase, the corporation issues new shares for which the (new or existing) subscribing shareholders make contributions either in cash or in kind. The ordinary capital increase requires a shareholder resolution with a majority of 75% of the share capital represented at the stockholders' meeting or such

[97] See Sec. 67 AktG.

majority as provided for in the articles of association.[98] The resolution has to cover the material issues of the capital increase, such as amount of increase, numbers of shares, and the initial price of each share. Additional special resolutions may be necessary if the corporation has issued more than one class of shares.

2.3.3.2 Contingent Capital Increase

The stockholders' meeting may authorize the management board to issue new shares on the condition of certain events. According to the AktG such contingent capital increase (*bedingte Kapitalerhöhung*) is only permitted in connection with (1) the issue of certain financial instruments (convertible bonds or similar securities), (2) in order to prepare for a merger of enterprises and (3) in order to grant specific subscription rights to employees and members of the management board (such as stock-options).[99]

The stockholder resolution authorizing the management board to execute the contingent capital increase requires a 75% majority and has to indicate the purpose of the capital increase, the specific event upon which new stocks may be issued, as well as the persons entitled to subscribe to such stocks and the issue price (or a basis on which the price is to be computed). The amount of the contingent capital increase may under no circumstances exceed 50% of the existing capital stock as of the date when the increase was approved. Usually, the amount is based on the number of stocks to be converted or purchased through subscription rights of the bondholders.

When the relevant event occurs, e.g. if bondholders exercise their call-options, the management board may (similar to the situation of a capital increase from authorized capital) issue new stock without another involvement of the stockholders' meeting.

2.3.3.3 Capital Increase from Authorized Capital

As outlined above, in case of an ordinary capital increase all essential issues are decided by the stockholders' meeting by way of resolution, which the management board must execute. While the regulatory framework for an ordinary capital increase provides for a maximum degree of protection of shareholders' interests it also considerably reduces the AG's ability to quickly adapt to changing market situations, thus restricting the company's scope for action. Given the lengthy and highly formalized process of validly calling and conducting a stockholders' meeting, the AG runs the risk of missing interesting business opportunities.

To provide the management board with more flexibility, the AktG thus acknowledges a procedure called 'authorized capital' (*genehmigtes Kapital*).[100] It allows the stockholders' meeting to approve of a capital increase in advance, already before

[98] See Sec. 182 AktG.

[99] See Secs. 192 *et seq.* AktG.

[100] This specific (German) term is not to be confused with the Anglo-American concept of 'authorized share capital', which refers to the maximum amount of share capital that the company is authorized under its constitutional documents to issue to shareholders (also referred to as 'nominal capital').

such approval is actually required: the management board may be authorized for a period of time not exceeding five years to carry out a future capital increase at a time of its own choosing, and without the need for further involvement of the stockholders' meeting.[101] In order to protect minority stockholders the authorizing resolution requires a 75% majority and is limited to a maximum amount of 50% of the existing share capital. Furthermore, the issue of stocks from authorized capital requires the consent of the supervisory board.

Within the framework of the stockholders' resolution authorizing the capital increase, the management board may, at its own discretion, decide the time, the conditions and the scope of issuing the new shares. The subscription rights of existing stockholders must be recognized (except in cases in which the authorizing stockholders' resolution has restricted such subscription rights or has delegated the power to restrict such rights to the management board).

2.3.3.4 Capital Increase from Retained Earnings

Finally, the AG may increase its stock capital by converting open reserves that are created by retained profits into capital stock.[102] In contrast to a capital increase against contributions, the AG does not acquire additional funds from outside resources. Existing stockholders receive so-called bonus stocks in relation to their participation.

2.3.4 Capital Reductions

Capital reductions usually serve one of two purposes. First, a capital reduction (*Kapitalherabsetzung*) may be undertaken in order to repay a part of the registered share capital. Second, and far more important in practice, capital reductions are used to compensate for losses, i.e. in order to avoid a negative position in the balance-sheet: by reducing the capital figures to the lower equity, financial soundness can be restored.

Capital reductions are indicated as a separate item in the profit-and-loss statement and may be conducted in one of three different forms: so-called ordinary capital reduction (*ordentliche Kapitalherabsetzung*), simplified capital reduction (*vereinfachte Kapitalherabsetzung*) and capital reduction by redemption of shares (*Kapitalherabsetzung durch Einziehung von Aktien*).

2.3.4.1 Ordinary Capital Reduction

An ordinary capital reduction requires a resolution of a 75% majority of the capital represented at the stockholders' meeting.[103] The articles may provide for stricter, but not for laxer requirements. The resolution must stipulate the purpose of the reduc-

[101] See Secs. 202 *et seq.* AktG.

[102] See Secs. 207 *et seq.* AktG.

[103] See Secs. 222 *et seq.* AktG.

tion (distribution of assets, compensation of losses, establishing free reserves) and has to be filed with the Commercial Register to become effective.

The ordinary capital increase is effectuated by a reduction of the registered share capital of the AG. In the case of an AG having issued par value stocks, the par value of the existing stocks is reduced. Where the par value is already set at the legal minimum of EUR 1.00, a consolidation or redemption of stocks is necessary.

For the protection of creditors, payments to the stockholders resulting from an ordinary capital reduction may only be made after six months. During this period, creditors who cannot demand immediate consideration of their claims must be given security payments.[104]

2.3.4.2 Simplified Capital Reduction

A simplified procedure, i.e. one without the aforementioned creditor protection mechanisms, is available if the capital reduction only serves to compensate for a decrease in the value of the AG, offset other losses, or allocate resources to the company's reserves.[105] Distribution of the free capital obtained in the process may only be used for these purposes; in particular, any distribution to the shareholders is prohibited.

As the primary purpose of this procedure is to restore financial soundness of the company during a crisis, it is only permissible after the AG has appropriated its profits and reversed its reserves to cover the losses. As a means of creditor protection, the distribution of dividends is limited for a period of two years after the simplified capital reduction has been conducted.[106]

2.3.4.3 Capital Reduction by Way of Redemption of Stocks

A capital reduction by redemption of stocks takes place either after the company has bought back its own stocks or by way of compulsory redemption of stocks.[107] In the latter case, stockholders are required to hand over their stocks to the company, whereupon the stocks are cancelled. A capital reduction by compulsory redemption is permissible only if it is provided for in the articles of association.[108]

2.3.5 Capital Preservation

One of the core principles of German stock corporation law is the principle of capital preservation: the registered stock capital, as stipulated by the articles of association, has to be paid in and may not be repaid to the stockholders. This key concept is expressed in numerous forms in the AktG.

---

104 See Sec. 225 AktG.

105 See Secs. 229 *et seq.* AktG.

106 See Sec. 233 AktG.

107 See Secs. 237 *et seq.* AktG.

108 See Sec. 237 para. 1 sentence 2 AktG.

First, as a general rule, capital contributions by the stockholders should be made in cash.[109] Any non-cash contributions (so-called contributions in kind) are considered an exception and are subject to specific auditing requirements confirming the value of the asset contributed.[110]

Second, the contribution stocks have to at least equal the par value of the stocks. Stocks must not be issued for an amount below the portion of the registered stock capital attributable to them (*Verbot der Unter-Pari-Emission*).[111]

Third, the contribution stocks have to be made in a timely manner. A stockholder who fails to pay in her/his contribution owed will be granted a grace period. But in case of her/his continued failure to pay her/his contribution following the expiry of such period, her/his stocks and any contribution already made will be forfeited.[112] In addition, any predecessor of such stockholder may be held liable for the remaining amount if the expelled stockholder is unable to pay.[113] The company may neither release the stockholder nor its predecessor from their contribution obligations.

Fourth, contributions may principally not be repaid to the stockholders. This includes any payments made by the company to one of its stockholders, which do not consist of a distribution of balance sheet profits according to a valid distribution resolution of the stockholders' meeting, or for which the company, in return, does not receive at least equal consideration.[114]

Finally, the AG may acquire its own stocks only pursuant to a stockholders' resolution and only up to an amount of 10% of the total stock capital. The costs of such acquisition have to be covered by free reserves, i.e. assets which otherwise would have been available for distribution to the stockholders (distributable profit, profit reserves and profits carried forward).[115] To prevent a circumvention of these rules, the AktG provides for any transaction to be null and void by which the AG grants any advance payment, loan or security to a third party for the purpose of acquiring stocks in such company.[116]

2.4 Formation, Dissolution and Liquidation of the AG

2.4.1 Formation

An AG may be established by one or more natural or juristic persons for any legal purpose. The formation procedure of an AG is quite similar to that of a GmbH.

[109] See Sec. 54 para. 2 AktG.

[110] See Sec. 34 para. 1 no. 2 AktG.

[111] See Sec. 9 para. 1 AktG.

[112] See Sec. 64 AktG.

[113] See Sec. 65 AktG.

[114] See Sec. 57 AktG.

[115] See Sec. 71 AktG.

[116] See Sec. 71a AktG.

It takes several steps beginning with drafting the articles of association and ending with applying for registration of the AG into the Commercial Register; this entry is the prerequisite (as in the case of the GmbH) for the AG to come into legal existence.

The first step to establish an AG is to draft the initial articles of association, which must include, *inter alia*, the corporate name, the registered office, the purpose of the company, and the amount of the registered stock capital.[117] As in the case of the GmbH, the articles have to be established in the form of a notarial deed.

In addition to the legal requirements for the GmbH, the AktG further stipulates an obligation to set-up a notarized deed of formation (*Gründungsurkunde*), which states the founders, the paid up amount of the registered stock capital, as well as the class and volume of the stocks to be subscribed by each founder.[118] As the actual subscription (*Übernahme der Einlagen*) [119] has to be notarized as well, it is included in the formation deed.[120]

Having subscribed to the stocks, the founders then have to appoint the first supervisory board and the first auditor.[121] These appointments shall be made in the form of a notarial deed. The supervisory board then, in turn, appoints the initial management board. The period of office for both initial bodies expires automatically by operation of law at the first stockholders' meeting.

As the next step, the founders have to pay in the stock capital contributions subscribed to in the deed of formation.[122] In case of cash contributions, at least 25% of the lowest issue price has to be paid.[123] Non-cash contributions (contributions in kind) have to be made in full.[124]

The founders must also prepare a specific formation report (*Gründungsbericht*), explaining the formation procedure.[125] In particular, the formation report shall provide details as to the fair value of any contributions in kind made. Based upon, but not limited to, the findings of the formation report the management board and the supervisory board shall audit the formation procedure. If a member of one of the boards has subscribed to stocks of the AG or if contributions in kind were involved, an additional formation audit by independent formation auditors (*Gründungsprüfer*) is required.[126]

After the AG has made an application for registration in the Commercial Register, which has to include, *inter alia*, the notarized articles of association, the deed of formation and the report concerning the formation audit, the court will examine

[117] See Sec. 23 para. 3 AktG.

[118] See Sec. 23 para. 2 AktG.

[119] See Sec. 29 AktG.

[120] See Sec. 23 para. 2 no. 2 AktG.

[121] See Sec. 30 AktG.

[122] See Secs. 36, 54 AktG.

[123] See Sec. 36a para. 1 AktG.

[124] See Sec. 36a para. 2 AktG.

[125] See Sec. 32 AktG.

[126] See Sec. 33 para. 2 AktG.

whether all necessary formation requirements have been met.[127] If the court comes to the conclusion that the AG has been duly established, it will register the company in the Commercial Register. Upon registration, the AG will come into legal existence.

2.4.2 Dissolution and Liquidation

2.4.2.1 Dissolution

An AG may be dissolved for one of the following legal reasons for dissolution (*Auflösungsgrund*) set forth in Sec. 262 AktG:

- Expiration of the 'lifetime' of the AG as according to the time period stipulated in the articles of association;
- Resolution of the stockholders' meeting deciding to dissolve the company;
- Initiation of insolvency proceedings;
- Final court rejection to initiate insolvency proceedings due to lack of sufficient assets pursuant to Sec. 394 of the Act on Legal Proceedings in Family Law Matters and in Non-Contentious Jurisdiction (*FamFG*);
- Declaration of the Commercial Register court that the articles of association have been found to be incomplete or defective in essential points;
- Order of deletion due to a complete lack of assets (*Vermögenslosigkeit*).

Furthermore, the AG may be dissolved due to a declaration by the courts resulting from an action of a stockholder or the management board to declare the company null and void.[128] Such action may be brought on grounds that essential provisions of the articles of association are missing or defective, and is only permissible within three years after the company has been registered in the Commercial Register.

2.4.2.2 Liquidation

From the moment of dissolution the AG's remaining existence exclusively serves the purpose of liquidating its assets, satisfying its creditors from the proceeds and distributing the remains to the stockholders.

As a general rule, members of the management board will act as liquidators.[129] They are responsible for taking the necessary steps to wind up the AG, e.g. to execute contracts, to satisfy creditor claims and to sell and dispose of company assets. Similar to the procedure in insolvency proceedings, creditors will be requested by way of publication to register their claims. Any proceeds that remain after all registered claims have been satisfied and after the liquidators have received their remuneration shall be distributed among the stockholders according to their share in the registered stock capital.[130] The liquidation procedure is concluded by deletion of the AG from the Commercial Register.[131]

[127] See Sec. 38 AktG.

[128] See Sec. 275 AktG.

[129] See Sec. 265 para. 1 AktG.

[130] See Secs. 271 para. 1, 265 para. 4 and 5 AktG.

[131] See Sec. 273 AktG.

2.5 Employee Participation

The term 'employee participation' describes methods and concepts utilized to ensure a certain degree of influence of employees in industrial relations. To this means the three strategies that may be distinguished are (1) collective bargaining, (2) shop-level co-determination and (3) board-level co-determination.[132]

2.5.1 Collective Bargaining and the Role of Labor Unions

Labor unions (and with them collective bargaining) have a long and substantial tradition in Germany. The history of collective bargaining in Germany dates back to the second half of the nineteenth century century. In the aftermath of the revolution of 1848 national labor organizations, the labor unions, were founded, the first being the unions of cigar workers (1865), book-printers (1866) and tailors (1867). It was the book-printers who in 1873 succeeded in accomplishing the first collective bargaining agreement (*Tarifvertrag*) in Germany: the book-printers' union and the association of employers in the printing business agreed that future employment of workers by the employers should be subject to the conditions negotiated by the two groups.[133]

Attempts of the Bismarck-regime to prevent the rise of the labor union movement remained futile. When, after the death of Bismarck in 1890, the Anti-Socialist Act of 1878[134] was abolished, three large centralized labor unions (Socialist, Christian and Liberal) were established and grew rapidly in size. In 1913, the total number of members already approximated the three millions threshold,[135] with 13,500 collective bargaining agreements in force.

After the end of World War I, this development continued, not least due to governmental legislation, which for the first time recognized collective bargaining agreements as legally binding and even allowed for individual agreements to be made generally binding through a declaration of the Labor Ministry.[136] In 1919 the concept of 'free', i.e. without state intervention, collective bargaining was finally incorporated into the Weimar Constitution (*Weimarer Reichsverfassung*). However, divisions between the unions along their political and ideological orientation, as well as the economic crisis and subsequent mass-unemployment had a debilitating effect on the union movement. Under the Hitler regime both labor unions, as well

---

[132] Of course the legal rules governing employee participation also apply to the *GmbH*. However, since in particular mandatory board-level co-determination rules apply only to companies with a higher number of employees (500, 1,000 or 2,000 respectively), which typically are organized as stock corporations, for the purpose of this book employee participation is dealt with in the context of the AG.

[133] On the history of collective bargaining in Germany see Kronstein 1952, pp. 199 et seq.

[134] *Gesetz gegen die gemeingefährlichen Bestrebungen der Sozialdemokratie* as of 21 October 1878, *Reichsgesetzblatt* 1878, p. 351.

[135] Socialist: 2.5 million; Christian: 343.000; Liberal: 107.000; see Wehler 1994, p. 95.

[136] *Verordnung über Tarifverträge, Arbeiter- und Angestelltenausschüsse und Schlichtung von Arbeitsstreitigkeiten* as of 23 December 1918, *Reichsgesetzblatt* 1918, p. 1456.

as their counterparts—the employers' associations—were banned and thousands of union members were arrested or murdered. Instead of free collective bargaining, the Nazi regime introduced a centralized system of state control of labor conditions according to the *Führer* principle.[137]

In the early post-war years, labor participation mainly concentrated on the establishment level, flanked and promoted by the reinstatement of works councils by the occupying powers.[138] At the same time, efforts were made on the side of the readmitted[139] unions to overcome the ideological divisions which had weakened the trade unions in the Weimar republic. They finally led to an association of the sixteen largest unions under the auspices of the German Union Association (*Deutscher Gewerkschaftsbund, DGB*) in 1949, and, consequently, the formation of the Federal Union of German Employer Associations (*Bundesvereinigung deutscher Arbeitgeberverbände, BDA*) on employer side in 1950. Also regarding collective bargaining, the year 1949 brought two major milestones: since the Constitution for the Federal Republic of Germany (*Grundgesetz für die Bundesrepublik Deutschland, GG*), entered into force on 23 May of that year, its Art. 9 para. 3 guarantees the right of every individual to form associations to safeguard and improve working and economic conditions, so-called Freedom of Coalition (*Koalitionsfreiheit*). Measures taken by the public authorities to restrict or impair these rights, especially directed against industrial disputes, are prohibited. The main implication is the freedom of collective bargaining from any form of state intervention (*Tarifautonomie*). This was paralleled by the enactment of the Act on Collective Bargaining Agreements. (*Tarifvertragsgesetz*) on 9 April 1949, which was amended in 1969 and still constitutes the central legal basis for collective bargaining.

Under this legal framework and fueled by the historically grown political and social influence of labor unions, an extensive regime of collective bargaining agreements developed in post-war Germany. Furthermore, until the mid-1990s collective bargaining in Germany mainly occurred on a sectoral level. With large-scale regional or even nation-wide agreements covering a whole industrial sector (e.g. metalworking, chemicals and public services).[140]

However, with the growing global competition, changing working conditions resulting from technological innovations and, not least, as a side-effect of the unions' efforts to bring East-German wages up to the West-German level and the corresponding introduction of hardship and opening-clauses in collective agreements, a clear decentralization development towards company agreements. (*Firmentarifverträge*) began. Recent studies, therefore, show more of a mixed result of still prevailing

[137] *Gesetz zur Ordnung der nationalen Arbeit* as of 20 January 1943, *Reichsgesetzblatt* 1943 I, p. 45.

[138] Law No. 22 of the Allied Control Council as of 10 April 1946, Official Gazette of the Control Council in Germany, p. 133.

[139] Directive No. 31 of the Allied Control Council as of 3 June 1946, Official Gazette of the Control Council in Germany, p. 160.

[140] In doing so a high collective bargaining coverage was reached. Traditional estimations show a coverage rate of 90% for Germany; see *OECD*, Employment Outlook 1994, p. 173.

sectoral agreements on the one hand, and a clear decline in union membership and bargaining agreement coverage ratios on the other.[141]

2.5.2 Shop-Level Co-determination

The second cornerstone of employee participation in Germany is co-determination at 'shop-level' (*betriebliche Mitbestimmung*) as realized in so-called works councils (*Betriebsräte*).

The purpose of works councils is to provide an institutionalized set-up to enable employees to participate in decisions pertaining to the organization and management of the individual business unit (i.e. shop, plant or site) at which they are working. Although also pertaining to participation rights of employees, works agreements (*Betriebsvereinbarungen*) between works councils and employers are strictly separated from collective bargaining agreements as negotiated by the labor unions. While the latter mainly concern material working conditions, e.g. wages, the works councils are involved in decisions regarding the more formal working conditions, such as industrial safety. Furthermore, the management is obliged to consult the works council if it plans to dismiss an employee of the respective business unit.

Works councils in Germany are governed by the Works Constitution Act (*Betriebsverfassungsgesetz, BetrVG*) of 1972. The history of shop-level employee participation, however, dates back to the Weimar Republic, when the first Works Councils Act was enacted in 1920. Shortly after the end of World War II, the Allied Control Council reinstated the work councils, which had been abolished under the Nazi regime for being incompatible with the centralized Führer principle.[142] Although this re-installment primarily served the self-interest of the occupying powers, i.e. to provide a better supervision over German workers, many of which had played a dubious part under Hitler, this measure laid the foundation for the success story of shop-level employee participation in Germany.

The BetrVG applies to all private enterprises, regardless of their legal form. According to Sec. 1 BetrVG, a works council may be established in any business unit with at least five permanent employees of legal age, three of which have to have worked in the business for at least six months. If these conditions are met, the employees are entitled to form a works council, electing fellow employees as their representatives. The employer must refrain from any actions that could impede or interfere with the formation or work of a works council. A violation is considered a criminal offense under Sec. 119 BetrVG and is punishable with imprisonment up to one year.

The works council formed in a business unit represents only the employees who belong to that specific unit. The employer has to abstain from unlawful interference with its work and must not discriminate between employees elected to the works

[141] See e.g. Fitzenberger et al. 2008.

[142] Law No. 22 of the Allied Control Council as of 10 April 1946, Official Gazette of the Control Council in Germany, p. 133.

council and 'regular' employees. The works council, in return, must duly and properly exercise its functions and is not allowed to disturb the operation or compromise the peace of the workplace. Strikes and other means of industrial disputes are not allowed on the works-council level but are limited to trade unions.

The general functions of the works council are enumerated in Sec. 80 BetrVG. According to this provision, the works council, *inter alia*, shall ensure that the employer observes provisions set forth by statutes, regulations, collective bargaining agreements and works agreements, shall propose measures that benefit the business unit and the workforce and shall mediate between employers and employees.

To this purpose, the works council is vested with specific participation rights. Depending on the subject matter concerned, the works council may have:

- the right to obtain timely, complete and correct information from the employer and to inspect corresponding documents;
- the right to be consulted regarding a specific topic with the employer, e.g. prior to dismissals and new employments;
- the right to veto a decision made by the management until either an agreement is reached or a labor court overrules the veto;
- the right of co-determination, i.e. the employer cannot validly make a specific decision without the consent of the works council.

Co-determination rights arise in particular in connection with social matters and specific questions regarding working conditions. For example, according to Sec. 87 para. 1 no. 2 BetrVG, a direction or measure of the employer pertaining to the commencement and termination of the daily working hours, including breaks and the distribution of working hours among the days of the week, is invalid, unless an amicable agreement with the works council is reached. This provision, however, does not extend to the duration of daily or weekly working hours; these are subject to the individual working contracts and the collective bargaining agreements in place.

2.5.3 Board-Level Co-determination

With regard to corporate governance, board-level co-determination, the third pillar of employee participation, is the most relevant. It also is perhaps the most irritating feature of German corporate law for foreign entrepreneurs, in particular those with an Anglo-American background.

The term 'corporate governance' is used broadly to describe various issues of a company's structure, such as the relationship between a company's management, its shareholders and other stakeholders. Questions relating to how companies should be governed also include the roles, composition and duties of the company's statutory bodies (*Organe*). Depending on the relevant social and economic function, one can make a distinction between a shareholder-controlled corporation model (as is the case in many common law countries) and a model also recognizing the interests of non-shareholder constituencies of the company, especially the interests of employees. Germany is a good example of the latter model, with its detailed legislation on board-level employee co-determination.

Board-level co-determination (*unternehmerische Mitbestimmung*) refers to employee participation on corporate boards, i.e. participation in the company-wide entrepreneurial decision-making process. In the German two-tier board system, distinguishing between the management board and supervisory board, such representation on a board-level pertains to the latter. German law also provides for three regimes of board-level co-determination, which differ as to their scope of application, as well as to the extent of participation rights granted.

2.5.3.1 Coal and Steel Co-determination Act of 1951

The Coal and Steel Co-Determination Act (*Montan-Mitbestimmungsgesetz*) of 1951 applies exclusively to companies of the coal and steel industry in Germany with more than 1,000 employees. In such companies the supervisory board must consist of at least 11 members, five of which are (in effect) appointed by the employees and another five of which are appointed by the shareholders.[143] These ten board members together appoint a neutral chairman. Of the five employee representatives three are appointed by the relevant labor union, while the other two are appointed by the works councils of the respective company—with the labor union having a right of objection. Altogether, this act provides for a full parity of employees in the supervisory board. However, due to the steep decline of the German coal-mining industry since the 1960s, it has lost much of its importance.

2.5.3.2 One-Third Co-determination Act of 2004

The One-Third Co-Determination Act (*Drittelbeteiligungsgesetz*) of 2004 applies to incorporated companies, such as the AG and the GmbH, provided that they employ more than 500 and less than 2,000 employees.[144] In such corporations the employees, by way of election, shall appoint one-third of the members of the supervisory board. This also means that, although limited liability companies generally are not required to have a supervisory board under German corporate law, a GmbH employing more than 500 employees will have to establish such a board to make employee participation possible.

2.5.3.3 Co-determination Act of 1976

The Co-Determination Act (*Mitbestimmungsgesetz*) of 1976 applies to corporate entities outside of the coal and steel sector with more than 2,000 employees.[145]

[143] The Coal and Steel Co-Determination Act stipulates special requirements for the size of the supervisory board deviating from the general rules of Sec. 95 AktG.

[144] As a general rule the statute is applicable regardless of the specific business purpose of the company. However, within the scope of its applicability (more than 1,000 employees, coal and steel) the Coal and Steel Co-Determination Act takes precedence over the One-Third Co-Determination Act.

[145] For a more detailed review see Mertens and Schanze 1979, pp. 75 *et seq.*

In such companies, the supervisory board has to consist of an equal number of shareholders' representatives and employees' representatives.[146] Corporations (as the GmbH) lacking a supervisory board are obliged to establish such a board for the purpose of implementing co-determination.

The Co-Determination Act stipulates a complicated procedure for appointing the employee representatives. A special delegates' assembly has to be installed, the size of which depends on the total number of employees. As the delegates' assembly shall reflect the proportion of top-level executive personnel and lower-level employees in the company, each group sends a certain number of its own delegates. The delegates' assembly elects the employees' representatives. However, only a part of these representatives may be employees of the company; a certain number of the employees' seats has to be staffed with union representatives.[147]

Although, at first glance, this regime provides for a full parity of shareholders and employees, the shareholders are slightly superior. This is owed to fact that, in the (rare) situation of an equality of votes (*Stimmengleichheit*), the chairman of the board—to be elected by a two-thirds majority or by the shareholders' board members alone—has a casting vote. Therefore, this co-determination regime often is described as 'quasi-parity co-determination' (as opposed to the 'full-parity' regime of the Coal and Steel Co-Determination Act).

Finally, the Co-Determination Act also provides for a so-called 'labor director' (*Arbeitsdirektor*) either as an additional member of the management board or—in the case of the GmbH—as an additional managing director. In either case, the labor director is a full manager, enjoying equal rights, and is responsible for social and personal matters. Although, like any other member of the management board she/he is appointed or removed by the supervisory board, the labor director typically belongs to the 'side' of the employees and enjoys the confidence of the employees' representatives.

2.6 Capital Markets Law

Entrepreneurs with a mind to fully utilize the advantages of the legal form of an AG will consider listing the corporation on a stock exchange and/or issuing other kinds of securities in order to obtain new financial resources for further expansion of the business. In such cases, however, the AG is not only subject to the rules of the AktG

[146] By derogation from the general rules of Sec. 95 AktG, the size of the supervisory board depends on the number of employees: in companies with up to 10,000 employees, 12 representatives (six from each side) have to be elected; in companies with between 10,000 and 20,000 employees, 16 representatives (eight from each side) have to be elected and in companies with more than 20,000 employees, 20 representatives (ten from each side) must be elected.

[147] For instance in an AG with 11,000 employees, six members of the supervisory board will be elected by the shareholders' meeting, four by the employees and two members will be appointed by the labor union.

but also has to adhere to the rules and regulations governing the capital markets, the so-called capital markets law. The following section will give some orientation in this complicated subject matter by introducing the basic concepts and sources of capital markets law and by providing three particularly important examples of German capital markets regulation.

2.6.1 Introduction

The term 'capital markets law' (*Kapitalmarktrecht*) refers to the legal rules governing capital markets. It encompasses the totality of all legal rules and principles that regulate the flow of financial means between the investors and the undertakings. The investors supply capital to the undertakings, which supply corporate, governmental or private securities (*Wertpapiere*) in return. Apart from this basic definition, the exact scope of capital markets law is difficult to determine as both the terms 'capital' and 'security' are used in economics, legal and accounting with a variety of meanings, loosely describing different concepts at different times.[148] Moreover, modern capital markets law is subject to constant and often fast-paced changes in order to adapt to the highly dynamic nature of its subject matter. Thus, although the essence of capital markets law is fairly concrete, its boundaries are not at all clear-cut.

2.6.1.1 Objectives of Capital Markets Law

Commonly, there are two different objectives of capital markets.[149]

Ensuring Market Functionality

Capital markets law aims at an effective protection of the functionality of the market as a whole (*Funktionsschutz*). In the interest of the economy as a whole, legislature has to ensure the systemic stability and general efficiency of capital markets as such. In order to safeguard an efficient functioning of a market, legislative means have to secure that it is:

- institutionally efficient, i.e. suitable market institutions exist, to which market actors have unhindered access and which are governed by a set of basic rules providing for its long-term integrity and stability;
- allocationally efficient, i.e. that invested capital is distributed to those undertakings which—from an overall public wealth point of view—need it the most and simultaneously create the highest yield for the investor. Such allocative efficiency implies an adequate degree of transparency and competition in the respective market;
- operationally efficient, i.e. that economic hindrances to an effective market functioning, especially transaction costs, are minimized.

[148] See Davies 1997, p. 234.

[149] For more detail see Heiser 2000, pp. 60 *et seq.*

Protecting Investors

Furthermore, capital markets law also aims at protecting investors (*Anlegerschutz*), which also has two aspects.

First, a capital market 'works' only if and insofar as investors have confidence in its integrity, stability and fairness. Therefore, legislature has to protect the investing public as a whole in order to accomplish an institutional functionality of capital markets. This so-called 'institutional investor protection' (*institutioneller Anlegerschutz*) is primarily effectuated by transparency requirements, e.g. mandatory *ad-hoc* publicity in case of market-relevant developments in the company. Rules pertaining to institutional investor protection frequently are safeguarded by criminal sanctions.

Second, investor protection also refers to legal rules protecting the interests of individual shareholders. Investors are protected as individuals without considering them in their function in the market. This 'individual investor protection' (*individueller Anlegerschutz*) in Germany originates from the practice of German courts which began in the 1970s to award damages to individual investors for malpractice of their market counterparts. In recent decades, however, an increasing number of statutory claims for damages can also be observed.

The boundaries between both aspects, i.e. institutional and individual protection, is often far from being clear-cut. For instance, statutory rules primarily protecting the investing public as a whole may entitle an individual shareholder to damages under Sec. 823 para. 2 BGB if such rules can be considered to at least 'also' serve the individual interests of the materially damaged person. The increasing emphasis of the 'ethical' approach towards investor protection has made the borderlines between the two aspects even more fragile.

2.6.1.2 Sources of German Capital Markets Law

In Germany a single codification of capital markets law does not exist. The relevant rules are spread in a variety of acts of which the Securities Trading Act (*Wertpapierhandelsgesetz, WpHG*) and the Stock Exchange Act (*Börsengesetz, BörsG*) are the most important.[150]

Securities Trading Act

The WpHG contains the fundamental principles and requirements governing transactions on and the behavior of the market participants in the capital markets. The act distinguishes between different 'markets' or 'trading segments' and stipulates special requirements for each segment. The trading segments governed by the WpHG encompass the so-called 'regulated market' (stock exchanges), multi-lateral trading facilities (MTF) (successful examples for such MTFs are *Chi-X* and *Turqouise*), the privately organized open market (e.g. the 'entry-standard' of the *Deutsche Börse AG*) and, finally, the so-called 'systematic internalizers', i.e. traders who regularly and systematically engage in security trading outside of a regulated exchange or MTFs, i.e. over-the-counter (OTC) trading. As a general rule, the WpHG does

[150] An English translation of the most important supervisory legislation is available at www.bafin.de.

not apply to the so-called 'gray' capital market (*grauer Kapitalmarkt*). The gray market is a German specific and is not a capital market in the strict sense, since it is neither coherently organized nor used to trade fungible securitized investments. Financial products commonly traded on the gray market are shares in limited commercial partnerships (*Kommanditgesellschaften*).

Stock Exchange Act

The BörsG mainly contains organizational rules governing the structure of stock exchanges and its trading segments (regulated market, open market). In contrast to the WpHG, the scope of application of the BörsG is limited to the secondary markets: while the WpHG also applies to the pre-IPO and IPO phase of an initial emission of securities, the BörsG is limited to the post-IPO trading of stocks and bonds already placed in the market.

Other National Sources of Law

Further important statutes of German capital markets law encompass the Securities Acquisition and Takeover Act (*Wertpapier- und Übernahmegesetz, WpÜG*), which is of particular importance in the context of M&A transactions and will be explained in more detail later on[151], as well as the Investment Act (*Investmentgesetz, InvG*), the Securities Deposit Act (*Depotgesetz, DepotG*), the Act on the Prospectus for Securities Offered to Sale (*Verkaufsprospektgesetz, VerkProspG*) and the Securities Prospectus Act (*Wertpapierprospektgesetz, WpPG*). Statutory requirements regarding or influencing market behavior are also contained in general statutes. For example, the accounting standards stipulated in Secs. 238 *et seq.* HGB can be considered a part of capital markets law, as they create transparency, thus, enhancing the trust of investors.

Sources of capital markets law ranking below formal acts of the Federal parliament comprise numerous ordinances (*Verordnungen*) clarifying the details of such acts, e.g. the Federal Securities Trading Reporting and Insider List Ordinance (*Wertpapierhandelsanzeige- und Insiderverzeichnisverordnung, WpAIV*) which specifies in detail the pre-requisites and procedure of the notification requirements under the WpHG. Other important sources are the trading regulations issued by the stock exchanges. Finally, in practice, decrees and announcements issued by the German Federal Security Supervisory Authority (*Bundesanstalt für Finanzdienstleistungaufsicht, BaFin*) are of particular importance. Although many of these announcements do not, as such, have an immediate legal effect, they clarify the opinion of BaFin, thus serving as a guideline for issuers and investors.

EU Law

In capital markets law, European legal sources are of particular relevance[152] More than 80% of German capital markets regulations are estimated to be based on EU

[151] See *infra*, Sect. 4.5.

[152] For further detail on the following see Möllers 2010, pp. 133 *et seq.*

legislation.[153] The WpHG, for instance, has mainly been pre-determined by EU Directives.

The purpose of such EU legislation is to further the freedom of capital and the freedom to provide services within the common market. From the introduction of these freedoms in the 1958 Treaty of Rome until the mid-1980s harmonization in this area was left to the European Court of Justice and remained fragmentary. In 1985 the European Commission in its White Paper on the Internal Market declared a shift of focus away from court-led approximation of Member State law based on primary EU law to secondary EU legislation. To this purpose, until 1998 several EU Directives were adopted, including, *inter alia*, the Investment Services Directive which introduced the so-called passport principle, according to which investment firms and banks could provide specified financial services in other Member States on the basis of home state authorization and supervision. These legislative measures mostly adhered to the principle of 'minimum harmonization', i.e. the Member States were obliged to implement the minimum standard as set forth in the Directives but also allowed to stipulate stricter rules in the interest of market participants.

The European Commission in 1999 issued the Financial Services Action Plan, which addressed remaining deficiencies, such as differences between the Member States in several areas due to different national implementing legislation. To assess possibilities of further improving market integration and removing remaining hindrances for the free movement of capital within the Common Market, the Commission instated the so-called 'Committee of the Wise Men', which in 2001 delivered its final report (commonly referred to as 'Lamfalussy report' after the committee's chairman *Alexandre Lamfalussy*).

The Lamfalussy report recommended the introduction of a new four-level 'fast-track' legislative procedure (the so-called 'Lamfalussy process') and the establishment of two committees: a European Security Committee (ESC) and a Committee of European Securities Regulators (CESR) with advisory functions. The main element of the Lamfalussy process is that only the key political decisions are made by the European Council and the European Parliament and are stipulated in a general framework (Level 1), while EU level implementing measures containing the details are implemented by the European Commission with ESC and CESR providing advice (Level 2). Thus, the legislative procedure has been sped-up considerably.[154] In Level 3, the Member States implement the EU rules into national law upon consultation with CESR. The final Level 4 of the Lamfalussy process serves the supervision and fine-tuning of the national implementation and the enforcement of enacted legislation.

[153] See *Frankfurter Allgemeine Zeitung* as of 9 April 2009, p. 11.

[154] An average of 20 months was required to pass the four Level 1 Directives as opposed to an average of nine years for the enactment of a Directive prior to the introduction of the Lamfalussy process; see European Commission, The Application of the Lamfalussy Process to EU Securities Markets Legislation—A preliminary assessment by the Commission services, Commission Staff Working Document as of 15 November 2004.

The Lamfalussy process has led to the adoption and implementation of four central Level 1 Directives: the Market Abuse Directive[155], the Markets in Financial Instruments Directive[156], the Transparency Directive[157], and the Prospectus Directive[158], and numerous Level 2 directives. The result is a dense European legislation which approximates full harmonization and has, in large part, established a level playing field in capital markets regulation. Given the positive experiences, the Lamfalussy process has also been extended to related legislative fields, such as the supervision of banking services, insurances and pension funds and financial conglomerates.

2.6.2 Prohibition of Insider Trading

According to Sec. 14 WpHG market participants must not (1) trade with insider securities on the basis of inside information, (2) disclose or make available such inside information to another person without the authority to do so and (3) recommend another person to trade with insider securities on the basis of their own knowledge of the inside information, i.e. recommending such securities without actually disclosing the information.

'Insider securities' are securities admitted to trading on a German organized market, an organized market in another EU/EEA Member State or which are traded on the open market (*Freiverkehr*).[159] Furthermore, the insider trading rules also apply to other financial derivatives such as stock options, cash-settled equity swaps, financial forward contracts and other forward contracts entailing a commitment to acquire or dispose of securities if both the derivatives/forward contracts and the corresponding securities are admitted to trading on an organized market within the EU or EEA or are traded in the open market.

According to the legal definition of Sec. 13 WpHG, 'inside information' is specific information relating to insider securities or an issuer of insider securities, if such information has not yet been published but would be likely to have a significant effect on the price of the insider security if it were. Information is deemed likely to have such effect if a reasonable investor would take the information into

---

155 Directive 2003/6/EC of the European Parliament and of the Council of 28 January 2003 on insider dealing and market manipulation, OJ 2003 L 96/16.

156 Directive 2004/39/EC of the European Parliament and of the Council of 21 April 2004 on markets in financial instruments, OJ 2004 L 145/1.

157 Directive 2004/109/EC of the European Parliament and of the Council of 15 December 2004 on the harmonization of transparency requirements in relation to information about issuers whose securities are admitted to trading on a regulated market, OJ 2005 L 390/38.

158 Directive 2003/71/EC of the European Parliament and of the Council of 4 November 2003 on the prospectus to be published when securities are offered to the public or admitted to trading, OJ 2003 L 345/64.

159 See Sec. 12 WpHG; an 'organized market' within the meaning of the WpHG is a market which is regulated and supervised by state-approved bodies, is held on a regular basis and is directly or indirectly accessible to the public, see Sec. 2 para. 5 WpHG.

account for investment decisions. A valuation based solely on information about publicly known circumstances is not inside information, even if it could have a significant effect on the price of insider securities.

Naturally, the exact scope and limits of inside information and the prohibition of insider trading can be difficult to determine. In M&A transactions, for example, usually a due diligence review takes place in the course of which the vendor discloses internal documents to the potential buyer. Such disclosure could well be assessed as a violation of Sec. 14 para. 1 no. 2 WpHG (disclosure of inside information to third parties). However, most scholars would argue that such disclosure in the course of a due diligence review does not constitute a disclosure 'without the authority to do so' within the meaning of said provision, since it serves the interest of the company and does not jeopardize the functionality of the market.

2.6.3 Publication of Inside Information

According to Sec. 15 para. 1 sentence 1 WpHG, inside information, which directly concerns a domestic issuer of financial instruments, shall be published without undue delay, i.e. as soon as reasonably possible. The purpose of this so-called '*ad-hoc* disclosure requirement' is to ensure that the public receives the respective information as soon as possible to make insider trading impossible. An issuer is deemed 'directly concerned' within the meaning of this provision if the inside information relates to the developments within the issuer's sphere of activity, e.g. the company enters an M&A transaction. After having published the inside information, the issuer is also obliged to file the information with the competent Commercial Register.

A failure to make a publication in contravention of Sec. 15 para. 1 sentence 1 WpHG, i.e. incompletely, incorrectly or not timely, constitutes an administrative offence under Sec. 39 para. 2 no. 5 lit. a WpHG, punishable by a fine of up to EUR 500,000.00. Furthermore, individual shareholders may be entitled to damages if the information was not published (Sec. 37b WpHG) or the publication was incorrect (Sec. 37c WpHG).

Especially with regard to negotiations in the run-up to M&A transactions, it can be difficult to determine whether and when concrete information is given that triggers the *ad-hoc* disclosure obligation. Of course, the fact that the issuer enters such negotiations does not necessarily mean that an agreement can be reached and that the transaction will actually take place. However, depending on the size of the transaction, the fact that the issuer entered into negotiations can, as such, already be likely to have a significant effect on the stock exchange or market price of the issuer's securities. Moreover, according to Sec. 13 para. 1 sentence 3 WpHG the definition of inside information also applies to future circumstances, e.g. the signing of the M&A contract, if such circumstances may reasonably be expected to come into existence in the future.

In order to protect legitimate business interests, Sec. 15 para. 3 WpHG allows an issuing company to exempt itself from immediate disclosure (*Selbstbefreiung*). According to this provision, the issuer is exempt from the publication requirement if and as long as such exemption is necessary to protect its legitimate interests, provided there is no reason to expect a misleading of the public and the issuer is able to ensure that the inside information will remain confidential. As soon as such necessity is no longer given, the issuer has to effect the publication without undue delay. For instance, the issuer may withhold a publication if otherwise current negotiations would be adversely affected and thus interests of shareholders and investors would be compromised.[160]

2.6.4 Share Ownership Notification Rules

Shareholders of a listed stock corporation whose home county is Germany are required to notify the Federal Security Supervisory Authority and the corporation if they acquire or dispose of shares of that company and their shareholding hereby reaches, exceeds or falls below certain thresholds.[161] According to Sec. 21 para. 1 WpHG the relevant thresholds are 3, 5, 10, 15, 20, 25, 30, 50 and 75% of the total voting rights existing in the company. The notification has to be made without undue delay and within four trading days at the latest. The notification period begins at the point when the shareholder learns (or in consideration of the circumstances must have learned) that her/his percentage of voting rights has reached, exceeded or fallen below the above-mentioned thresholds. Since the law assumes that the shareholder learns of this two trading days after reaching, exceeding or falling below the threshold, a maximum period of six trading days applies. The notification must also be published and filed with the Commercial Register.[162]

In determining whether or not a shareholder reaches, exceeds of falls below a threshold,. voting-rights held by third parties may, under certain circumstances, be attributed to the shareholder in question.[163] For example, according to Sec. 22 para. 1 WpHG shareholdings of subsidiaries are attributed to the parent company for the purpose of the notification requirement; shareholdings of the parent company and the subsidiary are added. The reason for such attribution is to prevent the shareholder from circumventing the notification requirements by means, which—from a strictly formal legal perspective—do not or do not yet constitute a direct shareholding but which have a similar or identical economic effect. Otherwise, for instance, a shareholder holding only 2.9% of the shares of a corporation directly would not be obliged to make a notification although she/he might be entitled to another 27.1% by way of stock options or forward contracts with several banks. If such acquisition rights were not attributed to the shareholder[164], she/he would be able to 'silently' build up a controlling majority without the corporation or other market participants being forewarned.

---

[160] Detailed requirements for this self-exemption procedure are regulated in the WpAIV.

[161] For further detail see van Kann et al. 2007, pp. 255 *et seq.*

[162] See Sec. 26 WpHG.

[163] See Sec. 22 WpHG.

[164] See Sec. 22 para. 1 no. 5 WpHG.

Furthermore, a shareholder whose interests in the respective company reaches or exceeds 10% or more of the voting rights must, within 20 trading days, inform the issuer of the aims underlying the acquisition of the voting rights and of the origin of the funds used to purchase the voting rights.[165] The notification shall, *inter alia,* contain a declaration of whether the aims underlying the acquisition are of strategic or profit-oriented nature and whether the shareholder plans to acquire further voting rights within the next twelve months.[166]

A violation of the notification rules constitutes an administrative offense under Sec. 39 WpHG, punishable with an administrative fee of up to EUR 1 million. Furthermore, according to Sec. 28 WpHG a shareholder who violates the notification requirement looses the right to exercise her/his voting rights for the period of time for which the notification requirements have not been met. In case of a willful or grossly negligent violation and the shareholding concerned exceeding 10%, such loss of rights even extends to six months after the shareholder has finally made the required notification.[167] By implementing such an extended period (*verlängerte Sperrfrist*) the law makes it impossible for a shareholder to intentionally build up a hidden controlling or blocking majority prior to a shareholders' meeting and to exercise her/his voting rights in the meeting by disclosing her/his shareholding immediately before the meeting takes place.

References

Bayer W, Hoffmann T (2011) Die Verbreitung von Inhaberaktien von Deutschen Aktiengesellschaften. http://www.jura.uni-duesseldorf.de/dozenten/noack/Texte/Inhaber.PDF. Accessed 25 July 2011

Davies PL (1997) Gower's principles of modern company law, 6th edn. Sweet & Maxwell, London

Fitzenberger B, Kohn K, Lembcke A (2008) Union density and varieties of coverage: the anatomy of union wage effects in Germany. ZEW—centre for European economic research discussion paper no. 08–012. http://ssrn.com/abstract=1103466. Accessed 25 July 2011

Heiser K (2000) Can capital market law approaches be harmonised with essential principles of company law? Eur Bus Law Rev 11:60–82

Kann J van, Wiedemann K, Just C (2007) German securities trading law—new share ownership notification rules. GLJ 8:255–259

Kronstein H (1952) Collective bargaining in Germany: before 1933 and after 1945. Am J Comp Law 1:199–214

Mertens HJ, Schanze E (1979) The German codetermination act of 1976. J Comp Corp Law Secur Regul 2:75–88

Möllers TMJ (2010) European legal theory and legislation in capital market law. J Interdiscip Econ 20:133–151

Wehler HU (1994) Das Deutsche Kaiserreich 1871–1919. Vandenhoeck und Ruprecht, Göttingen

Wirth G, Arnold M, Morshäuser R, Greene M (2010) Corporate law in Germany. Beck, Munich

[165] See Sec. 27a para. 1 sentence 1 WpHG.

[166] See Sec. 27a para. 1 sentence 3 WpHG.

[167] See Sec. 28 para. 1 sentence 3 WpHG.

Limited Liability Company (*GmbH*) 3

Abstract

In the following chapter, we will present the German corporate form 'limited liability company' (*Gesellschaft mit beschränkter Haftung, GmbH*). We will start with a basic introduction, outline the general characteristics of a GmbH, provide a short historical overview, as well as present recent developments (in particular the company law revision of 2008) and discuss some advantages of the GmbH as a business vehicle. After a discussion of the legal requirements and procedure of establishing a GmbH, including the newly introduced simplified procedure using standard templates and the alternative company form of the 'entrepreneurial company' (*Unternehmergesellschaft, UG*), we will outline the internal organization of a GmbH, explaining the competencies and functioning of its corporate bodies. Following a detailed discussion of the duties and responsibilities of a GmbH's managing director, as well as the most important liability risks, we will turn to the statutory and contractual mechanisms available for protecting minority shareholders, giving several examples of common provisions in the articles of associate, which are used for this purpose in practice. We will conclude our presentation with a brief outline of the grounds and procedure for dissolution and liquidation of a GmbH.

Contents

M. Schulz, O. Wasmeier, *The Law of Business Organizations*,
DOI 10.1007/978-3-642-17793-4_3,

3.1 Introduction

3.1.1 Characteristics of the *GmbH*

The German limited liability company (*Gesellschaft mit beschränkter Haftung, GmbH*) is a highly flexible corporate form ideally suited for medium-sized closely-held enterprises, as well as for use within group structures.

The GmbH may be established by one or more natural or juristic persons. As a corporation (*Körperschaft*) the GmbH is a legal entity separate from its shareholders. Once the GmbH is registered with the Commercial Register—upon which the company comes into legal existence—and the share capital has been paid in, the shareholders may not be held liable for any obligation of the GmbH.[1]

The required statutory minimum share capital is EUR 25,000. There is no maximum amount. In an effort to maintain the GmbH's as an attractive business vehicle against increasing competition from other corporate forms in the European Union (and, in particular the Limited Liability Company from the UK), the German legislator has, however, introduced a new 'subspecies' of the GmbH, the entrepreneurial company (*Unternehmergesellschaft, UG*) which may be founded with a share capital of only EUR 1.00.[2]

In practice, no share certificates are issued and the shares of a GmbH are not publicly traded on the stock exchange. Instead, GmbH shares may be transferred by way of assignment in form of a notarial deed. A list of the shareholders has to be filed with the Commercial Register and is subject to public inspection.

[1] There are very few exceptions to this rule; see *infra*, Sect. 3.5.

[2] Of course, the correct abbreviation would be UG (*haftungsbeschränkt*) (entrepreneurial company (limited in liability)). Section 5a para 1 GmbHG expressly demands that the addition '*haftungsbeschränkt*' be used at all times when conducting business, intended to be a warning signal for third parties. However, for the sake of readability we will hereinafter use the less unwieldy 'UG'.

The GmbH must have at least one managing director (*Geschäftsführer*) who manages the company and represents it in and out of court. In contrast to a German AG, however, the shareholders' meeting is considered the principal decision-making authority: The shareholders' meeting may give binding instructions to the managing director even as to specific issues of day-to-day management. There is no general requirement for a GmbH to establish a supervisory board (*Aufsichtsrat*); however, the GmbH must establish a supervisory board if the company is subject to mandatory German co-determination rules which require that representatives of the workforce become members of the supervisory board. Furthermore, the shareholders may voluntarily stipulate a supervisory board in the articles of association (*Gesellschaftsvertrag*).

3.1.2 The Lasting Success of the *GmbH*—A Historical Overview

In Germany, the limited liability company is traditionally subject to specific regulation in form of the Act on German Limited Liability Companies (*GmbH-Gesetz, GmbHG*). This Act was passed in 1892 in order to fill the regulatory gap between the German AG (as the classic corporate form for large enterprises) on the one hand, and business associations like civil law partnerships (*BGB-Gesellschaften*) or commercial law partnerships (*OHG, KG*), on the other hand. The GmbH is typically designed for medium sized companies with a limited number of shareholders (in contrast to the AG) and with shares not being publicly traded.

As the most frequent company form in Germany, the GmbH has long been a success story, and other countries have adopted the German legislative model, enacting legal frameworks similar to the German GmbHG (e.g. Austria in 1906, England in 1907, France in 1925, Luxembourg in 1933, Belgium in 1935, Italy in 1942, Greece in 1955, and The Netherlands in 1971[3]). In Germany, the legal framework of the GmbH has been subject to numerous amendments by the legislator and has also been supplemented frequently by judge-made law. Thus, although the GmbH faces increasing competition from similar company forms from other European Member States, it still remains by far the most popular corporate form in Germany (Fig. 3.1).

3.1.3 Recent Developments: Reform of the Statutory Framework in 2008

The continuing success of the GmbH as a business vehicle is greatly due to constant legislative efforts to adapt its legal framework to the ever-changing economic circumstances. In recent times, the most significant reform has been the 'Act on the Modernization of the Limited Liability Company Law and the Prevention of

[3] See Beurskens and Noack 2008, p. 1070.

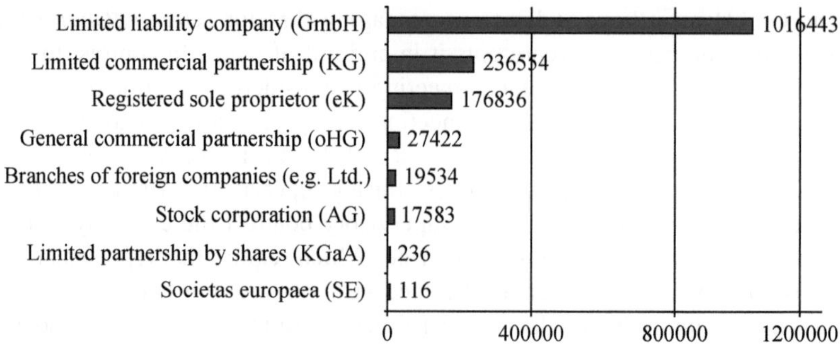

Fig. 3.1 Registered companies in Germany as of 1 January 2010. (Figures according to Kornblum 2010)

Abuses' (*Gesetz zur Modernisierung des GmbH-Rechts und zur Bekämpfung von Missbräuchen, MoMiG*), enacted in 2008.

As its name suggests, the MoMiG aimed at abolishing certain abusive forms of the GmbH (e.g. fraudulently damaging creditors) as well as introducing various new features. This was done in order to keep the GmbH an attractive business vehicle for entrepreneurs given the increasing competition of company forms within the EU.[4] The reform of the statutory framework included, *inter alia*, the following important amendments:

- *Simplifying and Accelerating the Formation and Registration process:* In order to achieve this goal, the formation procedure has been deregulated considerably. Among other steps, the requirement to obtain a governmental approval prior to registration with the Commercial Register (*Handelsregister*) in specific formation scenarios (e.g. forming a GmbH with a business purpose requiring a public license) has been waived. Furthermore, the legislature provided for an option to establish a GmbH by using a standard template form. Thus, the establishment can be achieved more quickly and less expensively because in standard scenarios some notarial costs can be saved.
- *Alternative Business Form:* In the competition of European corporate forms (following the decision of the European Court of Justice (ECJ) in the famous *Centros* case) the German legislature felt the need to improve the options for entrepreneurs regarding the comparatively high statutory minimum capital required to establish a German GmbH. But instead of simply reducing the statutory minimum capital from EUR 25,000 to EUR 10,000 (as was discussed during the legislative debates) or even to EUR 1.00, which would approximate the legal requirements for a private Limited Liability Company formed in England or Wales—the German legislature introduced a third, alternative option: The introduction of a new 'entry-level' GmbH subtype: the so-called entrepreneurial company (*Unternehmergesellschaft, UG*). Such an UG can be formed without complying with the minimum capital provisions applicable to a 'standard' GmbH, but is subject to certain other restrictions. Furthermore, by increasing

[4] For a discussion of this development see *infra*, Sect. 5.1.

the capital to at least EUR 25,000 an UG may, in the course of its existence, be changed to the 'standard' GmbH.

- *Facilitating Share Purchases:* To facilitate share purchases, the legislature has introduced a mechanism for *bona fide* acquisitions of shares from someone who is not the true owner of the shares. The company must file a list of shareholders with the Commercial Register, which is subject to public inspection. In regards to the GmbH, only a shareholder actually registered in this list will be considered a shareholder. The acquisition of shares from a person listed in this list will be considered valid even if such person has not been the correct shareholder for more than three years, or the incorrectness of the list is attributable to the real owner of the shares. Thus, for practical purposes, a potential buyer can rely on the list of shareholders for acquisition purposes if no objection has been raised to an incorrect entry on the list for the last three years.
- *Simplification of Capital Preservation Rules:* Until the MoMiG entered into force in 2008, the Federal Court of Justice (*Bundesgerichtshof, BGH*) took a rather extensive line of interpretation of the capital preservation rules for the GmbH. According to this view, any payment of the company to a shareholder reducing its statutory capital was prohibited, regardless of whether or not the payment was compensated by the company (e.g. by acquiring a fully recoverable claim of (re-)payment, *vollwertiger Gegenanspruch*). Due to this rather formalistic interpretation of the capital preservation rules by the BGH and the lower courts, the ability of a GmbH to extend loans to shareholders was restricted considerably. In practice, this was considered a major obstacle for corporate group financing, e.g. for so-called 'upstream loans' and also for cash pooling agreements. Under the MoMiG the legislature has now returned to the so-called balance sheet approach: payments made by the company to a shareholder are admissible if they are—from a balance-sheet point of view—fully covered by a claim for repayment. Thus, the GmbH may extend loans to a shareholder if the shareholder can objectively be expected to repay the loan. Accordingly, the MoMiG permits intra-group payments made by the GmbH pursuant to a domination agreement or a profit and loss absorption agreement, as well as upstream security provided in favor of a shareholder.
- *Facilitating Shareholder Loans:* Prior to the MoMiG reform, loans and other contributions by shareholders were treated as quasi-equity. Thus, they were prohibited from being repaid if they were given or retained in a crisis of the GmbH, i.e. in a situation in which the company would have been unable to obtain a loan from other creditors at regular market conditions. However, these strict rules had an adverse effect on corporate group financing. Through the MoMiG, the legislature has now considerably relaxed the former case-law regime by clarifying the scope of the statutory provisions: The company may grant shareholder loans at any time; the former distinction between equity-replacing and regular loans has been abolished.[5] However, in the interest of outside creditors, shareholder

[5] Loans of a minority shareholder who holds up to 10% of the shares and is not a director are not affected. Furthermore, there is no subordination of loans if the lender acquires shares of the company while it is already in financial distress as a means of restructuring the entity.

loans will always rank last in priority in the event of an insolvency of the company. The insolvency administrator may set aside repayments made to such loans within one year prior to the insolvency application and demand that the funds be returned to the insolvency estate.

- *Enabling the Relocation of the GmbH's Seat:* The MoMiG reform also provides for the relocation of the GmbH's administrative seat (head office) to another jurisdiction different from that of its registered office. This allows for the GmbH to be used as a business vehicle in other countries while preserving corporate group consistency. To prevent misuse, a valid domestic business address has to be registered with the competent Commercial Register to which mail for the GmbH can be delivered at all times. If a delivery fails, service will be replaced by public notice.
- *Increasing Protection against abusive Practices:* In order to strengthen creditor protection, the MoMiG provides for a number of amendments aimed against abusive practices, in particular in connection with an insolvency of the GmbH: To prevent deliberate withdrawal of assets in the face of impending insolvency, managing directors can now be held liable for payments made to shareholders if such payments led to illiquidity of the company. Furthermore, the reasons for disqualifying managing directors have been extended, now also including a violation of the obligation to file for insolvency, a failure to ensure registrations and notifications in due form, as well as former convictions for fraud, including convictions in other jurisdictions. Finally, in the event of an illiquidity or over-indebtedness of the GmbH, the managing director must immediately file an application for insolvency with the competent court. In order to avoid circumvention, this duty (as well as the resulting civil and criminal liability) passes over to any shareholder if the company at that time does not have/no longer has a managing director.

3.1.4 Advantages of the *GmbH* as a Business Vehicle

The GmbH combines the benefits of a flexible business vehicle suited for small and medium sized enterprises with the advantage of being a separate legal identity with limited liability of its shareholders.

In contrast to other forms of business organization (like sole proprietorship or a partnership) the GmbH has the advantage of limited liability of its founders and shareholders. Furthermore, a GmbH does not necessarily need to be represented by one of its members, but may be represented by external representatives (*Fremdorganschaft*).[6] On the other hand, compared to the German AG, the shareholders of a GmbH have a much stronger impact on management. For example, the shareholders of a GmbH appoint the managing director, but may also remove her/

[6] See Sec. 6 para 3 sentence 1 GmbHG.

him without any cause at any time.[7] Furthermore, the shareholders may issue binding instructions to the management, which are typically passed as so-called 'rules of procedure for the management' (*Geschäftsordnung für die Geschäftsführung*).[8] In addition, establishing a GmbH is less expensive and easier than establishing a German AG.

Another reason for the continuing popularity of the GmbH is the dispositive statutory framework which offers the founders and shareholders of a GmbH a great variety of possible organizational choices. Compared with the much stricter and often mandatory framework for the AG (*Satzungsstrenge*),[9] the GmbHG grants the shareholders a great amount of flexibility in designing and amending the company's articles of association. Thus, the articles and, in principle, all internal issues and relationships may be tailor-made to suit the shareholders' needs (*Satzungsautonomie*).[10]

In addition to the flexible statutory framework set out in the GmbHG, the German courts have developed a number of rules under case law which need to be observed, for example with regard to the liability of the shareholders and managing directors at the time prior to formation of the company (*Vorbelastungshaftung*), the acquisition and use of so-called 'shelf companies' (*Vorratsgesellschaften*), and the doctrine of 'piercing the corporate veil' (*Durchgriffshaftung*), which will be explained later on.[11]

Combining both benefits of flexibility and of limited liability, the GmbH is typically used for smaller or 'closely held' companies and for family businesses. It is also widely found in corporate group structures, since the influence of shareholders facilitates a close management regime throughout the whole group.

3.2 Formation

After the MoMiG reform in 2008, the GmbHG now provides for three options to establish a GmbH. In addition to the traditional 'regular' formation procedures, founders may also now choose to form a GmbH more easily and cost-effectively using a template form of articles of association. Furthermore, apart from founding a fully-fledged GmbH with a share capital of EUR 25,000, entrepreneurs now have the option of establishing a 'Mini-GmbH' (UG) instead.

[7] See Sec. 38 GmbHG.

[8] One example of such rules of procedure is contained in the appendices, see *infra*, Sect. 6.3.2.

[9] See Sec. 23 para 5 AktG.

[10] See Sec. 45 GmbHG.

[11] See *infra*, Sect. 3.5.2.

3.2.1 Regular Formation Procedure

As a corporation, the GmbH is a legal entity separate from its shareholders. A GmbH may be established by one or more natural or juristic persons with a minimum share capital of EUR 25,000. It may be formed by contributions in cash (*Bargründung*), by non-cash capital contribution (*Sachgründung*), by use of a 'shelf company' (so-called 'economic new formation', *wirtschaftliche Neugründung*), or by conversion from another form of business association, e.g. from an AG (*formwechselnde Umwandlung*).

In the first two scenarios, which clearly dominate in practice, a GmbH is formed upon notarization of the articles of association (*Satzung*) by a public notary.[12] The articles of association must contain the name of the company (*Firma*), the domicile or seat of the company (*Sitz*), the business purpose of the company (*Unternehmensgegenstand*), the amount of the share capital (*Stammkapital*), and the numbers and the nominal amounts of the shares subscribed by each founding shareholder (share capital contribution, *Stammeinlage*).[13] In practice, the articles of association are usually attached to the minutes of the notarial formation deed (*Gründungsprotokoll*). The notarial formation deed must be signed by all shareholders of the company.[14] The founding shareholders must subscribe for all share capital contributions of the company. The formation can be carried out by one or more persons.[15]

As in the case of the AG, the GmbH comes into existence as a legal entity separate from its shareholders upon registration in the Commercial Register. Once the GmbH is registered in the Commercial Register, the shareholders are, in principle, not liable for the GmbH's debts (except in exceptional circumstances of 'piercing the corporate veil').

It is permissible and also quite common in practice to establish a GmbH by authorized representatives (*Gründung durch Bevollmächtigte*), e.g. lawyers acting for the GmbH's shareholder(s). For example, if a business entity is considering establishing a GmbH (itself being the sole shareholder of the new company), it would grant a power of attorney to lawyers authorizing them to establish the GmbH on behalf of this business entity. Pursuant to Sec. 2 para 2 GmbHG, such power of attorney also needs to be notarized.[16] The representative(s) may then establish the GmbH on behalf of the founder(s) before a German notary.

[12] See Sec. 2 para 1 sentence 1 GmbHG.

[13] See Sec. 3 para 1 GmbHG.

[14] See Sec. 2 para 1 sentence 2 GmbHG; Secs. 9, 13 German Notarization Act (*Beurkundungsgesetz, BeurkG*).

[15] See Sec. 1 GmbHG.

[16] In case of notarization by a foreign notary or foreign court of law, an additional 'legalization' is required by a representative of the state in which the deed is to be used. This legalization is executed by the competent German consulate official. If a country is a party to the *Hague Convention of 5 October 1961* on the exemption from legalization of foreign public deeds, this legalization is replaced by an *Apostille* (recognition of authentication by the authorities of the state in which the notarization is to be carried out). According to some treaties, the legalization may not always be necessary as, for example, in the case of notarizations by notaries/courts of law in Belgium,

Following execution of the notarial deed, the share capital of the new GmbH has to be paid into a German bank account. The notarial deed will typically include a shareholder resolution regarding the appointment of the first managing director(s) of the company. The GmbHG provides for a minimum statutory share capital of EUR 25,000, of which at least an amount of EUR 12,500 has to be paid upon registration.[17] After the share capital has been paid, the managing director(s) of the GmbH will have to file for registration of the GmbH with the competent Commercial Register by submitting the registration application, the notarial deed, which includes the notarized articles of association and other necessary attachments (e.g. a list of all shareholders). The signatures of the managing directors must be notarized, as well.

In the application for registration of the GmbH, each managing director must confirm that the necessary share capital contributions are at her/his free and unrestricted disposal and that she/he is properly qualified to act as a managing director of a GmbH.[18] After the Act on Electronic Commercial, Cooperative and Company Registers (*Gesetz über elektronische Handelsregister und Genossenschaftsregister sowie das Unternehmensregister, EHUG*) entered into force on 1 January 2007, the necessary documents relating to the formation of a GmbH must be filed electronically with the Commercial Register and, accordingly, all respective registrations need to be published electronically.

3.2.2 Simplified Formation Procedure

The MoMiG has introduced the option of establishing a GmbH or UG in a simplified procedure using a standard template form if the company is formed by cash subscription. The standard form (included as an annex to the GmbHG) contains all necessary formalities for a formation by cash subscription, including formation deed, appointment of one managing director, the most basic provisions of the articles of association, and the list of shareholders.

This simplified formation procedure is intended to accelerate the formation procedure, as the required examination of the formation documents by the register court can be kept to a minimum. As the template form has to be notarized as well, possible cost advantages with regard to notary fees are rather limited.[19]

Denmark, France, Italy and Austria. In case minors participate in the formation of a GmbH, their legal representatives need the consent of the competent Guardianship Court (*Vormundschaftsgericht*) (see Sec. 1822 no. 3, no. 10 German Civil Code, *BGB*). If the legal representative (i.e. parent) is also a founding shareholder, then a special guardian needs to be appointed (Secs. 1629 para 2, 1795, 181, 1909 BGB).

[17] See Secs. 5, 7 GmbHG.

[18] See Sec. 8 paras. 2 and 3 GmbHG.

[19] Founders of a UG using a standard template form will save approximately EUR 150 compared to a regular formation with individual articles. In the event of formation of a regular GmbH through use of the template, there is no saving potential whatsoever.

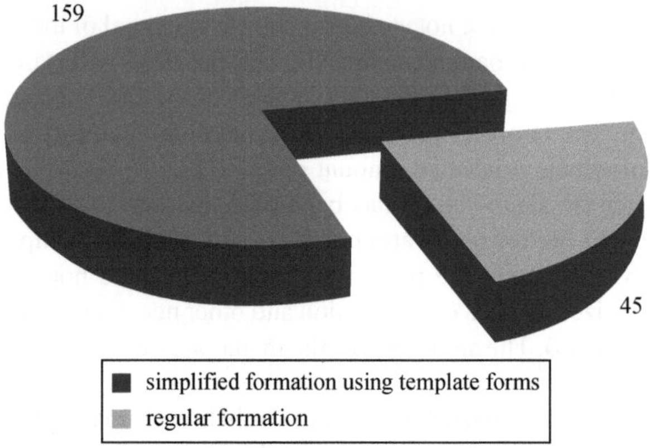

Fig. 3.2 Use of simplified formation procedure. (Figures relate to entrepreneurial companies incorporated in Thuringia as of 15 September 2009; data according to Bayer and Hoffmann 2009b, p. R225; Whether these figures are representative for the whole of Germany remains to be seen; for example Braun and Richter 2010 show that of 246 operating *UG*s formed in the district of the Commercial Register of Lüneburg. Lower Saxony, between November 2008 and May 2011 only 113 (ca. 45%) were established using the template forms.)

The major downturn of this simplified procedure, however, is its lack of flexibility. The content of the template form is compulsory: deviations are not allowed. Therefore, a GmbH formed in this manner may have a maximum number of three shareholders and only one managing director. Further customization, beyond inserting the company's name, its registered seat, its nominal capital and the company's purpose are not permitted.[20] Thus, founders using the template form who wish to make full use of the GmbH's flexibility and want to tailor-cut the articles of association to their specific needs are compelled to amend the articles subsequent to registration and such amendment has to be notarized and registered. Given this effort, shareholders should think twice before using the standard form documents and should consider using the regular formation procedure (Fig. 3.2).

3.2.3 Formation of an Entrepreneurial Company (*UG*)

One of the major new features of the MoMiG has been the introduction of a new company form, the so-called entrepreneurial company (*Unternehmergesellschaft, UG)*. This new sub-type of the GmbH is specifically designed for small and me-

[20] Thus common (and in nearly all cases desirable) provisions cannot be included in the initial articles, including among others, provisions regarding: termination of the company; appointment of more than one managing director; general rules regarding the power of representation of the managing directors, e.g. prohibition or admission of self-dealings; duties to obtain consent for the transfer or retraction of shares; inheritance and succession.

dium enterprises, a fact that has won it the name 'Mini-GmbH' or 'GmbH light'.[21] The UG is not an entirely new company form, but rather a sub-type of the GmbH. Therefore, except for special provisions regarding the minimum share capital,[22] the UG is subject to the same rules and regulations that are applicable to the 'regular' GmbH.

From the perspective of the German lawmaker, the UG can be seen as the German answer to the business form of the UK Limited Liability Company formed in accordance with the Companies Act of England and Wales (hereinafter: Ltd.). As a result of the decisions of the European Court of Justice (ECJ) regarding the Freedom of Establishment, German entrepreneurs have increasingly used the Ltd. as a vehicle for their business by way of incorporating domestic branches of Ltd. registered in the UK. Especially smaller enterprises without the need of significant capital investments have welcomed the new alternative business form, mainly for two reasons: A Ltd. can be established much more quickly and it does not require any minimum share capital.[23] Internet-based service providers actively advertising and offering assistance and translation tailor-cut for German entrepreneurs have promoted this development.[24] As a consequence, the Ltd. has become a business form to be frequently encountered in Germany, especially in the German services sector.[25]

The question of whether and how to deal with this trend has been subject to lengthy discussions both in German politics and academia. According to one view, the mandatory minimum capital requirement of the GmbH should be abolished, arguing that the required amount was arbitrary, since it applied to all companies regardless of their individual risk structure. Furthermore, capital preservation rules only prohibited a reduction of the share capital below the minimum figure by way of payments to shareholders but ordinary operating expenses are not prohibited. Therefore, there was no guarantee that the minimum share capital in its function as an 'equity cushion' was still in place when creditors need it most, i.e. in the case of insolvency.[26] Other commentators proposed at least a reduction of the statutory minimum capital to EUR 10,000, while still others pleaded to leave the minimum capital requirement in place, emphasizing its function for creditor protection and—especially—as a 'test of seriousness'.

[21] For the following, as well as for a detailed comparison between the entrepreneurial company (Unternehmergesellschaft) and the British limited, see Schmidt 2008, pp. 1093 *et seq.*

[22] See Sec. 5a GmbHG.

[23] Although establishment of a limited is considerably less expensive, cost advantages are insignificant as when setting up a branch the most important documents have to be translated and notarized before filing the application with the Commercial Register. When employing a service provider, further annual service fees (e.g. for maintenance of the UK registered office) will accrue.

[24] See for example www.go-limited.de; www.limited24.de; www.go-ahead.de

[25] For a comparison of both company forms see the table at Sec. 5.1.

[26] For the parallel discussion in The Netherlands see Barneveld 2009, pp. 87 *et seq.*

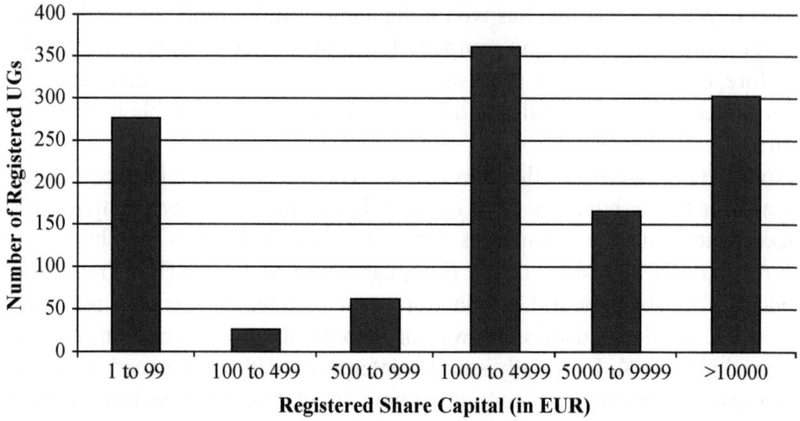

Fig. 3.3 Capitalization of registered entrepreneurial companies as of 31 December 2008. (Data according to Bayer and Hoffmann 2009a, p. 125.)

After a long debate, the German legislature finally opted for a third way. Instead of establishing a 'regular' GmbH with a minimum share capital of EUR 25,000 (half of which has to be paid prior to registration), entrepreneurs may choose to establish a UG for which they may stipulate any minimum capital in the articles from EUR 1[27] to EUR 24,999 (which has to be paid in full prior to registration[28]). The UG, however, must create a legal reserve in its balance sheet which amounts to at least 25% of its annual surplus.[29] Such reserve may not be distributed to the shareholders. If the accumulated reserve reaches the EUR 25,000 threshold the UG will turn into a 'fully-fledged' GmbH.[30] It may also keep the legal company name of *Unternehmergesellschaft* (Fig. 3.3).

So far, the registration numbers indicate that the introduction of the UG has been a success. The legislative aim to provide entrepreneurs with a German business vehicle as an alternative for entry-level businesses has been reached. Although introduced only at the end of 2008, in terms of registrations, the UG has already outpaced the Ltd (Fig. 3.4).

[27] In practice, however, a minimum capital of EUR 1 is rather a theoretical option, since, with a view to the formation costs, immediate insolvency would occur.

[28] See Sec. 5a para 2 GmbHG.

[29] See Sec. 5a para 3 GmbHG.

[30] See Sec. 5a para 5 GmbHG.

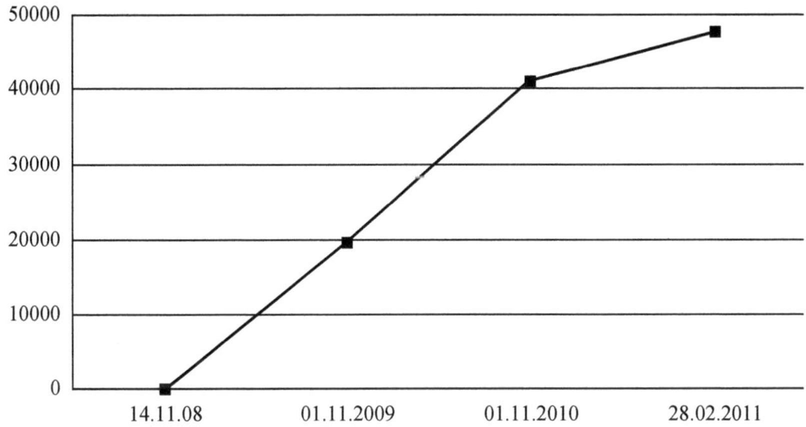

Fig. 3.4 Registered entrepreneurial companies (UG) in Germany. (Data according to *Institut für Rechtstatsachenforschung zum Deutschen und Europäischen Unternehmensrecht Jena*, available at: www.rewi.uni-jena.de.)

3.3 Internal Organization

As mentioned above, the GmbH is a highly flexible business vehicle. With only 87 sections, the GmbHG leaves many issues unregulated, thus leaving a considerable freedom for legal design. Therefore, the GmbH has been characterized as a laudable realization of the idea 'think small first'.[31] It is thus consistent that the rules governing the GmbH's internal organization are not nearly as complex and rigid as the tight legal framework applicable to a German AG.

The GmbH is required to have a shareholders' meeting (*Gesellschafterversammlung*) and at least one managing director (*Geschäftsführer*) as mandatory bodies (*Organe*). And, as indicated above, in certain instances the GmbH must also establish a supervisory board pursuant to specific German co-determination laws. If German co-determination rules do not apply, however, the implementation of a supervisory board is optional. In practice, also an optional advisory board (*Beirat*) is quite often created which, unlike the supervisory board, has less of a control function but rather assumes a more auxiliary, assisting role.

3.3.1 Shareholders' Meeting (*Gesellschafterversammlung*)

The shareholders' meeting has been coined the 'supreme body' of a GmbH.[32] It is the forum in which the shareholders—as owners of the company—meet and make the necessary decisions. Although decisions regarding everyday operative management in practice are often made directly by the managing director(s), certain matters

[31] See Bachmann 2008, p. 1065.

[32] See e.g. Dornseifer 2005, p. 126.

of general importance to the GmbH are reserved for decisions by the shareholders' meeting.[33] Furthermore, the GmbH's shareholders' meeting may closely control the managing directors by giving binding instructions which may regard all matters concerning the company.[34] In practice, managing directors are often bound by 'rules of procedure for the management' in which, among other things, certain management decisions require the prior approval of the shareholders' meeting.[35] The shareholders also have the right to revoke the appointment of managing directors at any time (subject to a restriction of this right in the articles of association).[36]

The shareholders' meeting is convened by the managing director(s) by registered letter with a notice of at least one week.[37] At least one annual meeting must take place to approve the annual account, formally approve the management, and—where applicable—distribute the profits.[38] Further (extraordinary) meetings shall be called whenever the situation of the company so requires.[39] Also, a minority of shareholders holding at least 10% of the total shares of the company may demand a convocation at any time.[40]

General decisions are made by the majority of votes cast[41], and amendments to the articles require a three-quarter majority.[42] Each EUR 1 of a capital share grants one vote to the respective shareholder.[43] Although, as a rule, decisions of the shareholders are made in the meeting, they are also free to decide in writing (letter, fax or email).[44]

---

[33] See Secs. 46, 53 GmbHG; such exclusive competencies include, among others: amendments to the articles of association (incl. capital increases and reductions), approval of annual account, appropriation of profits, appointment and dismissal of managing directors, measures to check and supervise the management, partition and redemption of shares.

[34] In contrast to the AktG, the GmbHG does not provide for an exclusive sphere of competence of the management body regarding day-to-day management; as the GmbH is specifically designed to suit the needs of closely held businesses, there is no mandatory separation of ownership and control.

[35] See Sec. 46 no. 6 GmbHG.

[36] See Sec. 46 no. 5 GmbHG.

[37] See Secs. 49 para 1, 51 para 1 GmbHG.

[38] See Sec. 46 nos. 1 and 5 GmbHG.

[39] See Sec. 49 para 2 GmbHG; such extraordinary convocation is mandatory especially if a balance sheet shows that half the company's share capital has been lost, Sec. 49 para 3 GmbHG. In case of an UG Sec. 5a para 4 GmbHG additionally requires a shareholders' meeting to be summoned if illiquidity is imminent.

[40] See Sec. 50 GmbHG.

[41] See Sec. 47 para 1 GmbHG.

[42] See Sec. 53 para 2 GmbHG.

[43] See Sec. 47 para 2 GmbHG.

[44] See Sec. 48 para 2 GmbHG.

3.3.2 Managing Director (*Geschäftsführer*)

The managing director (*Geschäftsführer*)[45] of the GmbH is responsible for the day-to-day management and representation of the corporation.[46] As such, the managing director carries out any legal measures or other necessary actions appropriate for realizing the purpose of the company. However, in contrast to the *Vorstand* of an AG, the managing director's position and competence is weaker and less comprehensive. The managing director of a GmbH has to comply with the instructions of the shareholders, which may be issued either on a case-by-case basis or more generally through corresponding by-law provisions or rules of procedure for the management. Furthermore, certain matters of critical importance are generally reserved for decisions made by the shareholders' meeting as mandated by law.

The managing director is appointed and removed by a resolution of the shareholders' meeting.[47] The GmbHG defines specific requirements as to the eligibility of persons to be appointed as managing directors: Only natural persons with full legal capacity may be appointed[48]; legal entities are not eligible.[49] In contrast to partnerships, the *Geschäftsführer* of a GmbH does not have to be a shareholder, but may be (and often is) an outsider with special business expertise (so-called *Prinzip der Fremdorganschaft*).[50] Furthermore, the law enumerates a catalogue of criteria which automatically (*ipso iure*) disqualify a person from becoming appointed managing director, such as a final sentence for fraud or similar offences in the last five years prior to her/his appointment.[51]

The managing director is the legal representative of the GmbH. In case of more than one managing director, the general rule is that the company has to be represented jointly by all managing directors.[52] Modifications of this principle, such as stipulating a power of sole representation for one of the managing directors in the articles of association, are quite common in practice. E.g., exemptions from the legal prohibition of self-contracting and multiple representation authority (Sec. 181 BGB) may be advisable, particularly in cases in which the same person is appointed as managing director of several entities in a group of companies. Restrictions of the power of representation have, as a general rule, no effect vis-à-vis third parties. However, if the managing director violates internal restrictions (e.g. she/he concludes a contract without the required prior approval of the shareholders' meeting) she/he may be liable for breach of duty.

[45] A GmbH must have at least one managing director (Sec. 6 para 1 GmbHG); there is no maximum number. For the sake of readability we will use to the singular unless otherwise appropriate.

[46] See Sec. 35 para 1 GmbHG.

[47] See Sec. 46 no 5 GmbHG.

[48] See Sec. 6 GmbHG.

[49] In corporate group structures it is therefore the CEO of the controlling entity, not the controlling entity itself who is appointed as *Geschäftsführer* of a subordinated GmbH.

[50] See Sec. 6 para 3 GmbHG.

[51] See Sec. 6 GmbHG.

[52] See Sec. 35 para 2 sentence 1 GmbHG.

3.3.3 Supervisory Board (*Aufsichtsrat*)

If the GmbH is subject to German co-determination rules, the establishment of a supervisory board is not optional, but mandatory.[53] In other cases, the GmbH may choose to have a supervisory board (*Aufsichtsrat*) by way of establishing this body in the articles of association.[54] Composition and procedure of such an optional supervisory board are regulated in the AktG; the shareholders may, however, exclude certain or all of these provisions and provide for their own rules in the articles of association.

In practice, many GmbHs also choose to have an optional advisory board (*Beirat*), an administrative board (*Verwaltungsrat*) or a shareholders' committee (*Gesellschafterausschuss*) consisting of shareholders' representatives or external experts (such as bankers, lawyers or auditors) appointed by the shareholders. Such boards may have a purely advisory function or may be designed to closely resemble supervisory boards.

3.4 Duties and Liability Risks of the Managing Director

The managing director of a GmbH has many duties and responsibilities to the company itself, to its shareholders and to its creditors. These duties result from statutory regulation, judge-made law, or can be provided for in the articles of association or in the managing director's service agreement with the company. In general, the managing director has to comply with all applicable statutory and judge-made rules, as well as with the instructions of the shareholders and must use her/his best efforts to act in the interests of the company. The following section provides an overview of some important duties and responsibilities of the managing director, as well as an outline of the most important liability risks.

3.4.1 Duties and Responsibilities of the Managing Director

3.4.1.1 Formation and Raising of the Share Capital

As a matter of principle, the shareholders are responsible for raising the registered share capital and the managing director may not be held responsible for any subscribed share capital contribution. However, when filing for registration of the company, the managing director must confirm that the required contributions for the shares (i.e. cash payments or contributions in kind), have been duly made and that they are at the free disposal of the managing directors. If false statements have been

[53] For an overview of the relevant co-determination statutes see *supra*, Sect. 2.5.3.

[54] See Sec. 52 GmbHG.

made in this respect, the managing director may have to pay the missing amounts himself or may be liable to pay compensation.[55]

3.4.1.2 Preservation of the Share Capital

The GmbHG contains strict rules regarding the preservation of the registered share capital which can be summarized as follows: a GmbH may not, neither directly nor indirectly, make payments to its shareholders without full consideration, and may not engage in any other activities which directly or indirectly benefit its shareholders, if such payments or activities would affect the registered share capital of the GmbH.

Although the MoMiG reform introduced certain exceptions to this rule, the general principle still applies. Therefore, every managing director should be familiar with the basic principles of the capital preservation rules as a violation of these provisions may lead to claims for damages by the GmbH and its creditors, and may even lead to criminal penalties under Sec. 266 of the German Criminal Code (*Strafgesetzbuch, StGB*).[56]

In contrast to the situation prior to the MoMiG reform, a payment made to a shareholder is not considered a violation of capital preservation rules provided that the payment is compensated by a full claim for repayment.[57] Accordingly, the managing director may no longer reject a payment to a shareholder by simply pointing out that the payment may cause or increase a deficit balance but rather needs to review the balance on an individual basis. In case of a lack of solvency of the receiver of the payment, the managing director must reject the claim.

Furthermore, the managing director must refrain from making payments to a shareholder if these would lead to the insolvency of the company.[58] Otherwise, the managing director will be liable in the amount of the payments made to the shareholder, unless the managing director—exercising the diligence of an orderly businessman—could not foresee that such payment would lead to the company's insolvency.

3.4.1.3 Accounting Duties

The managing director must ensure that the company's accounts follow proper accounting procedures.[59] The managing director may delegate the performance of the accounting duties to employees or third parties (such as public accountants) but she/he remains responsible for the careful selection and proper supervision of such persons. A violation of accounting duties may not only trigger a managing director's liability but may also be subject to criminal sanctions.

[55] See Sec. 9a para 1 GmbHG.

[56] See Secs. 30 *et seq*. GmbHG.

[57] See Sec. 30 para 1 sentence 2 GmbHG.

[58] See Sec. 64 sentence 3 GmbHG.

[59] The specific accounting duties are set out in Secs. 238 *et seq*. of the German Commercial Code (*Handelsgesetzbuch, HGB*) and Secs. 41 *et seq*. GmbHG.

3.4.1.4 Duty to Prepare and Submit the Annual Accounts

At the end of each fiscal year, the managing director must prepare the company's annual accounts (balance sheet, income statement and annex), as well as the management report.[60] Immediately following these preparations, the managing directors must submit the annual accounts to the shareholders for approval.[61] If the annual accounts are subject to auditing requirements, the managing directors must submit the audited accounts, along with the management report and the auditor's report to the shareholders; the submission has to be effectuated immediately upon receipt of the auditor's report.

The managing directors must electronically file the annual accounts, along with the auditor's qualified or unqualified opinion, with the electronic Federal Gazette (*Elektronischer Bundesanzeiger*)[62] immediately following submission to the shareholders; however, no later than the last day of the twelfth month of the fiscal year following the record date. The managing directors must also electronically file the management report, as well as the management's proposal and the shareholders' resolution regarding the use of profits including the GmbH's net income or net loss, unless such proposal and resolution are included in the annual accounts filed with the Commercial Register. Upon filing these documents with the Commercial Register, the managing directors must immediately publish a notice in the electronic Federal Gazette specifying the name of the Commercial Register and the number under which the documents have been filed.[63]

3.4.1.5 Duty to File Petition for Initiation of Insolvency Proceedings

The duties regarding proper accounting and annual accounts include a duty to closely monitor the financial situation of the GmbH. If the GmbH becomes insolvent or its liabilities exceed its assets, the managing directors must file a petition for initiation of insolvency proceedings or judicial composition proceedings without undue delay, but no later than three weeks following the date it is determined that the company is insolvent or its liabilities exceed its assets.[64]

3.4.1.6 Calling of the Shareholders' Meeting

The managing director must call a shareholders' meeting without undue delay if the balance sheet prepared at the end or in the course of a fiscal year shows that 50% (or more) of the company's registered share capital has been lost.[65]

[60] See Secs. 264 and 289 HGB. Requirements as to the form and contents of the annual accounts of a GmbH are set forth in Secs. 242–256 and 264–289 HGB and in Sec. 42 GmbHG.

[61] See Secs. 264 and 289 HGB. Requirements as to the form and contents of the annual accounts of a GmbH are set forth in Secs. 242–256 and 264–289 HGB and in Sec. 42 GmbHG.

[62] See Sec. 325 para 1 HGB.

[63] The above duties apply to so-called medium-sized corporations as defined in Sec. 267 para 2 HGB.

[64] See Sec. 15a para 1 Insolvency Code (*Insolvenzordnung, InsO*).

[65] See Sec. 49 para 3 GmbHG.

If an entrepreneurial company (UG) is formed with a registered share capital below the minimum registered share capital of EUR 25,000, the managing director must call a shareholders' meeting in case of the UG's imminent inability to pay its debts.[66]

The managing director must also call a shareholders' meeting whenever it appears to be reasonably necessary to protect the interests of the company.[67]

3.4.1.7 Duty of Disclosure towards the Shareholders

The managing director is obliged to provide information about the company's matters to every shareholder on request and to grant access to books and documents, unless there is a reasonable reason to believe that the shareholder will use the information in a harmful way and cause considerable disadvantages to the company.[68]

3.4.1.8 Duties Arising in Connection with Entries in the Commercial Register

The managing director also has numerous duties arising in connection with filings of the Commercial Register required by law. The managing director must file all applications to be entered in the Commercial Register on behalf of the GmbH, such as the application for registration of the company,[69] registration of the managing directors,[70] registration of any amendments to the articles of association,[71] registration of any capitalization measures,[72] registration of the dissolution of the company[73] and registration of the stipulations regarding legal representation of the GmbH.[74]

Furthermore, upon effect of each change in the identity of the shareholders or the size of their shareholding, the managing directors shall, without undue delay, submit to the Commercial Register a list of the shareholders signed by the managing directors, providing the surname, first name, date of birth and place of residence of the shareholders, as well as the nominal amounts and the serial numbers of their share capital contributions.[75] Managing directors who breach their duties are jointly and severally liable to the creditors of the company for the damages arising therefrom.

---

66 See Sec. 5a para 4 GmbHG.

67 See Sec. 49 para 2 GmbHG.

68 See Sec. 51a GmbHG.

69 See Sec. 7 GmbHG.

70 See Sec. 39 GmbHG.

71 See Sec. 54 GmbHG.

72 See Secs. 57 *et seq.* GmbHG.

73 See Sec. 65 GmbHG.

74 See Secs. 10 para 1 39 para 1 GmbHG.

75 See Sec. 40 para 1 sentence 1 GmbHG.

3.4.1.9 Duties Related to Social Security and Taxes

The managing director, among other things, is obliged to fulfill specific fiscal duties (e.g. monthly preliminary sales tax and wage tax returns) and to arrange for the timely preparation and filing of the annual tax return.[76] If the GmbH has employees for whom social security contributions have to be made, the managing director must also file and transfer the social security contributions properly and on time.

3.4.1.10 Information on the Business Letterhead

The managing director must ensure that the company's business letterhead contains the following information: the company's legal form and principal place of business, the court at which the Commercial Register is maintained and the Commercial Register number, the last name and at least one fully spelled-out first name of each managing director; if the GmbH has a supervisory board, the last name and at least one fully spelled-out first name of the chairman of the supervisory board.[77]

3.4.1.11 Other Duties

As far as the managing director is authorized to manage the company's business, it is her/his duty to manage it as appropriately and as beneficially as possible. The managing director shall keep himself informed about the company's situation and take appropriate organizational steps to enable her/him to be up to date concerning the economic and financial situation of the company at all times.

In addition to the specific legal duties outlined above, the managing director is also bound by certain fiduciary duties. For instance, she/he must take the company's interests into consideration and protect them (i.e. she/he may not use the company's assets solely for her/his private purposes nor is she/he allowed to take any personal advantages related to business activities, for example in the form of commissions or bribes). Such fiduciary duties also include duties of confidentiality, non-competition and the duty to make use of so-called 'corporate opportunities' only in the interest of the company.

3.4.2 Liability Risks of Managing Directors

The managing director has exposure to a variety of liability risks in connection with her/his duties to the GmbH and third parties. The most important liability scenarios are outlined below.

3.4.2.1 Liability to the Company

The managing director of a GmbH must exercise the care of a prudent businessman when managing the affairs of the company.[78] Managing directors who violate their duties are jointly and severally liable to the company for the resulting damages.[79]

[76] See Sec. 34 of the German Tax Code (*Abgabenordnung, AO*).

[77] See Sec. 36 GmbHG.

[78] See Sec. 43 GmbHG.

[79] See Sec. 43 para 2 GmbHG

There are two exceptions to this rule, the first (and practically more important) one being the so-called 'business judgment rule'. According to this rule, a managing director is not considered to have violated her/his duties when making a business decision if she/he (at the time of her/his decision) reasonably believed to be acting in the best interest of the company on the basis of sufficient information.[80] The second exception involves cases in which the managing director has followed the binding instructions of the shareholders' meeting.

If these exceptions do not apply, the managing directors are liable for damages, in particular, in the event of payment from funds necessary to preserve the registered share capital, or in the event of a forbidden purchase by the GmbH of its own shares.[81] In addition, the managing director must reimburse the company for any payments made in breach of duty following the date on which the GmbH becomes insolvent or the date on which it is determined that the GmbH is over-indebted.[82] The managing director is also liable for any payments made to shareholders which lead the company to becoming insolvent,[83] and the managing director can only avoid this liability if she/he constantly monitors the financial situation of the company.

Finally, the managing director of the GmbH may also be liable to the company for damages for illegal actions under the German law of torts (delicts).[84] Examples include committing criminal offences (e.g., for breach of fiduciary duty or fraud) or willfully causing damages to the company.

3.4.2.2 Liability to the Shareholders

The managing director is liable to the shareholders for any unauthorized repayments of capital contributions from the GmbH's registered share capital.[85] Managing directors are also liable if they violate the right of membership (*Mitgliedschaftsrecht*) of a shareholder, for instance by violating the competences of the shareholder's meeting or by ignoring the obligation of equal treatment owed towards the shareholders.[86]

Moreover, the managing director may be subject to liability under German tort law for providing false information at the time of formation of the company or at any time thereafter.[87] Thus, managing directors are liable for all emerging damages

---

[80] The business judgment rule is based on the decision of the Federal Court of Justice in the case ARAG v. Garmenbeck as of 21 April 1997, see BGHZ 135, 244.

[81] See Sec. 33 GmbHG.

[82] See Sec. 64 sentence 1 GmbHG. However, this liability does not apply to payments being made after this date if these payments have been made using the diligence of an orderly businessman, see Sec. 64 sentence 2 GmbHG.

[83] See Sec. 64 sentence 3 GmbHG

[84] See Secs. 823 *et seq*. BGB.

[85] See Sec. 31 para 6 GmbHG.

[86] See Sec. 823 para 1 BGB; the membership right of a shareholder is regarded as 'another absolute right' in the sense of the provision.

[87] See Sec. 9a para 1 GmbHG.

if they do not disclose a non-cash contribution which was planned as being covert when registering the GmbH.

Finally, if the managing director violates her/his duty to file a signed list of shareholders immediately after a change in shareholders has taken place or the amount of the respective shareholder's shares has been effected, she/he can be held liable by those shareholders whose shareholdings have changed.[88]

3.4.2.3 Liability to Creditors of the GmbH

The managing director may also be liable to creditors of the company, for example, in the following cases:

Liability by Estoppel based on Pretended Authority

If the managing director does not disclose in business negotiations that she/he is acting on behalf of the GmbH, she/he may be personally liable by virtue of her/his *prima facie* authority to be the contractual partner (*Rechtsschein*). The managing director may, for example, be subject to so-called liability by estoppel, if she/he gives her/his contractual partner the impression of acting as an independent businessman (instead of the GmbH she/he represents), and thereby induces her/his contractual partner to rely upon personal liability of a natural person.

Liability for *Culpa in Contrahendo*

The managing director may also be personally liable for a breach of specific precontractual duties (so-called *culpa in contrahendo*) when representing the GmbH in negotiations with third parties.[89] The principles of *culpa in contrahendo* would generally apply to the GmbH as the contracting party being represented by the managing director. However, under specific circumstances also managing directors may be held personally liable, if, e.g., during the negotiations of the contract, the managing director provided the other party with a personal guarantee for the correctness and completeness of her/his statements thereby causing the other party to place special reliance on her/him personally. For example, the managing director may be personally liable for damages incurred by a creditor, who relies upon incorrect representations of the managing director, entered into an agreement with the GmbH after the GmbH had already become insolvent. If the GmbH later fails to perform its obligations, the managing director may be held liable for so-called 'reliance damages'.

Belated Filing for Insolvency

If the managing director culpably breaches her/his duty to file a petition for initiation of insolvency proceedings, the managing director may be personally liable for damages to creditors of the company.[90]

[88] See Sec. 40 para 3 GmbHG; damages to these shareholders may occur from the possibility of *bona fide* purchase of shares by non-shareholders, introduced by MoMiG.

[89] See Secs. 311 para 3, 241 para 2, 280 para 1 BGB.

[90] Sec. 823 para 2 BGB in conjunction with Sec. 15a InsO.

Product Liability

If the GmbH manufactures products, the duties of proper design, manufacture, and instruction, as well as product monitoring duties generally apply to the GmbH as the manufacturer. The managing director, however, is personally subject to specific organizational duties. She/he must ensure that the company does not market defective products and is thus responsible for the organization of product safety and quality management procedures. The managing director is also responsible for providing appropriate product information and appropriate product monitoring procedures. The managing director may be personally liable for a violation of these organizational duties if she/he knew or should have known that the products were defective and failed to prevent, or failed to prevent the distribution of such products in a timely manner, or failed to recall such products when such recall was required.

3.4.2.4 Liability for Violations of Competition Laws by the GmbH

The managing director may also be held personally liable for anti-competitive practices of the GmbH if she/he personally breaches competition laws or if she/he participates in the breach or infringement of unfair competition, antitrust laws or intellectual property rights, either directly or indirectly. Even if the managing director did not actively participate in such violations, her/his personal liability may result if she/he had knowledge of and, thus, an opportunity to prevent the violations. The managing director further must ensure that other managing directors, employees and third parties acting on behalf of the company do not violate unfair competition or antitrust laws or infringe intellectual property rights.

3.4.2.5 Personal Liability under Tort Law

In addition to the reasons for liability described above, the managing director may also be subject to liability under German tort law vis-à-vis the company's creditors. The managing director may, for example, be held liable under Sec. 823 para 2 BGB together with certain provisions of the StGB which were specifically designed for the protection of business assets (fraud, breach of fiduciary duty, embezzlement) if the managing director recklessly causes damage to a business partner of the GmbH, e.g. by deceiving such a business partner with regard to a financial crisis of the company. In addition, if the managing director fails to comply with certain provisions of environmental law or with data protection laws, the managing director may be held liable under Sec. 823 para 2 BGB.

Pursuant to Sec. 826 BGB, the managing director may also be liable for willfully causing damage to a third party in a manner contrary to public policy. For example, if the managing partner intentionally deceives such third party with regard to the insolvency of the GmbH at the time the agreement is executed or intentionally delays filing the petition for initiation of insolvency proceedings, she/he will be personally liable to the creditors.[91]

[91] In case of a negligent belated filing she/he may be liable under Sec. 823 para 2 BGB in conjunction with Sec. 15a InsO instead.

3.4.2.6 Liability to Tax Authorities and Social Insurance Agencies

A managing director is also liable for any willful or grossly negligent violation of the company's duties to pay taxes and social insurance contributions. The managing director incurs liability, for example, if she/he fails to file the company's tax returns in a timely manner or if she/he fails to pay payroll taxes. The managing director is also liable if she/he fails to satisfy outstanding tax liabilities in the same proportion as other liabilities of the company in the event of the GmbH's insolvency.

The managing director is also liable for failing to pay social insurance contributions owed by employees to social insurance agencies. In addition, a failure to do so is considered a serious criminal offense.

3.4.3 Joint Responsibility/Joint and Several Liability

If several managing directors have been appointed, they are jointly and severally liable,[92] provided that each managing director meets the respective requirements for liability.[93] This is usually the case if a duty is breached by joint action or joint omission of the managing directors. If the managing director did not personally breach a duty, she/he is generally liable only if she/he has breached her/his duty of supervision with regard to the remaining managing directors. Each managing director has a duty to supervise the remaining managing directors in the performance of their responsibilities within their area of responsibility. Thus, each managing director is required to ascertain on a regular basis whether the other managing directors are properly performing the responsibilities assigned to them. If the reliability of one managing director is in doubt, each of the other managing directors is required to intervene and to return the relevant areas to the management board as a whole. To the extent that particular duties fall within the area of responsibility of one particular managing director, the other managing directors are, nevertheless, subject to particularly stringent and extensive duties of supervision and control. If they realize that a legal duty has been breached, they must immediately take the initiative and solve the problem.

If there is more than one managing director, there will often be a case assignment plan (*Geschäftsverteilungsplan*) describing the scope of duties and activities for each managing director. Such a case assignment plan may limit the liability risks of a managing director as long as she/he adheres to the duties described therein. However, she/he may still be liable for other duties if she/he has violated her/his duty of control regarding the performance of the other managing directors.

[92] See Sec. 43 para 2 GmbHG.

[93] E.g. in case of a liability under Sec. 826 BGB the respective shareholder would be required to have acted intentionally.

3.4.4 Statute of Limitations

Most claims asserted by the GmbH against the managing director are subject to a five-year limitation period.[94] It is irrelevant whether the breach in question was negligent or willful. The limitation period applies to claims based on a breach of duty arising under corporate law, as well as claims based on a breach of duty arising from the managing director's employment agreement.[95]

The five-year limitation period (specified in Sec. 43 GmbHG) begins as of the time the damage resulting from the breach of duty occurs, regardless of the company's knowledge. In contrast, the three-year limitation period (specified in Sec. 195 BGB) begins only as of the time the company gains knowledge of the damage and the party that has caused the damage.[96]

3.4.5 Summary—Managerial Duties and Liability Risks

Duties and responsibilities of the managing director of a GmbH in particular include:

- Monitoring raising and preserving the minimum share capital;
- Filing all necessary applications for the GmbH with the competent Commercial Register;
- Calling of shareholders' meetings;
- Monitoring the financial situation of the GmbH and, in the case of insolvency, filing for insolvency proceedings without undue delay;
- Fiduciary duties, in particular, confidentiality, non-competition, making use of 'corporate opportunities' in the interest of the GmbH.

Liability risks arise especially from:

- Claims of the GmbH;
- Claims of the GmbH's creditors;
- Claims for delayed insolvency proceedings;
- Claims for payments following the GmbH's insolvency;
- Claims of tax authorities/social insurance agencies.

3.5 Shareholders' Liability

The GmbH, as well as the AG are both corporate entities which are legally separate from their shareholders. Following registration with the competent Commercial Register, in principle only the respective company's assets may be used to satisfy

[94] See Secs. 9b para 2, 43 para 4 GmbHG.

[95] If a breach of duty also constitutes a tort, the tort claim is subject to the limitation provisions of Secs. 195, 199 BGB, even if the underlying tort involves a breach of duty arising under corporate law.

[96] See Sec. 199 para 1 BGB.

the claims of the company's creditors. Thus, the risk of shareholders being held personally liable is principally limited to their capital contribution; any other personal liability is excluded.

There are, however, some important exceptions from this general rule, which may roughly be divided into two categories: First, there are statutory provisions which explicitly stipulate a personal liability of a shareholder violating her/his duties and obligations under the law. Second, there are specific cases of 'piercing the corporate veil' developed by the German courts.

3.5.1 Statutory Provisions Stipulating Personal Liability

Statutory law may explicitly provide for a personal liability of a shareholder vis-à-vis the company or its creditors in cases in which a limitation of liability is unjustified since the shareholder has violated specific statutory obligations. The most important examples include:

- Tort liability for providing false or incomplete information at the time of formation of the company or at any time thereafter.[97]
- Compensation of damages which arise from the shareholder's willfully or grossly negligently impairing the company through contributions or start-up costs.[98]
- Reimbursement of payments received in violation of the capital maintenance rules of Sec. 30 GmbHG.[99]
- Contingent liability of all other shareholders in case a payment made to another shareholder in violation of the capital maintenance rules of Sec. 30 GmbHG cannot be retrieved from the recipient but is necessary to satisfy the company's creditors.[100]
- If the company no longer has a managing director, the obligation to file for insolvency immediately upon the company's becoming illiquid or over-indebted automatically passes on to the shareholders by operation of the law. In this case, the shareholders are liable for damages suffered by third parties resulting from a belated filing.[101]

[97] See Sec. 9a para 1 GmbHG; such false information may in particular relate to the value of a contribution in kind.

[98] See Sec. 9a para 2 GmbHG; examples are contributions in kind which are of no use to the company or stipulating excessively overrated start-up costs in the articles of association.

[99] See Sec. 31 para 1 GmbHG.

[100] See Sec. 31 para 3 GmbHG.

[101] See Secs. 64 GmbHG, 823 para 2 GmbHG, 15a InsO.

3.5.2 Piercing the Corporate Veil

The term 'piercing the corporate veil' relates to exceptions from the general rule that only the company may be held liable for its obligations vis-à-vis its creditors, i.e. cases in which the 'corporate veil' of the GmbH may be 'pierced' resulting in the shareholders being liable in person. Such personal liability is mainly relevant in cases where shareholders neglect their duties or abuse the limitation of liability offered by the statutory design of the GmbH.

Since there is no statutory provision which specifically provides for a 'piercing of the corporate veil', the relevant principles have been developed by the German courts on a case-by-case basis.

3.5.2.1 Substantial Undercapitalization (*Qualifizierte Unterkapitalisierung*)

The group of cases under the heading of 'substantial undercapitalization' comprises fact patterns in which companies have been utterly under-resourced, i.e. inadequately capitalized, by the shareholders. Even though various regulations regarding capital protection already exist in order to secure a creditor against loss, there is still a need to extend this creditor protection because the current regulations are not deemed to be adequate.

As a general rule, the shareholders can freely determine the amount of share capital, provided it is not less than EUR 25,000 in the case of a GmbH (Sec. 5 GmbHG), and not less than EUR 50,000 in the case of an AG (Sec. 7 AktG). Beyond these minimum share capital requirements, neither the AktG nor the GmbHG prescribes that a company should have adequate equity capital in proportion to the business purpose of the company. Due to the general difficulties of determining the appropriate capital of a company, the risk of inadequate capitalization has to be accepted.

However, under exceptional circumstances, namely if the share capital *a priori* or at a time after the formation of the GmbH proves to be utterly inadequate for the business purpose of the company, its size, and economic activities—as set out in the articles of association—then shareholders may be held personally liable if the company later becomes insolvent. Such personal liability is considered to be justified from the point of view that the shareholders have created the false impression of a sufficiently resourced business entity. Any contractual partner should be able to assume that a company actively engaged in market activities is equipped with sufficient financial assets.

However, claims for damages based on a scenario of 'substantial undercapitalization' will usually not prove to be successful in legal practice because so far no legal rules nor reliable economic methods exist to verifiably define what 'adequate capitalization' means for an individual business entity. Furthermore, only those shareholders who have recognized (or at least who could have been reasonably be expected to recognize) such undercapitalization and its potential consequences could be held liable. Therefore, a liability resulting from 'substantial undercapitalization' will be relevant only in exceptional, evident cases.

3.5.2.2 Commingling of Assets (*Vermögensvermischung*)

A so-called 'commingling' of the shareholders' and the company's assets may, under certain circumstances, also justify the personal liability of the shareholders.

The separation of corporate assets on the one hand and the assets of the shareholders on the other is an indispensable prerequisite for the limitation of liability. Thus, personal shareholder liability may be assumed if the two spheres of property cannot be separated from each other, for example, due to a false accounting practice. Besides that, opaque accounting or other tactics to manipulate the allocation of the assets may lead to the personal liability provided that such dubious tactics prevent the control of the compliance with regulations regarding capital protection. The 'corporate veil' is 'pierced' essentially only with regard to those shareholders who caused the confusion or at least had actual knowledge of it and only in cases where the satisfaction of creditors cannot be obtained by the company.

3.5.2.3 Abuse of the Corporate Form (*Rechtsformmissbrauch*)

Another (and probably the most important) factual pattern which has been considered by the courts to justify personal liability of the shareholders, is an abuse of the corporate form. It should be noted, however, that it is, in principle, legitimate for entrepreneurs to form a separate legal entity solely for the purpose of enjoying the benefit of limited liability. Therefore, further factual circumstances are required in order to pierce the corporate veil.

For instance, if companies are established only for the purpose of collecting debt in order to create a 'shield' against creditors' claims, the courts might well disregard such a structure and hold the shareholders of such a company personally liable for any claims of the company's creditors.

3.5.2.4 Destructive Interference (*Existenzvernichtender Eingriff*)

In some recent decisions, the German Federal Court of Justice has further elaborated the case law on 'piercing the corporate veil' by introducing a new group of cases dealing with a shareholder's destructive interference with the company (*existenzvernichtender Eingriff*). Broadly speaking, this new concept is based on the idea that a shareholder may neither abuse the separate corporate personality of the GmbH, nor the limited liability of the GmbH's shareholders.

While the German Federal Court of Justice had initially defined the liability on the grounds of destructive interference as a liability in and of itself, the Court recently explained the legal basis of this liability more precisely by stating that the liability would directly arise from an application of Sec. 826 BGB (conduct *contra bonos mores*).

Broadly speaking, such liability requires a wilful and harmful interference by the shareholder, i.e. any intentional conduct that results in the inability to pay off its debts. Under such circumstances, a shareholder may not claim the privilege of limited liability and, consequently may be held directly liable.

Examples of destructive interference include, for instance, (1) the transfer of material assets from the company to a shareholder, (2) allocating the risks or losses of a certain business operation to a certain group company while at the same time allocating all of the opportunities, benefits or profits to another group company, (3) cash-management within a group of companies depriving the subsidiary of the liquidity necessary to meet its obligations, and (4) measures in connection with the integration into a group of companies (e.g. transfer of material business operations to other group companies; upstream guarantees).

However, since this form of piercing the corporate veil has been designed as a narrow exception, its application is restricted to interferences involving risks and disadvantages for the GmbH which, from an *ex ante* point of view, are clearly disproportionate to the potential opportunities, profits or benefits to be gained, and are therefore highly likely to result in the destruction (i.e. insolvency) of the GmbH. Consequently, cases of mere mismanagement do not fulfil the requirement of a wilful and harmful destructive interference.

Summary: Cases of 'Piercing the Corporate Veil'

- Substantial undercapitalization (*qualifizierte Unterkapitalisierung*): In the case of substantial undercapitalization, companies have been utterly under-resourced by the shareholders.
- 'Commingling' of assets (*Vermögensvermischung*): Personal liability may be assumed if the corporate and personal spheres of property cannot be separated from each other.
- Abuse of the corporate form (*Rechtsformmissbrauch*): Evident abuse of corporate form to the detriment of the company's creditors.
- Destructive interference (*existenzvernichtender Eingriff*): Willful conduct *contra bonos mores* which foreseeably results in the destruction (i.e. insolvency) of the company to the detriment of its creditors.

3.6 Protection of Minority Shareholders

In this section we will look at some key issues of protecting minority shareholders (*Minderheitenschutz*), with special focus on the GmbH.

3.6.1 Articles of Association—General Issues

As indicated above, the legal framework of a GmbH offers much more flexibility than that of an AG. The articles of association (*Gesellschaftsvertrag*) of the GmbH may, in particular, be tailored to the specific needs of the shareholders, provided that the minimum statutory requirements regarding the content of the articles of association (set out in Sec. 3 GmbHG) are met. Pursuant to this provision, the articles of association must contain the name and registered office of the company, the objects of the company, the amount of the registered share capital and the amount of shares, as well as their nominal value subscribed by each shareholder. Besides the prescribed mandatory contents, the GmbHG leaves a great deal of leeway for further optional provisions, e.g. for establishing an advisory board or for specific clauses protecting minority shareholders.

3.6.2 Clauses to Protect Minority Shareholders

3.6.2.1 Need for Supplementary Protection

In contrast to the stockholders of an AG, shareholders of a German limited liability company do not have the same level of statutory minority protection. However, a similar need for minority protection rules often arises since many issues, such as the management of the GmbH (see Sec. 47, para 1 GmbHG) are subject to majority voting requirements. This means that a minority shareholder can be easily overruled.

On the other hand, compared to a stockholder in an AG, it is more difficult for a GmbH shareholder to leave the company. GmbH shares (unlike shares in partnerships) are, in principle, freely transferable.[102] Any sale of such shares does, however, require notarization.[103] Section 15 para 5 GmbHG defines special requirements necessary for the transfer of GmbH shares, in particular regarding approval. Such restrictions on the transferability of GmbH shares are, in practice, very popular (so-called *Vinkulierung*). In contrast to the transfer of stock of an AG, there is no organized public market or market price for GmbH shares (in contrast to a stock exchange where stock of an AG can be traded daily). A GmbH shareholder is, therefore, typically bound more strongly to the GmbH than the stockholder to the AG.

For this reason, it is often either desirable or advisable to implement additional protective measures for minority shareholders in the articles of association.

3.6.2.2 Overview of the Minority Protection Rules for GmbH Shareholders

Following is a brief outline of statutory and judge-made minority protection rules for GmbH shareholders.

Statutory Minority Protection

Section 50 GmbHG entitles shareholders, whose shares together amount to at least one tenth of the share capital, to request that a shareholders' meeting be called. If such request is not complied with, the minority shareholders may themselves convene the meeting pursuant to Sec. 50 para 3 GmbHG.

In addition, Secs. 51a and 51b of the GmbHG grant each shareholder the right to receive information on the affairs of the company to be provided by the managing directors, as well as a right to inspection of the company's books and records.

[102] Sec. 15 para 1 GmbHG.

[103] Sec. 15 paras. 3 and 4 GmbHG.

Finally, Sec. 53 GmbHG requires a majority of three quarters of the shareholders' votes cast for any amendment of the articles of association in order to protect minority shareholders; the regular 'simple majority' of Sec. 47 para 1 GmbHG is not applicable.

Minority Protection developed in Case Law

In addition to the statutory protection of minority shareholders outlined above, there also are minority protection rules developed by the German courts.

Since the so-called *ITT* decision of the German Federal Court of Justice[104], the courts have imposed a duty of loyalty on the majority shareholder to take the minority shareholder's interests into consideration. Thus, the shareholder majority may only intervene in the rights of minority shareholders if it is in the interest of the company; furthermore, they must balance the necessity and proportionality of such intervention. In effect, the courts have defined certain requirements for majority intervention into minority shareholder rights.

3.6.2.3 Minority Protection through Clauses in the Articles of Association

Finally, minority shareholder protection can also be achieved by a variety of drafting options in the articles of association, some examples of which are outlined below (with 'Shareholder A' being used as a minority shareholder).

Restriction on the Transferability of GmbH Shares

Restrictions on the transferability of GmbH shares (*Vinkulierung*) are a popular way of making a change to the existing GmbH shareholders difficult (thereby also protecting minority shareholders if their consent is required). As a result, the transferability of such GmbH shares is made subject to the approval of the shareholders' meeting or other executive bodies.

Example

'Each disposal of shares or parts thereof, including the sale, assignment in trust (*treuhänderische Übertragung*) and each other encumbrance is only permissible with the prior approval of the shareholders' meeting with unanimous consent. Any disposal occurring without such approval shall be null and void.'

Restriction on the Revocation of Managing Directors

Pursuant to Sec. 38 para 1 GmbHG, the appointment of a managing director is revocable at any time. The articles of association may, however, restrict the right of revocation of the managing director.

[104] BGHZ 65, 15, 5 June 1975, II ZR 23/74– *ITT*.

Example

'The managing directors may only be removed from their office for cause.'

Example

'Shareholder A is appointed as managing director for life [until the age of 65]. His removal can only take place for cause.'

Position of Managing Director as a Special Privilege

The minority shareholder may be assigned the position of managing director by virtue of a special right or privilege[105], which may only be withdrawn with her/his personal consent.

Example

'Shareholder A is managing director by virtue of a special privilege. This privilege shall [not] pass to A's legal successor. Shareholder A can only be removed from office for cause.'

Special Privilege for Sole Management or Representation

In addition, to the position as managing director, the minority shareholder may also be assigned the power of sole representation or sole management of the GmbH as a special privilege.

Example

'Shareholder A is entitled as a special privilege to *manage* the company alone for as long as A is managing director of the company. This privilege shall [not] pass to A's legal successor. Shareholder A is entitled as a special privilege to *represent* the company alone for as long as A is managing director of the company. This privilege shall [not] pass to A's legal successor.'

Right to Appoint or Nominate Managing Directors

If the minority shareholder himself/herself does not wish to become managing director herself/himself, but would like to exercise influence on the person chosen as managing director, then a 'right of appointment' (*Bestellungsrecht*) or a 'right of nomination' (*Benennungsrecht*) can be included in the articles of association.

---

[105] See Sec. 35 BGB.

Right of Appointment

The 'right of appointment' (*Bestellungsrecht*) gives the minority shareholder the right to appoint the managing director directly himself without the need for a shareholders' resolution.

Example

'By virtue of a special privilege, Shareholder A may suggest a candidate to be appointed as managing director. Shareholder A alone is responsible for the removal of the person elected by her/him, unless an important reason within the meaning of Sec. 38 para 2 GmbHG exists to warrant the removal from office of this managing director.'

Right of Nomination

In the case of the so-called 'right of nomination' the minority shareholder is granted a binding right of nomination to propose a managing director. The appointment of the managing director then takes place on the basis of a shareholders' resolution. The co-shareholders are, however, normally obliged to vote in favor of the person nominated.

Example

'By virtue of a special privilege, Shareholder A may suggest a candidate to be appointed as managing director. The appointment takes place on the basis of a shareholders' resolution. With respect to this shareholders' resolution, the co-shareholders are obliged to vote in favor of the person nominated by Shareholder A, unless an important reason exists to the contrary within the meaning of Sec. 38 para 2 GmbHG.'

Example

The co-shareholders may only withhold their vote in favor of the nominated person for reasons relevant to and in the interest of the company.

Consent Requirements in Favor of the Minority Shareholder

Despite not being directly involved in the management of the company, minority shareholders can be kept informed about important business matters by means of consent requirements set out in the articles of association (*Zustimmungsvorbehalte)*. The advantage of having such consent requirements is that any amendment to, or termination of, such consent requirements requires a shareholders' resolution with a majority of three quarters of the votes cast (Sec. 53 para 2 sentence 1 GmbHG).

Consent requirements may also be laid down in separate rules of procedure for the management.

Example

'The shareholders can only release a managing director from the limitations of Sec. 181 BGB by means of a unanimous shareholders' resolution.'

Example

'The managing directors are obliged to follow the instructions of the shareholders and, in particular, to comply with any Rules of Procedure introduced by them and to carry out any business requiring the shareholders' approval only with such approval.'

Increase of Number of Votes

Irrespective of the amount of the nominal value of her/his share in the company, a (minority) shareholder may be granted a (special) right to exercise a certain number of votes.

Example

'Each EUR 1 of a share carries one vote. Notwithstanding the foregoing, each EUR 1 of the shares held by Shareholder A carries [•] votes.'

Veto Right

(Minority) Shareholders may—again as a special company law privilege—be granted a veto right for certain decisions.

Example

'The management needs the express prior approval of the shareholders' meeting for all business transactions which go beyond the ordinary course of business. This must be resolved with simple majority of the votes cast but, in any case, with the consent of Shareholder A.'

Casting Vote

Individual (minority) shareholders may also be granted the casting vote in the case of a tie.

Example

'In the event of a tie, where resolutions are to be passed with a simple majority of the votes cast and result in a tie (*Patt-Situation*), Shareholder A shall be entitled to cast a second vote.'

3.7 Dissolution and Liquidation

The legal reasons for dissolution of a GmbH, as well as the procedural rules regarding its liquidation are almost identical to those applicable to an AG. According to Sec. 60 GmbHG, a GmbH has to be dissolved if one of the following reasons apply:

- Expiration of the 'lifetime' of the company as stipulated in the articles of association;
- Resolution of the shareholders' meeting deciding to dissolve the company;
- Initiation of insolvency proceedings;
- Rejection to initiate insolvency proceedings due to a lack of assets;
- Declaration of the Commercial Register court that the articles of association have been found to be incomplete or invalid in essential points;
- Order of deletion due to a complete lack of assets.

The dissolution has to be registered in the Commercial Register and is published by the liquidators and the register court. The notice is combined with an invitation to outstanding creditors to file their claims with the liquidators.

From the moment of dissolution, the corporation's remaining existence serves the exclusive purpose of liquidating its assets, satisfying its creditors from the proceeds, and distributing the remains to the shareholders. According to Sec. 70 GmbHG the liquidators are responsible for winding up the company, i.e. to terminate current transactions, to discharge and perform all liabilities and obligations and to turn its assets into cash. For this purpose the liquidators acquire full and exclusive power of representation by operation of the law.

Creditor protection is ensured by Sec. 73 GmbHG which determines that the so-called 'waiting year' (*Sperrjahr*) has to be observed: no liquidation proceeds may be distributed until at least one year after the third and final notification of the creditors was published. After all claims have been satisfied, the liquidator's remuneration has been paid and any remaining proceeds have been distributed to the shareholders, the company is deleted from the Commercial Register, whereby the liquidation is completed and the GmbH 's legal existence finally comes to an end.

References

Bachmann G (2008) Introductory editorial: renovating the German private limited company—special issue on the reform of the GmbH. GLJ 8:1063–1068

Barneveld J (2009) Legal capacity and creditor protection—some comparative remarks. In: Zaman et al (eds) The European private company (SPE): a critical analysis of the EU draft statute. Intersentia, Antwerpen, pp 81–102

Bayer W, Hoffmann T (2009a) Die Unternehmergesellschaft (haftungsbeschränkt)—eine erste Bilanz. GmbH-Rundschau, pp 124–125

Bayer W, Hoffmann T (2009b) Die Musterprotokoll-Unternehmergesellschaft (haftungsbeschränkt). GmbH-Rundschau, pp R225–R226

Beurskens M, Noack U (2008) The reform of German private limited company: is the GmbH ready for the 21st century? GLJ 9:1069–1092

Braun S, Richter J (2010) Gründungsaktivitäten im Handelsregisterbezirk Lüneburg: Eine empirische Studie zur Unternehmergesellschaft. http://www.gmlg.de/32.0.html. Accessed 25 July 2011

Dornseifer F (2005) Germany. In: Dornseifer F (ed) Corporate business forms in Europe. Sellier, Munich, pp 211–294

Kornblum U (2010) Bundesweite Rechtstatsachen zum Unternehmens- und Gesellschaftsrecht. GmbH-Rundschau, pp 739–748

Schmidt J (2008) The new Unternehmergesellschaft (Entrepreneurial Company) and the Limited —a comparison. GLJ 9:1093–1108

Corporate Acquisitions in Germany

4

Abstract

In this section, we will provide a brief overview of mergers and corporate acquisitions (M&A) in Germany. First, we will outline so-called 'private' M&A transactions, focusing, in particular, on the acquisition of shares of a German limited liability company (*GmbH*). To this purpose, after introducing the possible types of transaction, we will describe the typical steps in such acquisition process and discuss briefly specific problems, which an entrepreneur intending such transaction should be aware of. Thereupon, we will turn to the so-called 'public' M&A transactions, outlining the typical procedure and the most important requirements of the Securities Acquisition and Takeover Act (*Wertpapiererwerbs- und Übernahmegesetz*). We will conclude our presentation with an overview of the German rules on the squeeze-out of minority stockholders, as a typical and major topic in public M&A transactions.

Contents

M. Schulz, O. Wasmeier, *The Law of Business Organizations*,
DOI 10.1007/978-3-642-17793-4_4, © Springer-Verlag Berlin Heidelberg 2012

4.1 Introduction

Compared to Anglo-Saxon countries, relatively few German companies are listed on a stock exchange. Many companies, notably the famous *Mittelstand* entities, are owned by families, foundations, other groups of individuals, financial investors or other companies. Most of these companies are in the legal form of a limited liability company (*GmbH*), which—unlike a stock corporation (*AG*)—cannot be listed on a stock exchange. Due to this structure, most corporate acquisitions in Germany choose the form of private M&A rather than public M&A.

The term 'mergers and acquisitions' (M&A) is a general term used for all different types of corporate acquisitions, including management buy-outs, joint ventures etc. M&A can be divided into two main categories: private M&A, where the buyer negotiates with the seller (or several known sellers) the acquisition of a business. In contrast, a public M&A transaction refers to the acquisition of a stock-exchange listed company.

There are no specific statutes governing private M&A. The general legal framework for the acquisition of goods regulated in the German Civil Code (*Bürgerliches Gesetzbuch, BGB*) will apply. In addition, as far as possible, the parties to an M&A transaction will try to develop their own set of rules within the framework of the sale and transfer agreement.

4.1.1 Case Study

Case Study

Following extensive market research, B has discovered that *M-GmbH*, a German limited liability company, registered and domiciled in Munich, is producing car components (mainly for the German car industry) which appear to be quite similar to those manufactured by A. B therefore thinks that *M-GmbH* would complement A's business portfolio perfectly and that a takeover of *M-GmbH* would be a significant way of getting a foot in the German market.

B asks C to develop a takeover strategy for *M-GmbH*, including detailed comments on the following issues:

- What type of transaction would appear advisable?
- What are typical steps in the acquisition process?
- B also wants to know the procedure and potential problems associated with a due diligence of *M-GmbH*. He wants C not only to explain the purpose and procedure of a due diligence for *M-GmbH*, but also wants to know about any risks associated with a due diligence and any possible ways of protecting himself from such risks.

4.2 Types of Transaction

From a buyer's perspective, the acquisition of a company is often carried out in order to improve the buyer's competitive position and strengthen its position in the market (e.g. improving its strategic position, entering into a new market etc.). From a seller's perspective, on the other hand, reasons for selling a company can include streamlining the portfolio (e.g. by selling group companies outside of the core business areas), plans for restructuring within the group or, in the case of family-owned businesses, problems regarding successors.

Principally, there are two ways in which to acquire the business of an existing German GmbH: the purchaser may buy the shares of the GmbH (a 'share deal'; this term is actually also used in the German language) or she/he may acquire the company's assets (an 'asset deal'). In the case of a share deal, the buyer will, within the corporate frame of the existing GmbH, automatically acquire all of the target company's assets, liabilities, obligations etc. when purchasing the shares. In the case of an asset deal, the buyer will only acquire the specific assets, liabilities etc., as identified and described individually in the Share Purchase Agreement.

4.2.1 Share Deal

A share deal is a much simpler method of acquisition compared to that of an asset deal, the latter requiring much more detailed documentation. In a share deal, all assets, rights and liabilities of the target company remain in the target company which passes to the buyer with the transfer of shares. In the case of shares of a GmbH, there is a statutory notarization requirement (see Sec. 15 paras. 3, 4 Limited Liability Companies Act, *GmbHG*). Therefore, if the target is a GmbH, the sale and purchase (along with all side agreements), as well as the actual transfer of the shares must be notarized.

Under statutory law, the transfer of shares in a GmbH does not require the consent of the other shareholders or the company. However, the articles of association may provide that the consent of all or certain shareholders or a majority of shareholders or the company must be obtained. If the articles provide that the consent of the company is needed (*Vinkulierung*), then the consent is granted by the directors. This is done to allow the GmbH—and its shareholders—control over who will become a new shareholder.

4.2.2 Asset Deal

An asset deal, by which the purchaser acquires all assets agreed upon of the target company, may sometimes be preferable for tax reasons. Furthermore, the buyer may wish to acquire only certain assets of the target company and be able to exclude certain liabilities of the target company. However, negotiating, concluding and carrying out an asset deal can be quite a complex procedure. Under German law, a great degree of detail is required since all assets, rights, liabilities etc. have to be very accurately described in the sale and purchase agreement. If moveable assets are sold, each item must be accurately listed. If claims have to be transferred, the underlying transaction and the name of the debtor have to be designated. All other rights and obligations and also any intangible assets, such as goodwill etc., have to be listed as accurately as possible. In each case, all assets, rights and liabilities require individual specification and transfer.

Furthermore, the transfer of any contract or liability requires the consent of the other contractual party. Since a business is likely to have concluded a multitude of ongoing contracts—from the important lease agreement for the factory halls to the rather less relevant supply agreement for the office coffee machine—both seller and buyer have to agree with all the relevant contractual parties that the agreement will be transferred to the buyer, including all rights and obligations such as warranty claims, payment obligations etc.

Pursuant to Sec. 613a of the German Civil Code, when acquiring a business, the purchaser automatically takes over all of the employees unless they exercise their right to object to the transfer of their employment contract. This means that neither the seller, nor the purchaser of the business may terminate existing employment contracts merely as a result of the transfer of the business.

The buyer automatically assumes all rights and obligations of the existing employment relationships at the time of the transfer. However, slavery having been abolished some time ago, each employee can object to her/his transfer to the buyer. In order to enable the employees to exercise their right to object to the transfer of business, the seller or the buyer must notify the employees prior to the business transfer. An employee who wishes to exercise her/his right of objection to the business transfer must notify her/his employer by no later than one month following receipt of this notification of transfer. If she/he objects, her/his employment relationship will not be transferred to the buyer and will remain with the seller. In this case, the seller may terminate the employment contract if there is no other vacant position for the employee. It is, therefore, particularly important that the prospective buyer review all labor law issues before signing the sale and transfer agreement.

4.3 Typical Steps in the Acquisition Process

For all but the smallest companies, there is an established process for selling companies in order to get a high price for the seller. This so-called 'limited auction process' is described below. This is followed by a description of the process where the seller only negotiates with one individual buyer.

4.3.1 Auction Process

4.3.1.1 Initial Phase

In a limited auction process, the seller—often with the help of a financial advisor—first identifies potential buyers of the business. These are approached with a short (often only two-page) document called 'teaser' to gauge whether they are interested in an acquisition, essentially based on publicly available information at that time. If the potential bidder indicates interest, she/he has to sign a confidentiality agreement which ensures that any information about the target company and the sales process will remain confidential.

4.3.1.2 Information Memorandum

In order to keep some competition for the target, the seller usually allows several bidders into this phase. Only when the confidentiality agreement is executed will the bidder get access to additional information about the target. First, the bidders receive a so-called 'information memorandum' which contains detailed financial information about the target company, including some of the recent financial statements and also the planned financials for the coming years. The information memorandum also includes a detailed description of the company's business and market. The purpose of the information memorandum is to put the bidder into the position to decide, on the assumption that the information memorandum is correct, on the purchase price it is prepared to offer.

Following the distribution of the information memorandum, the seller expects information from each bidder regarding the indicative purchase price such bidder is prepared to pay. Then, the seller will allow a limited number of bidders into the next stage of the process. This decision will be based, of course, on the indicative purchase price offered, but also on other parameters such as the plans for the business, the certainty that such bidder will ultimately agree to acquire the target, and any special terms and conditions such bidder requires for the share purchase agreement.

4.3.1.3 Due Diligence

The bidders which make it into the next round enter the due diligence phase. The buyer regularly carries out a so-called 'due diligence procedure'. This process is also Anglo-American by descent but, again, has become common practice in M&A transactions even in Germany.

'Due diligence' describes a process of information-gathering and detailed preparatory review of a target company, by which the buyer aims to get a clear idea of the potential chances and risks involved in the purchase of the target company. Since the buyer often requires a very detailed insight for the due diligence exercise, it is paramount for the seller that the information about the target remains confidential; this is another purpose of the confidentiality agreement already signed by the parties at the initial phase of the process.

From the buyer's perspective, the due diligence should serve the following purposes:

- Gathering and verifying information about the target company;
- Analysis of the relevant risks of the transaction/deficiencies of the target company;
- Deciding whether to continue or abandon the negotiations;
- Estimating the value of the target company. Basis for negotiating the purchase price;
- Forming the basis for negotiations of warranties to be given by the seller;
- Forming the basis for negotiations with banks if the purchase price has to be financed.

The due diligence procedure typically involves a detailed review of all relevant data of the target company, including the following:

- Review of the target company's economic situation ('Commercial Due Diligence');
- Review of the financial situation ('Financial Due Diligence');
- Review of the tax situation ('Tax Due Diligence');
- Review of the legal situation ('Legal Due Diligence');
- Review of any other relevant circumstances (e.g. environmental risks, 'Environmental Due Diligence').

The resulting 'Due Diligence Report' will then form the basis for the sale and purchase agreement.

4.3.2 Negotiations with One Bidder Only

If there is only one potential buyer, there is less need for a structured sale process. Seller and potential buyer may already know each other, or get to know each other without the help of an investment bank. Usually, seller and buyer will also execute a confidentiality agreement. In some cases, however, the seller commits to exclusivity in favor of the buyer, i.e., the seller promises not to negotiate with any other potential buyer for a specified period of time. Such exclusivity may induce a buyer to spend time and effort on due diligence and negotiations.

A seller typically makes her/his choice of purchaser by way of a so-called 'Letter of Intent'. This legal concept, originating from the Anglo-American legal system, has become common practice in transactions in the USA. It sets out the results of negotiations already reached between a potential buyer and the seller and contains a 'declaration of intention', in other words, a Letter of Intent by the buyer regarding the acquisition of the target company. The Letter of Intent often forms the basis for later contracts.

Following the Letter of Intent, the buyer usually commences the respective due diligence exercise (see above).

4.3.3 Key Elements of the Share Sale and Transfer Agreement

The sale and transfer of the shares is regulated by a share sale and transfer agreement. Depending on the complexity of the transaction, the share sale and transfer agreement will often be quite a voluminous document. In any case, the share sale and transfer agreement will contain the following key elements:

- Agreement by which the seller offers to sell and transfer the shares (including all ancillary rights of the shares) to the buyer with effect from a certain date and acceptance of such offer by the buyer.
- Amount of the purchase price and specification of the time when the purchase price shall be due (see Sect. 4.3.3.1 below).
- Warranties and indemnifications given by the seller (see Sect. 4.3.3.2 below).
- Any covenants given by either party (see Sect. 4.3.3.3 below).

4.3.3.1 Purchase Price

The purchase price may be a specific figure. In this case, the purchase price is usually based on the last balance sheet date, and all profits and losses after such balance sheet date are taken over by the buyer. This means that the target company shall be transferred to the buyer in such state as it was at the last balance sheet date, i.e. without any dividend payments or capital measures following such date. For the seller who still owns it between the last balance sheet date and completion date, the target company is thus treated like a locked box—which is why this purchase price structure is called a 'locked box' structure.

Often, however, the purchase price is agreed only as a formula, containing a base purchase price and a method of calculation by which the base purchase price is to be adjusted. This is often used when the purchase price reflects the correct market value at the time the transaction is completed, which is usually later than when the share purchase agreement is signed. In this case, the parties agree that they will establish a balance sheet of the target company at the time of completion (so-called 'closing balance sheet'), with the base purchase price being increased or decreased by certain positions from such balance sheet. Obviously, such closing balance sheet does not exist at the time of signing of the share purchase agreement; the agreement, therefore, needs to carefully spell out the exact parameters for the closing balance sheet including a mechanism for resolving disputes.

In some cases, notably when seller and buyer cannot agree on the prospects of the business, an earn-out is agreed. In this case, the purchase price will be increased if the target company performs at a certain level following the transfer of shares.

4.3.3.2 Warranties and Indemnities

The warranties and indemnifications given by the seller are a particularly important issue during the negotiation process and also in the process of drafting the share sale and transfer agreement. The share purchase agreement almost always excludes all statutory warranty provisions; therefore, the contractual warranties and indemnities are essentially the only comfort for the buyer. Typical warranties and indemnities include:

- Warranty that the shares are validly owned by the seller, free from any third party rights and freely transferable (this warranty is almost always given).
- Warranty that no insolvency of the target is pending or threatened.
- Warranty that the last financial statements were set up in accordance with generally accepted accounting principles and statutory law (weak balance sheet warranty) and give a true and fair view of the financial and earnings situation of the target (strong balance sheet warranty).
- Warranty that certain information regarding assets, material contracts, employees, intellectual property rights, litigation and compliance is correct.
- Warranty that the data room on which the due diligence of the buyer was based is correct and does not omit material information.
- Indemnity for all taxes prior to completion of the transaction.
- Indemnity for environmental risks.

Which of these warranties and indemnities (other than the first one) are agreed upon depends on the target company and the negotiation position of the parties. In any case, the share purchase agreement limits the financial exposure of the seller from these warranties to a certain amount and also specifies a time period when the warranties will lapse. Knowledge of the purchaser about defects, including the knowledge which the purchaser may have learned from its due diligence or from the financial statements, may void warranty claims with respect to such defects.

4.3.3.3 Covenants

The covenants usually contain the provision that the seller commits to certain behavior with the target for the time until completion of the transaction. Usually, this is essential to carry on the business in the ordinary course, where specified extraordinary measures require the consent by the buyer. The buyer, on the other hand, covenants to procure any necessary approvals (notably merger control approval) of the transaction.

4.3.4 Completion of the Transaction (Closing)

Some time will pass between the conclusion of the sale and transfer agreement and its completion, i.e. transfer of shares or assets, payment of the purchase price, meeting of conditions specified in the sale and transfer agreement etc. The sale and transfer agreement typically specifies the date of completion (*Übertragungsstichtag*, closing date), i.e. the date when all rights and obligations pass from the seller to the buyer and vice versa.

The steps necessary to complete the transaction may cover a wide range of issues such as the receipt of approvals (e.g. by the supervisory board, public authorities such as the Cartel Office etc.), the spin-off of subsidiaries, the termination of cash pooling agreements etc. These measures are often defined as 'conditions precedent' of the agreement and the transaction will only be completed if these conditions precedent have been fulfilled.

4.3.5 Post-Closing Integration/Restructuring

Post-closing integration is a more difficult issue in the case of an asset deal, where every individual asset and liability has to be transferred to the buyer. In particular, with respect to contracts, this may become a lengthy process. In both share and asset deals, the buyer will have to monitor the deadlines for representations and warranties given by the seller.

4.4 Specific Problems

4.4.1 Financing

Not all buyers have the necessary cash to pay for an acquisition. In particular, financial investors, but also other buyers, draw on debt financing to pay the purchase price for a company. In this case, the seller has a vital interest that the buyer will eventually be in the position to pay the purchase price—this means that the debt financing already has to be agreed upon when the share purchase agreement is signed.

4.4.2 Merger Control Issues

A prospective buyer must also take potential merger control issues into consideration. Depending on the size/volume of the transaction, a corporate acquisition may, under merger control law, be subject to approval by public authorities, e.g. the Federal Cartel Office (*Bundeskartellamt*). Under the Act Against Restrictive Trade Practices (*Gesetz gegen Wettbewerbsbeschränkungen, GWB*) German premerger control requires that the Federal Cartel Office must be informed of a merger before its completion. By way of an informal notification, the Federal Cartel Office will approve proposed mergers giving no cause for concern within a period of one month from their notification.

Buyer and seller are not allowed to complete the transaction (e.g. merger) before the end of the investigation by the Federal Cartel Office. In the case of cartel law infringements, the transaction will be considered void and the Federal Cartel Office may impose a fine on each party. Signing the sale and transfer agreement will not be treated as an infringement if the agreement is subject to a 'condition precedent' and the Federal Cartel Office is notified of the planned transaction, and it does not prohibit it. Therefore, the potential buyer (or her/his advisors) will also have to closely examine the applicability of anti-trust regulations in preparation for the sale and transfer agreement.

Provided that certain turnover thresholds are met, some transactions may fall under the remit of the EU Commission for merger approval instead of the German Federal Cartel Office. The process is, in principle, similar on the European level. Furthermore, businesses which are active in several countries may require merger control approval in all such countries, which can require serious efforts of the anti-trust specialists involved.

At completion, the bank providing the debt financing often requires collateral from the target group.

4.4.3 Other Regulatory Matters

Depending on the business sector of the target, the acquisition—in particular when done by way of an asset deal—may require additional public approvals. In the case of an asset deal, some public permits will automatically transfer to the new owner, i.e. the buyer, but others will not. Some branches such as banks and financial institutions will need to have their shareholders approved by the regulator, which means that a buyer has to get approval prior to acquiring the relevant business. Buyers from outside Germany may in theory be blocked if the acquisition poses a threat to public order and security—but in practice, no acquisition has ever been blocked on these grounds.

4.5 Introduction to Public Takeovers

We would like to conclude our outline on corporate acquisitions in Germany with a brief introduction to public takeovers, i.e. the German legal regime for takeovers of publicly listed companies. Public takeovers in Germany are regulated by the Securities Acquisition and Takeover Act (*WpÜG, Wertpapier- und Übernahmegesetz*, hereinafter 'Public Takeover Act'), which came into effect on 1 January 2002. In 2006, Germany passed amendments to the Public Takeover Act when implementing the EU Takeover Directive[1]. Among other things, the German implementation regulation permits target companies to opt in to the EU rules on the prohibition of frustrating actions (i.e. any action of the management board or the supervisory board which could prevent the success of the offer), and introduced new takeover-related squeeze-out and sell-out procedures. Minor amendments, especially regarding the

[1] Directive 2004/25/EC of the European Parliament and of the Council of 21 April 2004 on takeover bids, OJ L 142/12 as of 30 April 2004.

scope of acting in concert, came into force in August 2008; further changes regarding notification requirements will come into effect on 1 February 2012.

The Public Takeover Act contains detailed rules on public offers, the obligation to launch a mandatory offer, exemptions from that rule and the supervision of public offers and acquisitions of control over German listed companies by the German authorities. A public offer/bid is mandatory if a bidder has acquired a controlling interest of more than 30% in the target company). The Public Takeover Act is supplemented by a number of ordinances (*Verordnungen*) such as the Public Takeover Act Offer Ordinance (*WpÜG-Angebotsverordnung*), containing rules for supplementary information to be provided in offer documents and pricing rules for takeover offers and mandatory offers. In addition, certain provisions from the German Stock Corporation Act (*Aktiengesetz, AktG*) and the German Securities Trading Act (*Wertpapierhandelsgesetz, WpHG*), dealing with insider issues, are of relevance for public takeovers.

4.5.1 Scope of the Public Takeover Act

The Public Takeover Act generally applies to all public offers for shares in German stock corporations (*Aktiengesellschaften, AGs*) or (though much less frequently) for shares in German partnerships limited by shares (*Kommanditgesellschaften auf Aktien, KGaAs*) whose shares are listed on a regulated stock exchange in Germany or a Member State of the EU.[2] Under certain circumstances, the Public Takeover Act also applies to public offers for shares of companies incorporated in the European Economic Area (EEA) whose shares are listed in Germany but not in their home jurisdiction.

The Public Takeover Act not only regulates so-called takeover bids, i.e. bids for listed companies targeted at the acquisition of control, in other words at least 30% of the shares of the target company, 'acquisition of control'.[3] Rather, it also applies to all other bids for listed companies where the bidder intends to acquire only part of the shares and mandatory bids. All these public offers must comply with certain minimum requirements regarding, e.g., transparency, content, offer price, disclosure requirements and the equal treatment of stockholders in the target company.

4.5.2 Requirements for the Bidding Process

4.5.2.1 Mandatory Offer

The main purpose of a mandatory offer pursuant to the Public Takeover Act is to protect the minority stockholders of the target company against a new owner who might use its controlling interest to the detriment of the minority. The mandatory

[2] See Sec. 1 Public Takeover Act.

[3] See Sec. 29 Public Takeover Act.

offer gives the minority stockholders the opportunity to sell their shares at a certain minimum price. As stated above, a mandatory offer to all stockholders is always triggered if the bidder acquires a 'controlling' interest in the target company.[4] The Public Takeover Act defines 'controlling interest' as having been achieved if a bidder acquires, directly or indirectly, at least 30% of the voting rights.[5] When calculating the 30% threshold, the bidder's own voting rights, and such voting rights attributed to the bidder according to the Public Takeover Act, must be taken into account.[6]

Pursuant to the Public Takeover Act, a stockholder must publish the fact that it has acquired control of a target vis-à-vis the target company and the Federal Financial Supervisory Authority (*Bundesanstalt für Finanzdienstleistungsaufsicht, BaFin*). Such publication must be made without undue delay but, in any case, by no later than seven calendar days after the stockholder(s) became aware of the acquisition of control.[7]

4.5.2.2 Offer Document

In the offer document, which is a necessary part of the bidding process, the bidder must provide the stockholders of the target company with all information necessary to decide whether or not to accept the bid.[8] The framework for the content of the offer document is set out in the Public Takeover Act and the Public Takeover Act Offer Ordinance including, e.g., details of the bidder and the target company, the acceptance period, the consideration to be given, how the bid is to be financed, conditions of the bid and the bidder's future plans for the business.[9] This information must be true and complete and the issuers of the offer document are held liable for any incorrect, misleading or incomplete statements in the offer document.[10] The offer document must be approved by the Federal Financial Supervisory Authority.[11]

After the offer document has been published, the management board (*Vorstand*) and the supervisory board (*Aufsichtsrat*) of the target company must each issue a detailed statement evaluating the offer.[12] The management board must append to its own statement any statement on the offer issued by the target's work council.[13] The members of the management board of the target company must pass their statement on to the relevant works council (*Betriebsrat*) without delay. If no works council exists, then the statement must be provided to the employees directly.[14]

---

[4] See Sec. 35 para. 2 Public Takeover Act.

[5] See Sec. 29 para. 2 Public Takeover Act.

[6] See Sec. 30 Public Takeover Act.

[7] See Sec. 35 para. 1 Public Takeover Act.

[8] See Sec. 11 para. 1 Public Takeover Act.

[9] See Sec. 11 para. 2 and 3 Public Takeover Act.

[10] See Sec. 12 Public Takeover Act.

[11] See Sec. 15 Public Takeover Act.

[12] See Sec. 27 para. 1 Public Takeover Act.

[13] See Sec. 27 para. 2 Public Takeover Act.

[14] See Sec. 27 para. 3 Public Takeover Act.

4.5.2.3 Financing the Bid

Prior to the publication of the offer document, the bidder must meet all necessary requirements to satisfy the offer when the consideration becomes due. For example, in the case of a cash offer, proof must be provided that sufficient funds are available; for every cash offer an independent financial institution must confirm in writing that the bidder is indeed capable of financing the bid even if all issued shares are tendered. This confirmation must be attached to the offer document.[15]

In the event that a stockholder accepts the offer but then suffers a loss due to the bidder's inability to satisfy the offer, she/he can hold the financial institution liable for any losses incurred unless, in turn, the financial institution can prove it did not know that the issued statements were incorrect, misleading or incomplete.[16]

4.5.2.4 Time Limits and Procedures for Notifying BaFin

Within four weeks of the publication of the decision to launch a bid or publication of the acquisition of 'control', the bidder must file the offer document with BaFin.[17] This time-limit can, however, be extended by BaFin by up to a total of eight weeks if the bidder is unable to comply with the original time-limit, e.g. due to a cross-border offer or the necessity of a capital increase.[18] Following approval of the offer document by BaFin, the document must be published on the Internet and in the electronic Federal Gazette.[19] Approval can be assumed if the BaFin has not prohibited the bid within ten working days of the bidder's submission of the offer document.[20]

4.5.3 Evaluation of the Bid by the Target Company

After the offer document has been published, the management board and the supervisory board of the target company must each issue a detailed statement evaluating the offer.[21] Such statement(s) must comment on the type and amount of the consideration being offered by the bidder, the possible impact of the bid on the interests of the target company and its employees or their representative bodies, and the aims of the bidder. Furthermore, both boards must indicate whether or not any of their members intend to accept the bid.[22] Usually, the board(s) indicate(s) if a recommendation to accept the offer to the stockholders will be issued or not.

The management board must append to its own statement any statement on the offer issued by the target's work council.[23] The members of the management board

[15] See Sec. 13 para. 1 Public Takeover Act.

[16] See Sec. 13 paras. 1 and 3 and Sec. 12 paras. 2–6 Public Takeover Act.

[17] See Sec. 14 para. 1 sentence 1 Public Takeover Act.

[18] See Sec. 14 para. 1 sentence 3 Public Takeover Act.

[19] See Sec. 14 para. 3 Public Takeover Act.

[20] See Sec. 14 para. 2 Public Takeover Act.

[21] See Sec. 27 para. 1 sentence 1 Public Takeover Act.

[22] See Sec. 27 para. 1 sentence 2 Public Takeover Act.

[23] See Sec. 27 para. 2 Public Takeover Act.

of the target company must pass their statement on to the relevant works council without delay. If no works council exists, then the statement must be provided to the employees directly.[24]

4.5.4 Consideration: Cash Offers and Exchange Offers (Share for Share)

4.5.4.1 Types of Consideration

Under the Public Takeover Act, the bidder is, in principle, free to choose whether it will offer cash or shares as consideration to the stockholders of the target company. In the case of shares, they must be traded in a liquid market and admitted to trading on an organized market within the European Economic Area.[25] A cash offer is required, however, if, within the six month period prior to publication of the decision to launch a takeover bid, or the publication of the attainment of control, the bidder has acquired, in return for cash payment, at least 5% of the shares in the target or shares which represent at least 5% of the voting rights of the target.[26] The vast majority of German public offers since 2002 have offered cash as consideration due to the fact that share-for-share offers are rather complicated under German law.

4.5.4.2 Determination of the Offer Price/Consideration

As already mentioned, the consideration offered must be adequate.[27] When determining the amount of the consideration, the following two issues must be kept in mind: the average weighted stock exchange price of the target's shares during the three months leading up to the announcement of the offer, and prior acquisitions of shares in the target company by the bidder within the six months before publication of the offer document. The Public Takeover Act and the Public Takeover Act Offer Ordinance also prescribe how to determine the price, taking the volatility of the market (if possible pre-offer acquisitions by the bidder) into consideration. The rules in the Public Takeover Act and the Public Takeover Act Offer Ordinance apply to both mandatory and voluntary offers (however, only if they are targeted at the acquisition of control, so-called 'takeover bids').

4.5.5 Duty of Neutrality and Defence Measures

The Public Takeover Act establishes a general duty of neutrality on the part of both the management board and the supervisory board of the target company during the

[24] See Sec. 27 para. 3 Public Takeover Act.

[25] See Sec. 31 para. 2 Public Takeover Act.

[26] See Sec. 31 para. 3 Public Takeover Act.

[27] See Sec. 31 para. 1 Public Takeover Act.

takeover bid process. However, certain defence measures are permitted. After the amendments to the Public Takeover Act by Germany's implementation of the EU Takeover Directive, German law now provides for two different sets of defence measures:

On the one hand, the existing rules on frustrating a bid remain in place if the target company does not opt for the EU regulation on frustrating the bid. Under the relevant German takeover rules, as a general principle, the management board and the supervisory board of the target company are required to act in the best interests of the target company, and, after a decision to launch a bid has been published, the target company's management board may not take actions which could prevent the success of the offer.[28] However, this prohibition does not apply to actions which a prudent manager (not being subject to a public bid) would have taken. Nor does it apply to any search for a competing bid (looking for the 'white knight'). Furthermore, this prohibition does not apply to any actions approved by the supervisory board of the target or to any actions subject to stockholders' approval.[29] The stockholders' meeting of the target may authorize the management board to frustrate the offer.[30] However, such authority will expire no later than eighteen months after the date of the stockholders' resolution.

On the other hand, if the target company's articles of association specify that the above-mentioned rules do not apply, the target company will be considered to have automatically opted in to the following rules implementing Art. 9 of the EU Takeover Directive: Under these rules, after a decision to launch an offer has been published, the management board and the supervisory board of the target company are prohibited from taking any action which could prevent the success of the offer, with the exception of actions approved by the stockholders' meeting after the decision to launch an offer has been published, actions within the normal business operations of the target company, other actions if they are intended to implement measures commenced before the publication of the decision to launch a bid and the search for an alternative bid.

Since these rules are more restrictive than the rules of German national law, German companies have so far been reluctant to rely on the EU rules in actions that might prevent a successful bid. To date, no major German-listed company has amended its articles to this effect.

4.5.6 Role of BaFin

Adherence to the rules of the Public Takeover Act is supervised by the Federal Financial Supervisory Authority BaFin. In the event that the bidder or any other

[28] See Sec. 33 para. 1 sentence 1 Public Takeover Act.

[29] See Sec. 33 para. 1 sentence 2 Public Takeover Act.

[30] See Sec. 33 para. 2 Public Takeover Act.

person breaches its obligations under the Public Takeover Act, BaFin may impose sanctions, including fines of up to one million Euro.[31]

Any decisions made by BaFin may be challenged by way of an appeals procedure under administrative law. An appeals committee (*Widerspruchsausschuss*) will decide on objections against decisions of BaFin. These decisions of the appeals committee are subject to appeal (*Beschwerde*) to the Higher Regional Court (*Oberlandesgericht*) in Frankfurt am Main.[32]

4.6 Squeeze-out of Minority Stockholders

At the same time as the Public Takeover Act entered into force (January 2002), a new rule on the squeeze-out of minority stockholders was introduced. This rule has not, however, been incorporated into the Public Takeover Act, but has been implemented in the AktG. Therefore, it applies to all stock corporations whether publicly listed or not. In addition, a squeeze-out of minority stockholders does not require a public bid in advance.

However, when implementing the EU Takeover Directive, Germany has also introduced a new takeover-related squeeze-out procedure which will be briefly described in Sect. 4.6.3 below.

4.6.1 Overview

Secs. 327a–327f of the AktG provide for a procedure for the squeeze-out of minority stockholders in return for cash compensation in the event that a stockholder holds at least 95% of the target company's share capital ('principal stockholder'). The target company must be a stock corporation or a partnership limited by shares incorporated in Germany. The shares of the target company do not need to be listed on a stock exchange.

The principal stockholder must provide a written report to the general meeting of the stockholders explaining the requirements for the squeeze-out and the fairness of the cash compensation. Moreover, a fairness opinion regarding the proposed cash compensation is required from independent auditors who will be appointed by a court upon application of the principal stockholder. The amount of the cash compensation may be subject to court review in a specific proceeding pursuant to the *Spruchverfahrensgesetz* (Appraisal Proceedings Act).

---

[31] See Secs. 60, 61 Public Takeover Act.

[32] The *Oberlandesgericht* Frankfurt am Main has exclusive jurisdiction in this subject matter for the whole of Germany.

4.6.2 Steps of the Squeeze-out Procedure

The squeeze-out procedure comprises the following steps:

- The principal stockholder determines the amount of cash compensation, which usually requires a valuation of the target by an independent auditor (such auditor to be appointed by the competent court upon application by the principal stockholder).
- Prior to the stockholders' meeting which will decide on the squeeze-out, the principal stockholder must provide the management board of the target with a declaration from a bank stating that the bank guarantees the fulfilment of the principal stockholder's obligation to pay the cash compensation to the minority stockholders.
- The principal stockholder must provide the stockholders' meeting of the target company with a written report explaining the pre-conditions for the transfer of shares to the principal stockholder (such report also to be reviewed by the expert auditor). Moreover, it must explain and substantiate the appropriateness of the cash compensation.
- As from the time of convening the stockholders' meeting, the following documents must be on display at the business premises of the target for inspection by the stockholders of the target company:
  - Draft of the share transfer resolution;
  - Annual accounts and management reports for the last three financial years;
  - Above-mentioned report of the principal stockholder;
  - Above-mentioned review by the expert auditor.
- Each stockholder must, upon request, be provided with a copy of the above-mentioned documents without undue delay and free of charge.
- The resolution of the stockholders' meeting requires a majority vote of at least three-quarters of the share capital represented at the passing of the resolution.
- The management board of the target company must apply for registration of the transfer resolution in the Commercial Register. Such application requires notarization.
- If no action to set aside the transfer resolution (*Anfechtungsklage*) has been filed within one month of the adoption of the resolution, the management board of the target company must notify the Commercial Register thereof in a so-called 'negative declaration' (*Negativerklärung*). Based on such declaration the transfer resolution will be entered into the Commercial Register and the stocks automatically transferred to the principal stockholder.
- Following the registration of the transfer resolution in the Commercial Register, the cash compensation must be paid to the minority stockholder by the principal stockholder.

A minority stockholder has the right to have the appropriateness of the cash compensation reviewed by a court in a specific appraisal proceeding (*Spruchverfahren*). Such procedure may also be initiated if the principal stockholder has not offered, or has not properly offered, any cash compensation and an action to set aside the transfer resolution based thereon has not been commenced within the avoidance period, has been withdrawn, or has been conclusively rejected. The application for such procedure may only be filed within three months of the registration of the transfer resolution in the Commercial Register.

4.6.3 The Takeover-Related Squeeze-out Procedure as an Alternative

In addition to the general squeeze-out rules under the AktG described above, a new takeover-related squeeze-out procedure has been introduced implementing Art. 15 of the EU Takeover Directive.[33] If, following its bid, a bidder holds at least 95% of the target company's voting rights, the bidder will be able to acquire the remaining shares at a fair price. In order to achieve this, the bidder may apply for a squeeze-out of the minority stockholders in return for compensation within three months of the end of the period allowed for acceptance of the offer. In contrast to the squeeze-out procedure under the AktG, no stockholders' resolution is necessary. The takeover-related squeeze-out becomes effective upon the court decision which will be binding on all remaining stockholders of the target company.

[33] See Secs. 93 *et seq*. Public Takeover Act.

Cross-Border Corporate Activities 5

Abstract

In the following chapter, we present various aspects of the legal framework governing cross-border corporate activities in Germany and the European Union (EU). First, we will deal with the complex and controversial issue of a cross-border transfer of a company's seat and the conflict-of-laws issues resulting from such transfer. Then we will provide an introduction into the topic and outline the past and current legal framework of German conflict-of-laws rules on companies and legal entities. In this context we will discuss in detail the impact of European law, in particular the Freedom of Establishment as provided by Art. 49, 54 Treaty on the Functioning of the European Union (TFEU) and interpreted by the European Court of Justice (ECJ). Then, we will explain the consequences in German legal practice, and cover the government proposal on a revision of the German conflict-of-laws rules on companies and legal entities. After a presentation of the European company and the European private company as possible alternatives for cross-border economic activities in the European market, we will turn to the European cross-border mergers directive, outlining its implementation in Germany, as well as providing a list of key issues to be considered in a cross-border merger proceeding. The presentation will be concluded with a brief outline of the reasons for and key issues of international joint ventures.

Contents

M. Schulz, O. Wasmeier, *The Law of Business Organizations*,
DOI 10.1007/978-3-642-17793-4_5, © Springer-Verlag Berlin Heidelberg 2012

5.1 Cross-Border Transfer of Corporate Seat and Applicable Law

5.1.1 Case Study

Case Study

In order to further the expansion of **A**'s business activities in the German market, B recognizes the need to establish a number of subsidiaries in Germany. Having visited a conference on new business opportunities in Europe, **B** has heard about a new 'competition of company forms in Europe', in which the legal form of the private limited company as provided by Companies Act of England and Wales (hereinafter: Ltd.) plays an important role. Without learning all the details, **B** has found out, however, that due to a series of decisions of the European Court of Justice, any EU company is now generally allowed to operate in other member states. Being more familiar with the Ltd. than with the German GmbH, **B** asks **C**: Is it possible to either establish or buy a Ltd. and operate in the German market using the corporate form of a Ltd.? Which advantages/disadvantages does the Ltd. have compared to the GmbH regarding an operation in the German market?

5.1.2 Introduction

Cross-border activities of companies and entrepreneurs are far from being a new development. Since the *Vereenigde Oostindische Compagnie*[1] sailed the seven seas, making available rare Indian spices to European merchants, companies have often

[1] Dutch East-India Company. The VOC was established in 1602 and is said to be the first company ever to issue tradeable stock certificates.

taken the opportunity of cross-border trading in order to maximize their profits. Today, businessmen, company representatives and workers are crossing borders on a daily basis; goods are more or less freely traded within the borders of the EU and beyond; and companies, as well as globally active corporate groups are setting up branches and subsidiaries in other countries.

Cross-border activities are a vital factor of economic integration at the European level, fuelling the establishment of new markets, thus creating innovation, job opportunities and a gain in overall welfare. Nonetheless, the issue of a company crossing borders causes a number of specific legal problems, resulting from the special 'nature' of a company.

Naturally, a company does not, in itself, have a physical substance, but is a legal fiction, embodying the factors of production, the people, the capital and the sum of assets together forming 'the company' as a business unit. From an economic point of view, a company, therefore, represents a nexus of contracts between independent market actors working together to pursue a common goal set on an institutionalized basis.[2] Companies in general and corporations in particular, are, therefore, ultimately creatures of the law, i.e. the national law under which they are formed.[3]

That being said, the problem of a company crossing borders becomes apparent. Because companies are legal constructs, it has to be determined what consequences arise from such a legal construct of State A moving into the jurisdiction of State B. What rules apply to a company doing so, and what consequences does this decision have for the structure and organization of the company?

Although it is one of the fundamental goals of the European Union to provide for a Common Market in which an unrestricted exchange of goods, services and capital shall be possible, this aim has not yet been achieved. EU legislation and other measures to harmonize the national legal systems have only been partially successful and are limited in scope. The subject matter of cross-border migration of companies is one example where EU rules are incomplete and depend on national legislation to fill in the gaps. The cross-border movement of companies is governed by the applicable national corporate laws as determined by the national conflict of laws rules. As there are still no unified conflict-of-law rules for cross-border transfers of a company's seat, the outcome depends on the national rules.

5.1.3 German Conflict-of-Law Rules for Corporations

As already outlined above[4], German conflict-of-laws questions are generally codified in the German Introductory Law of the Civil Code (*Einführungsgesetz zum Bürgerlichen Gesetzbuch, EGBGB*). However, this act (up until now) contains no provisions for cross-border corporate law questions. Traditionally the German conflict-of-laws of companies and legal entities is not codified but merely dealt with

[2] On this concept see Cheffins 1997, p. 33.

[3] ECJ Case C-81/87 *Daily Mail and General Trust* [1988] ECR 5483, para. 19.

[4] See *supra*, Sect. 1.1.3.3, Relevance of Conflict of Laws.

on a case-law basis.[5] Before the relevant ECJ decisions were made, the German courts and legal commentators almost unanimously followed the so-called 'real seat doctrine'. This doctrine takes as a connecting factor (i.e. the factor relevant for the connection of a cross-border case and the national law to be applied) the factual seat of the administration of the company (*siège rèel*). The basic assumption of this doctrine is the following: the place where a company's administrative center is located is, as a general rule, the place where a company also conducts business; and thus, typically, is the place where there will be the most interests affected by the company's business, such as those of employees or creditors. Hence, the law of the state of the company's real seat should be authoritative to protect those third-parties.

The real seat doctrine was codified the first time in Belgium in 1873[6] and has its philosophical roots in the theory of nationalism predominant at that time. Legal entities and commercial companies were—analogous to natural persons—to be governed solely by the rule of the sovereign ruling the country in which they were attending their business. This was in line with the evolving theory regarding the nature of legal entities: Since they were now seen as mere creatures of the national law which granted them their existence, they would naturally need to be recognized when moving into other legal systems. The main intention of the real seat doctrine—at least in its self-perception—was to prevent foreign laxer company law from undermining the well-reflected system of creditor and third party protection provided by the German substantive law, e.g. statutory minimum capital requirements and rules regarding capital maintenance.

In Germany, the real seat doctrine was applied in two different forms. Both forms have in common that they take as the relevant connecting factor the 'real administrative seat' of the company, which is commonly defined as the "place where the essential decisions of the directors are transferred into specific acts of management"[7]. Therefore, both forms apply domestic national law to foreign companies relocating all or most of their business into the German jurisdiction. However, both forms of the real seat doctrine differ as to their outcome.

The first and stricter form of the real seat doctrine was introduced by the German Imperial Court (*Reichsgericht*) and continued by the German Federal Court of Justice (*Bundesgerichtshof*) up until 2002. Its main consequence was that a foreign company moving into the German jurisdiction was to be judged under domestic law and—not being effectively founded under this law—was considered completely lacking legal capacity.[8] This outright denial of legal capacity means that the foreign company could not acquire rights or be a party to legal proceedings in Germany.

---

[5] Although the first draft for the German Civil Code (*Bürgerliches Gesetzbuch*) contained the proposal "The legal persistency of a legal entity is governed by the law which is authoritative at the place of its seat", it did not state whether this 'seat' was meant to be the company's real seat or rather its place of incorporation.

[6] *Loi du 18 mai 1873 sur les sociétés commerciales en Belgique.*

[7] This definition is known as so-called '*Sandrock* formula'; see Sandrock 1979, p. 683.

[8] The situation in Austria has been the same; see Secs. 10 and 12 of the Austrian Act on Conflict-of-Laws.

Additionally, the shareholders' limitation on liability was disregarded and the shareholders could potentially be held personally liable.

Under the impression of the ECJ's ruling in the *Centros* case and the pending case of *Überseering,* the *Bundesgerichtshof* in 2002 reconsidered this harsh consequence.[9] The BGH modified the original real seat doctrine and decided that the foreign company would not be a limited liability company, but that since it would still be a cooperation of individuals to achieve a common goal under a common contractual framework, it could be considered as a general partnership (*Gesellschaft bürgerlichen Rechts, GbR*) or—depending on size, complexity and objective—a general commercial partnership (*offene Handelsgesellschaft, oHG*) under German law (this may be called the 'second form' of the real seat doctrine as applied by the German courts). As a result, the foreign company lost its privilege of limited liability but kept its legal existence, its identity and its legal capacity. Thus, the foreign company remained able to sue or be sued in a German court and remained capable of conducting court proceedings in its own name. This modified interpretation of the real seat doctrine was meant to allay concerns regarding the fact that the stricter first alternative of the real seat doctrine, although initially meant to protect the company's creditors, achieved the exact opposite in its effect: by neglecting the company's legal capacity it had become impossible for the creditors to sue the company.

5.1.4 The Decisions of the European Court of Justice

Although—as mentioned above—so far no uniform, harmonized rules on the cross-border transfer of a company's seat exist in Europe, the EU Treaties provide for a number of fundamental freedoms in order to further the development of a Common Market. As one of these freedoms, the TFEU stipulates in its Art. 49–55 the so-called 'Freedom of Establishment'. This freedom includes the right of EU citizens to take up and pursue activities as self-employed persons and to set up and manage entrepreneurial undertakings, in particular companies and firms, in other Member States.

As regards the cross-border migration of companies, the ECJ has rendered a number of important decisions in recent decades, which have clarified the meaning and scope of application of Art. 49–55 TFEU in this context. These decisions have led to a controversy in German academia, in the course of which the prevailing opinion in Germany has radically shifted from supporting the 'real seat doctrine' to a general approval of the so-called 'theory of incorporation' (*Gründungstheorie*), which is often considered its counterpart.

5.1.4.1 The Segers Decision (1986)

In June 1981 Mr. Segers, a Dutch citizen, took over the 'Slenderose Limited Company', a limited liability company formed in accordance with the Companies Act

[9] BGH, Judgment of 1 July 2002, II ZR 380/00.

of England and Wales[10] in April 1981. He incorporated into this company as a subsidiary his one-man-business, the 'Free Promotion International', whose registered office was located in the Netherlands. Afterwards, all of Slenderose's business has been conducted solely by its subsidiary in the Netherlands.

In July 1981, in order to obtain certain sickness insurance benefits, Mr. Segers registered as being ill with the *Bedrijfsvereniging voor Bank- en Verzekeringswesen, Groothandel en vrije Beroepen* (Banking, Insurance, Wholesale Trade and Professions' Association), because the *Ziektewet* (Dutch law establishing a general sickness insurance) provides that any person who is working in a subordinate position in relation to another person is insured by law. The Association, however, refused to grant Mr. Segers the desired benefits of health insurance arguing, *inter alia*, that he might not be considered as a subordinate to his own company, as the relevant rules only applied to companies whose registered office was in the Netherlands and not to a company incorporated under foreign law.

The ECJ decided that the Freedom of Establishment

> must be seen as prohibiting the competent authorities of a member state from excluding a director of a company from national sickness insurance benefit scheme solely on the ground that the company in question was formed in accordance with the law of another member state, where it also has its registered office, even though it does not conduct any business there.[11]

Perhaps the most noteworthy fact of this judgment is that the ECJ stated the fact that Slenderose Ltd. conducted its business solely through its subsidiary and was, therefore, a so-called 'U-Turn construction'[12] which did not hinder the application of the Freedom of Establishment. Its application required only that the company

> be formed in accordance with the law of a member state and have their registered office, central administration or principal place of business within the Community. Provided that those requirements are satisfied, the fact that the company conducts its business [solely; addition by the authors] through an agency, branch or subsidiary in another member state is immaterial.[13]

The question of whether a so-called 'U-Turn construction' would prevent an application of the Freedom of Establishment was also a crucial issue in the case *Centros* more than one decade later.

5.1.4.2 The Daily Mail Decision (1988)

The Daily Mail and General Trust plc., a public limited company incorporated in accordance with the English Companies Act, planned to transfer its central management to the Netherlands in order to avoid tax payments in the UK. These taxes would arise from the company's selling a significant part of its non-permanent as-

[10] Hereinafter—for the sake of readability—referred to as 'UK Ltd.'.

[11] ECJ, case 79/85, *Segers* [1986] ECR 2375, para. 19.

[12] Term according to Kjellgren 2000, p. 179.

[13] ECJ, case 79/85 *Segers* [1986] ECR 2375, para. 16.

sets and, in particular, the substantial capital gains on the assets which the company proposed to sell. Section 482 (1) (a) of the UK Income and Corporation Taxes Act 1970 prohibited companies which were resident only for tax purposes in the UK from ceasing to be resident without the consent of the Royal Treasury. This authority refused its consent if Daily Mail plc. would not be prepared to sell at least part of its assets before transferring its residence for tax purposes to the Netherlands.

The ECJ answered the question whether such attitude violated the Freedom of Establishment referred to it by the High Court of Justice, Queen's Bench Division, for a preliminary ruling as follows:

> Articles 52 and 58 of the Treaty [now Art. 49 and 54 TFEU] cannot be interpreted as conferring on companies incorporated under the law of a Member State a right to transfer their central management and control and their central administration to another Member State while retaining their status as companies incorporated under the legislation of the first Member State.[14]

It reasoned that

> unlike natural persons, companies are creatures of the law and, in the present state of Community law, creatures of national law. They exist only by virtue of the varying national legislation which determines their incorporation and functioning.[15]

The prevailing opinion in Germany deducted from this decision a general *obiter dictum*[16] by the ECJ confirming that the real seat doctrine did not violate the Freedom of Establishment since, if companies were creatures of national law and existed only by virtue of national legislation, then it could be concluded that a company ceased to exist whenever leaving the territory of this national jurisdiction. However, a famous line of ECJ decisions, starting in 1999, has shown that this conclusion proved to be invalid.

5.1.4.3 The Centros Decision (1999)

The *Centros* decision involved a Danish couple, Marianne and Tonny Bryde, being the sole shareholders of the Centros Ltd., a private limited company incorporated in accordance with English Company Law. The address of Centros Ltd's. registered office was that of a friend of Mr. Bryde, the company's share capital, (amounting to GBP 100), had not actually been paid in and was kept in a cash-box at Mr. Bryde's home.

Mr. and Mrs. Bryde did not intend to conduct any business in the UK but wanted to carry out their business solely by a branch located in Denmark. The obvious

---

[14] ECJ, case C-81/87 *Daily Mail and General Trust* [1988] ECR 5483, para. 23.

[15] ECJ, case C-81/87 *Daily Mail and General Trust* [1988] ECR 5483, para. 19.

[16] An obiter dictum (lat.: said in passing) is a remark or observation made by the court which is included in the body of the court's opinion but which is not a necessary part of the court's decision in the particular case. The ECJ uses obiter dicta to clarify the legal situation and provide general guidelines for questions which—although not decisive for the individual case—are closely related to the problems of the case and which it deems particularly important.

purpose of this 'U-Turn-Construction' was to avoid the Dutch regulations regarding the required statutory minimum capital.[17] According to Dutch law,[18] private limited companies and foreign companies having similar legal forms which are established in a Member State of the European Community may conduct business in Denmark through a branch which has to be registered by the *Erhvervs- og Selskabsstyrelsen* (Trade and Companies Board). This Board refused to register a branch of Centros Ltd. arguing that since Centros Ltd. neither conducted any actual business in the UK nor was intended to do so, the business in question was not a branch but rather the principal place of business.

However, when the *Centros* case was brought to the ECJ, the court upheld its decision made in the Segers case and decided that it is contrary to the Freedom of Establishment

> for a Member State to refuse to register a branch of a company formed in accordance with the law of another Member State in which it has its registered office but in which it conducts no business where the branch is intended to enable the company in question to carry on its entire business in the State in which that branch is to be created, while avoiding the need to form a company there, thus evading application of the rules governing the formation of companies which, in that State, are more restrictive as regards the paying up of a minimum share capital.[19]

In addition to the *Segers* decision, the ECJ introduced a standard describing under what circumstances a restriction of the Freedom of Establishment of companies can be justified. The ECJ applied for the first time its so-called 'four condition test' as developed initially for the Free Trade of Goods.[20] Restrictions of the Freedom of Establishment can only be justified if they fulfill the following four conditions:

- they must be applied in a non-discriminatory manner;
- they must be justified by imperative requirements in the general interest;
- they must be suitable for securing the attainment of the objective which they pursue and
- they must not go beyond what is necessary in order to attain it.

In the *Centros* case, however, the Court considered that the refusal of the Danish authorities to register a branch did not meet these requirements. The Danish government argued that the Danish regulations concerning the higher amount and stricter regulations regarding the minimum capital were necessary to protect the Danish creditors of the company. However, the ECJ did not agree with these arguments for two reasons: First, even if Centros Ltd. would have conducted business in the United Kingdom and consequently the Dutch branch would have been registered,

[17] The Opinion of Advocate General *La Pergola* as of 16 July 1998 states in para. 3: "Appearing as a witness in the proceedings before the competent Dutch court (the *Højesteret*), Mr. Bryde said he did not know if the purchase of Centros and the subsequent establishment of a branch in Denmark could be called a circumvention of Danish law but admitted that 'it is certainly easier to find GBP 100 than DKK 200,000'".

[18] In particular Sec. 117 *Anpartsselskabslov.*

[19] ECJ, case C-212/97 *Centros* ECR [1999] I-1459, para. 39.

[20] On this see ECJ, case 120/78 *Cassis de Dijon* ECR [1979] 649, para. 8.

its Dutch creditors would have been exposed to the same risk. Second, and perhaps more noteworthy, the ECJ expressed its doubts regarding the necessity of protecting Dutch creditors. The Court stated that, since

> the company [...] holds itself out as a company governed by the law of England and Wales and not as a company governed by Danish law, its creditors are on notice that it is covered by laws different from those which govern the formation of private limited companies in Denmark.[21]

5.1.4.4 The Überseering Decision (2002)

In the case of *Überseering,* the German real seat doctrine itself came under the ECJ's scrutiny.[22] The Dutch Überseering BV, a limited liability company formed in accordance with Dutch law (*Besloten Vennootschap met beperkte aansprakelijkheid*) and registered in Amsterdam and Haarlem, owned a piece of land in Düsseldorf, Germany. In 1992 Überseering BV had hired a company, the NCC, to refurbish a motel and a garage located on the site. Two years later, two German Nationals residing in Düsseldorf acquired all shares of Überseering BV. In a legal dispute arising between NCC and Überseering BV, the latter filed an action with the District Court (*Landgericht*) Düsseldorf and, upon appeal, with the Higher Regional Court (*Oberlandesgericht*).

The Higher Regional Court dismissed the action on the grounds that Überseering BV obviously had transferred its administrative center (i.e. its real seat) to Germany. Therefore, under the 'real seat doctrine', German company law would apply to it. But since the firm was not formed in accordance with German corporate law, it was considered null and void under German law and, therefore, lacked the capacity to bring any legal proceedings under the German Act on Civil Procedure (*Zivilprozessordnung*).

The ECJ decided

> that, where a company formed in accordance with the law of a Member State ('A') in which it has its registered office is deemed, under the law of another Member State ('B'), to have moved its actual center of administration to Member State B, Articles 43 EC and 48 EC [now: Artt. 49, 54 TFEU] preclude Member State B from denying the company legal capacity and, consequently, the capacity to bring legal proceedings before its national courts for the purpose of enforcing rights under a contract with a company established in Member State B.[23]

The Court made clear that the 'creatures of the law doctrine' as employed in *Daily Mail* only applied to such national restrictions regarding the movement of a company's center of administration that were imposed on it by the state of its incorporation. Thus, the Member States were not to be seen as

> having the power, vis-à-vis companies validly incorporated in other Member States and found by it to have transferred their seat to its territory, to subject those companies' effec-

---

[21] ECJ, case C-212/97 *Centros* ECR [1999] I-1459, para. 35.

[22] See Schulz and Sester 2002, pp. 545 *et seq.*

[23] ECJ, case C-208/00 *Überseering* ECR [2002] I-9919, para. 94.

tive exercise in its territory of the freedom of establishment to compliance with its domestic company law.[24]

Once again, the ECJ repeated that restrictions of the Freedom of Establishment in principle could be justified by imperative requirements in the general interest and stated that such requirements may well be seen in the protection of the interests of creditors, minority shareholders, employees and even the taxation authorities. In the *Überseering* case, however, the ECJ held that such objectives could neither justify denying the legal capacity, nor the capacity to be a party to legal proceedings of a company which was properly incorporated in another Member State in which it had its registered office. The ECJ regarded such a treatment of Überseeing as tantamount to an outright negation of the Freedom of Establishment conferred on companies by the EU Treaties.

5.1.4.5 The Inspire Art Decision (2003)

Inspire Art Ltd. was a limited liability company formed in 2000 under English Company Law, with its registered office located in Folkstone, England, and its sole director resident in the Netherlands. Similar to the cases *Segers* and *Centros* it again was a so-called 'U-Turn construction' that neither conducted any business within the UK nor was ever intended to do so.

In October 2000 the *Kamer van Koophandel en Fabrieken voor Amsterdam* (Chamber of Commerce and Industry of Amsterdam) applied to the *Kantongerecht te Amsterdam* (Amsterdam Cantonal Court) for an order that a statement should be added to Inspire Art Ltd.'s registration in the commercial register that it was a so-called 'formally foreign company' in accordance with Art. 1 of the Dutch Act on Formally Foreign Companies.[25] This Act provided for 'an incorporated company formed under laws other than those of the Netherlands and having legal personality, which carries on its activities entirely or almost entirely in the Netherlands and does not have any real connection with the State within which the law under which the company was formed applies'[26] (formally foreign company) to be subject to specific Dutch regulations regarding disclosure requirements, annual reports and minimum capital requirements. Pursuant to Art. 4 para. 1 of said Act, the subscribed capital of a formally foreign company had to equal the minimum amount required of regular Netherlands limited companies. If a formally foreign company failed to meet these requirements, the Act sanctioned this by a personal liability of its shareholders.

The application of said Act in the case of Inspire Art Ltd. created two problems:

Although the Act was supposed to implement the regulations of the Eleventh Council Directive (aimed to harmonize disclosure requirements in the EU Member

---

[24] ECJ, case C-208/00 *Überseering* ECR [2002] I-9919, para. 72.

[25] Wet van 17 December 1997, houdende regels met betrekking tot naar buitenlands recht opgerichte, rechtspersoonlijkheid bezittende kapitaalvennootschappen die hun werkzaamheid geheel of nagenoeg geheel in Nederland verrichten en geen werkelijke band hebben met de staat naar welks recht zij zijn opgericht, Staatsblad 1997, 697.

[26] Definition according to Art. 1 of said Act.

States) it actually exceeded the requirements of this Directive in some points, such as recording in the commercial register the fact that the company may be 'formally foreign'. In this matter, the ECJ stated that the harmonization of the disclosure to be made by branches, as regulated by the Eleventh Directive, was exhaustive. Any further disclosure obligations imposed on the branch of a company not provided for by that directive were contrary to (secondary) European law.[27]

As a consequence, only those provisions of the Act that did not fall within the scope of the Eleventh Directive were subject to control of the Freedom of Establishment, including the requirements regarding the amount of subscribed capital and the resulting 'penalty' of personal liability for violating them. The ECJ decided that, although the Member States are in principle

> entitled to take measures designed to prevent certain of its nationals from attempting improperly to circumvent their national legislation or to prevent individuals from improperly or fraudulently taking advantage of provisions of Community law.[28]

In the *Inspire Art* case no such behavior was evident. Although the company was formed under the law of another Member State solely for the purpose of evading the stricter Netherlands rules, the Freedom of Establishment was intended specifically to enable companies formed in accordance with the law of one member state to pursue activities in another one, and consequently enabled an entrepreneur to choose among the Member States' company law-rules those which seemed the least restrictive to him.

The ECJ further reasoned that neither the protection of Netherlands creditors nor the protection of fairness in business-dealings justified a national restriction of this freedom in the specific case. Creditors were

> on sufficient notice that it [Inspire Art Ltd.] is covered by legislation other than that regulating the formation in the Netherlands of limited liability companies and, in particular, laying down rules in respect of minimum capital and directors' liability.[29]

5.1.4.6 The Cartesio Decision (2008)

Cartesio Oktató és Szolgáltató (hereinafter: Cartesio) is a limited liability partnership (*betéti társa—sag*) formed in accordance with the Company Law of Hungary. Cartesio intended to move its head office from Hungary to Italy while maintaining its Hungarian legal form, and filed an application with the *Bács-Kiskun Megyei Bíróság* (Regional Court of Bács-Kiskun), sitting as a *Cégbíróság* (commercial court), for registration of such transfer. By a decision of 24 January 2006 the application was rejected on the grounds that the Hungarian conflict-of-laws rules[30] did not allow a company incorporated in Hungary to transfer its seat abroad while continuing to be subject to Hungarian law as its personal law.

---

[27] ECJ, case C-167/01 *Inspire Art* ECR [2003] I-10155, para. 72.

[28] ECJ, case C-167/01 *Inspire Art* ECR [2003] I-10155, para. 136.

[29] ECJ, case C-167/01 *Inspire Art* ECR [2003] I-10155, para. 135.

[30] Art. 18 of Decree-Law No 13 of 1979 on private international law rules (*a nemzetközi magánjogról szóló 1979. évi 13. törvényerejű rendelet*).

When asked whether this rejection was compatible with the Freedom of Establishment the ECJ decided that

> as Community law now stands, Articles 43 EC and 48 EC [today: Art. 49, 54 TFEU] are to be interpreted as not precluding legislation of a Member State under which a company incorporated under the law of that Member State may not transfer its seat to another Member State whilst retaining its status as a company governed by the law of the Member State of incorporation.[31]

The ECJ reasoned that the question of whether the Freedom of Establishment applied to a company which seeks to rely on the fundamental freedom enshrined in that article—like the question whether a natural person was a national of a Member State, hence entitled to enjoy that freedom—was a preliminary matter which, as Community law now stands, can only be resolved by the applicable national law. The ECJ, therefore, respected the competence of the Member States to determine independently the requirements necessary to form a company under its national law, as well as the requirements such a company has to fulfill to remain in this national legal form. In effect, that decision confirmed the distinction (introduced in *Daily Mail*) between restrictions imposed by the company's country of origin and such obstacles arising from national measures of the host state.

As a consequence for the controversial debate in Germany (and other countries), whether or not the *Überseering* and *Inspire Art* decisions could also apply to cases in which a company transfers its place of management from Germany to another Member State ('*Wegzugsfälle*'), it is now clear that the Freedom of Establishment does not protect such a transfer.[32]

In an *obiter dictum*, however, the Court stated that its ruling only applied to restrictions of the movement of a company by the state of its incorporation if the company intended to emigrate while maintaining its legal status as a company of this state. If the company was willing to combine the transfer of its seat with a change of its legal form, i.e. converted into a legal form provided by the law of the state of immigration, restrictions imposed by the state of emigration, such as the need of a winding-up or liquidation, were prohibited under the EU Treaties.[33]

5.1.5 Status-quo of German Conflict-of-Laws Rules for Companies

The decisions of the ECJ (especially *Centros, Überseering* and *Inspire Art*) led to a paradigm shift in Germany regarding the compatibility of the 'real seat doctrine' with the EU Treaties. With only a few exceptions, the prevailing opinion today is that as far as companies which were formed in accordance with the rules of a European Member State are concerned, the 'theory of incorporation' (*Gründung-*

---

[31] ECJ, case C-210/06 *Cartesio* ECR I-9641 [2008] I-9641, para. 124.

[32] The German legislature, however, has made such transfer possible for the GmbH by amending Sec. 4a GmbHG in the course of the MoMiG; see *supra*, Sect. 3.1.

[33] ECJ, case C-210/06 *Cartesio* ECR I-9641 [2008] I-9641, paras. 112 *et seq*.

stheorie) must be applied. In contrast to the 'real seat doctrine' the 'theory of incorporation' determines the applicable law for corporations according to their place of incorporation, i.e. the legal system chosen by the founders of the company.

However, the German courts have not yet abandoned the 'real seat doctrine' completely. It still remains the general rule, which is only superseded by the Fundamental Freedoms if and insofar as they apply to the case.[34] Therefore, the *Bundes gerichtshof* decided that only companies '*protected* by the Freedom of Establishment' are governed by the law of their state of incorporation.[35] In relation to companies incorporated in states which are not a member of the EU or EEA, the 'real seat doctrine' (in its modified form) is still applied.[36] Consequently, the BGH has recently decided that a stock corporation incorporated under Swiss Law[37] has to be regarded as a limited commercial partnership by German courts.[38]

5.1.6 Legislative Proposals

To remedy this somewhat complex and unsatisfying situation, the German legislature in January 2008 passed a draft proposal for a revision of the German conflict-of-laws rules on companies and legal entities (hereinafter: the Draft). The Draft embodies the first codification of conflict-of-laws rules on companies and other business entities in Germany by way of a revision of the EGBGB and shall be outlined briefly.[39]

5.1.6.1 Connecting Factors

According to Art. 10 para. 1 EGBGB of the Draft, there shall be two relevant connecting factors for companies: First, for registered companies the law of their respective state of registration shall be applicable, as this state is considered to be identical with the state of the incorporation. Second, for companies which are not registered, the law under which they have been organized shall apply.

While the registration is a relatively clear connecting factor, the law under which a company is organized is somewhat more difficult to determine. In this regard the explanatory statement of the Draft argues that in most cases creditors can infer the

[34] For a more detailed discussion see Schulz and Wasmeier 2010, pp. 657 *et seq.*

[35] Phrase used explicitly in BGHZ 154, 185 (185); translation made and emphasis added by the authors.

[36] This is not true in relation to such states privileged by special international treaties, e.g. the United States of America, which is privileged under the Treaty of Friendship, Commerce, and Navigation, signed in Washington on 29 October 1954; for MERCOSUR countries see Sester and Cárdenas 2005, pp. 398 *et seq.*

[37] Art. 620 and 629 Swiss Code of Obligations (*Obligationenrecht*).

[38] BGH, Judgment of 27.10.2008—II ZR 158/06; the case became known as 'Trabrennbahn'.

[39] The Draft was prepared by an academic proposal of a special committee for international company law of the Deutscher Rat for International Private Law (*Deutscher Rat für Internationales Privatrecht*) which also contained a proposal for a EU Regulation. The proposals are avilabele in English at Sonnenberger and Bauer 2007, pp. 65 *et seq.*

relevant organization from the market appearance of the company. The company itself, however, could prove this conclusion wrong, e.g. by presenting documents of its incorporation in a different state.

In such cases, i.e. where the market appearance does not match the real situation, creditors and contractual partners shall be protected by Art. 12 EGBGB of the Draft. According to this provision, the law which the creditor has considered *bona fide* shall apply, meaning that he neither knew about the fact that the company was incorporated in a state different from the impression created by its market appearance, nor that his ignorance can be considered as negligence.

Regarding companies which are neither registered nor possess a relevant internal organization, the Draft determines the *lex contractus* to be applicable (Art. 27 EGBGB).

It is noteworthy that the Draft does not distinguish between companies incorporated in EU/EEA Member States and in other countries, but that the relevant cases are treated in the same way. The current distinction between 'privileged' European companies and 'regular' foreign companies is thereby abolished.

5.1.6.2 Scope of Application

Such national law as determined pursuant to Art. 10 para. 1 EGBG of the Draft shall apply to all phases of the company's existence (i.e. from its formation until and including its liquidation) and for all questions which are—in Germany—traditionally considered as being part of company law.

The applicable law shall govern in particular:

- the company's legal nature, its legal capacity and its capacity to cause legal effects by its own actions;
- the company's formation and all questions arising from its winding-up and liquidation outside of insolvency proceedings;
- issues arising from the company's legal name which are not concerning its registrability or are subject to restrictions pursuant to competition law;
- the company's internal organization and financial structure, including the relationships between the company, its shareholders, its directors and other statutory bodies, as well as the protection of minority shareholders and the financial structure and of the company, e.g. capital requirements;
- the representative power of the company's statutory organs which are empowered by company law to represent the company;
- the acquisition and loss of memberships and all related rights and obligations, including transfer of shares insofar as there are no other preceding rules (e.g. securities law) and including the question of the legitimacy of contracts between shareholders regarding their rights and duties, e.g. voting agreements (while the contracts themselves are subject to the *lex contractus*);
- the liability of the company itself, its shareholders and members of its statutory organs for liabilities of the company, including the question of limited liability and rules regarding a 'piercing of the corporate veil';
- the liability for violating duties arising from the respective company law.

5.1.6.3 Expected Consequences for Corporate Mobility

Transfer of Effective Place of Business

As, according to the Draft, the location of the effective place of business, the central administration or head office office is no longer a relevant connecting factor, the 'immigration' of companies formed in accordance with the rules of another state does not lead to a change of the law governing the company and is, therefore, at least as far as conflict of laws is concerned—no longer a problem. Immigrating companies remain governed by the company law chosen by their founders.

In principle, the same rules apply for 'emigrating' German companies, i.e. German companies transferring their head office from Germany into a foreign country. This means that as far as German conflict-of-laws rules are concerned, a company formed in accordance with German law, as a general rule, will remain a German company governed by German company law. To this purpose, a former hindrance in this regard (a provision in Sec. 4a GmbHG, which required that the company's registered office be in Germany) was also abolished by the MoMiG.

Framework for Cross-Border Restructuring

The requirements, proceedings and effects of cross-border restructurings by way of merger, demerger and (complete) transfer of assets are governed by the respective law of incorporation applicable according to Art. 10 para. 1 EGBGB of the Draft for each of the companies involved in the transaction. Following the example of the EU Directive on cross-border mergers of limited liability companies,[40] the national laws of both states involved are to be applied cumulatively.

Therefore, companies willing to merge have to comply with the national laws of all jurisdictions involved, e.g. rules regarding the necessary shareholder resolution or rules for the protection of creditors and minority shareholders.

As the Draft is limited to conflict-of-laws, so far no substantive rules on cross-border-mergers have been implemented. Although the EU Cross-Border Mergers Directive was implemented in the German Act on Corporate Restructuring (*Umwandlungsgesetz*) in April 2007, this implementation is restricted to mergers involving companies incorporated in the EU and the EEA. German substantive law, therefore, still lacks rules on mergers involving states from Non-EU/EEA states, regarding mergers of non-registered partnerships and regarding all other sorts of cross-border restructuring measures.

Framework for Cross-Border Conversions

According to Art. 10b EGBGB of the Draft, the applicable law shall change as soon as the company becomes registered in a state different from the state of its incorporation, provided both of the national laws involved (the one applicable at the former place of registration; as well as the law governing the company's new state of reg-

[40] For further detail on this directive see *infra*, Sect. 5.4.

istration) allow such a re-registration and that both their respective prerequisites are fulfilled cumulatively.

This provision allows companies to 'convert', i.e. change their legal form into a company governed by the law of another state without prior winding-up or liquidation and enabling them to maintain their legal personality. Thus, a German GmbH could change its legal form into that of a UK Ltd. while still remaining the 'same company'. The UK Ltd. would be considered the legal successor of the GmbH, being entitled to all rights of the GmbH; as well as obliged by all of the latter's obligations. Contracts concluded between the GmbH and another party would, by operation of the law, remain valid, now also binding the UK Ltd.

In sum, such a 'cross-border conversion' allows the shareholders a choice of the applicable company law *ex-post*. Those commentators arguing in favor of a competition of national company laws in Europe consider the option of such an *ex-post* choice of law as a fundamental part of a functioning market for company law. However, whether or not companies will exercise this option to change into the legal form provided by another jurisdiction remains to be seen.

In this context it should be noted, that in 1997, the EU Commission had already initiated an informal proposal for a EU Directive on the cross-border transfer of the registered office of limited liability companies.[41] In 2002, the so-called High-Level Group of Company Law Experts urged the EU Commission to consider adopting a proposal for such a EU Directive.[42] The EU Commission, in its Action Plan of 2003, undertook to adopt a proposal for a directive in the near future, considering this to be one of its top priorities[43] and a public consultation in 2004 showed a need on the part of the market actors towards such a possibility.[44] However, none of these projects so far proved to be successful. Presently, the EU Commission has postponed its plans for such a directive for an undetermined period of time.[45] However, with a view to the complicated procedure and high incurring costs of a cross-border merger, the so-called 'Reflection Group on the Future of EU Company Law' has, recently once again advised the EU Commission to take legislative actions in

[41] The text of said proposal is not available on the website of the EU Commission anymore; German-speaking readers, however, may find the proposal published at ZIP 1997, p. 1721 *et seq*. and ZGR 1999, p. 157.

[42] Report of the High-Level Group of Company Law Experts on a Modern Regulatory Framework for Company Law in Europe as of 4 November 2002.

[43] Commission communication to the Council and the European Parliament on modernizing company law and enhancing corporate governance in the European Union—A plan to move forward (COM (2003) 284 final).

[44] Results are available at http://ec.europa.eu/yourvoice/results/transfer/index_en.htm (last checked 1 July 2011). It has to be noted, however, that this consultation has to be considered with caution, for only 127 responses were given.

[45] Former Commissioner Charlie McCreevy justified this decision with inconclusive economic data, as well as the possibility for companies to transfer their registered offices by using the possibilities offered by the European Company Statute in addition to—more interestingly for small medium-sized enterprises—the possibility of a cross-border merger into a shell subsidiary in another Member State as provided by the Cross-Border Mergers Directive; see Speech at the European Parliament's Legal Affairs Committee on 3 October 2007, Speech/07/592.

this field.[46] Furthermore, the EU Parliament has adopted a non-legislative resolution with recommendations to the EU Commission regarding this subject matter in March 2009.[47]

In any case, it has to be noted that the conflict-of-laws rule of Art. 10b EGBGB of the Draft remains an empty shell. Up until now, there is no substantive law governing a re-incorporation in Germany, its requirements or its proceedings.

5.1.7 Competition of Corporate Forms—GmbH vs. Limited

5.1.7.1 Competition of Corporate Laws—Some Comments

Following the ECJ's decisions in *Centros, Überseering* and *Inspire Art*, outlined above[48], German commentators now agree that the 'real seat doctrine' can no longer be applied to companies from other EU/EEA Member States. A company's legal capacity and identity validly established in another EU/EEA Member State must be recognized in all other Member States. However, it remains controversial if and to what extent German national rules protecting specific interests (such as those of creditors and employees) can still legitimately be applied to foreign companies. Furthermore, it is interesting to consider the long-term effects of the ECJ case law on the prospective further harmonization of Member States' law in the EU. In Germany, the 'real seat doctrine' had often been justified arguing that it prevented a purported negative competition of laws ('race to the bottom'). According to this view, under a competition of legal systems, the legal system with the weakest level of protection for certain interest groups (i.e. creditors and employees) would prevail. In this respect, reference was often made to developments in US company law, where the 'theory of incorporation' has a long tradition and companies enjoy an almost unrestricted freedom of establishment. When referring to the US experience, German commentators often alleged that, due to the 'theory of incorporation', a negative race of legal systems took place in US law. However, given the success story of Delaware, the most popular state for the incorporation of American companies, such skepticism has not been proved by way of empirical investigation. On the contrary, in the US, the bleak prospect of a 'race to the bottom' has been confronted by several commentators with the bright vision of a 'race to the top'.[49] For various reasons, Delaware law is considered to be a driving force for progress in US corporate law. For example, Delaware offers a simple and unbureaucratic incorporation process and, with its Court of Chancery, Delaware has established a court system with specialized judges for company law disputes. This specialization and the expertise of the Delaware judiciary ensure legal stability and, in the case of legal disputes, enable an analysis of the risks of litigation and result in faster

[46] Report of the Reflection Group on the Future of EU Company Law as of 5 April 2011, p. 19.

[47] See European Parliament resolution of 10 March 2009 with recommendations to the Commission on the cross-border transfer of the registered office of a company (2008/2196(INI)).

[48] See *supra*, Sect. 5.1.4.

[49] See Schulz 2006, pp. 153 *et seq.*

legal proceedings in Delaware compared to those in other federal states. Thus, the negative German perception of corporate law competition in the US may be unjustified. A closer look at the US seems to indicate that perhaps there is no need to be afraid of a 'race to the bottom' as a result of the recent ECJ jurisprudence on the EU Freedom of Establishment. Within Europe, it seems unlikely that a competition of legal systems will occur on the same scale as in the US, as the conditions for a market of company laws in Europe are different: the company laws of the Member States are still only partially harmonized and, in contrast to the US, there is no common language and culture in Europe which would facilitate a competition of legal systems.[50] In addition, within its strict guidelines for national restrictions on the freedom of establishment, the ECJ has left enough room for the legitimate application of national laws, thereby preventing an unrestricted freedom of establishment. These European law guidelines may ultimately serve as a safeguard against a 'race to the bottom'.

5.1.7.2 Check List—Advantages and Disadvantages of a UK Ltd. Compared to a German GmbH

Advantages of a UK Ltd.	Disadvantages of a UK Ltd.
A popular and commonly used legal corporate form, legal advice easy to find; Quick and easy formation process, low startup costs; no notarization requirements; No minimum share capital requirement; No regulations regarding formation by non-cash capital contribution No liability of the founders for net asset positions falling below the amount of the registered share capital (*Unterbilanzhaftung*); No restrictions on the acquisition of shelf companies; In the absence of a supervisory board no statutory board-level co-determination; Amendments to the articles of association do not require notarization; No notarization necessary for the transfer of company shares, written form sufficient.	UK legal advisors necessary, in particular with respect to complex issues (e.g. book keeping, accounting etc.); Running costs high (e.g. for legal and tax advice, translation expenses etc.); Dual Regulation: UK Ltd. remains obliged to keep records and remains subject to accounting duties in the UK; Rules on preservation of company assets (*Vermögensbindung*) complex and even stricter than for the GmbH. Distributions may only take place out of the profits; Acquisition of own shares in principle may only be made out of the profits of the company; Liability risks of managing directors in the case of insolvency in accordance with 'wrongful trading' rule and 'fraudulent trading rule'; 'Piercing the corporate veil' of the company in certain cases.

[50] Also see Kieninger 2004, pp. 765 *et seq.*

5.2 The European Company (SE)

5.2.1 Case Study

Case Study

Seeing his activities in Germany as part of a long-term business strategy for the European market, **B** is interested in cross-border restructuring options of companies operating in the EU. In this context **B** wants to know more about the European Company ('*Societas Europaea*', *SE*) as a new European company form, which, in his view would be a convenient option for A to do business throughout Europe. In particular, he wants to know what advantages the SE has and how it can be established.

5.2.2 General Background

Since October 2004 the European Company (*Societas Europaea, SE*) is available as a new transnational company form within the EU. This new company form was created by the European legislature in order to overcome the numerous legal constraints existing for companies engaged in cross-border transactions. The legal framework for the SE is set out in the Regulation on the Statute for a European Company (hereinafter: SE Regulation)[51], which is complemented by a EU Directive on questions relating to the involvement of employees (hereinafter: SE Directive).[52] In Germany, this European requirements have been transposed into national law by the SE Implementation Statute (*SE-Ausführungsgesetz, SEAG*) and the SE Participation Statute (*SE-Beteiligungsgesetz, SEBG*). This framework provides rules for certain key issues (such as minimum capital, management structure and shareholder meetings), but with regard to many other questions, the SE is still subject to the relevant national company laws of the member state in which it has its registered office. This means that a SE will be subject to a variety of different rules stemming from the SE Regulation. These rules were passed to implement the associated EC Directives (such as the SEBG), as well as 'regular' national company law provisions (such as rules from the German Stock Corporation Act, *AktG*) for matters which are not yet determined by the SE Regulation and, finally, the provisions of the SE's constitutional documents (in particular the articles of association).[53]

The SE is intended to enable companies which are established in more than one EU member state to merge and operate throughout the EU on the basis of a single set of rules and a unified management and reporting system. By using a SE as a business vehicle, enterprises engaged in cross-border activities can now restructure

[51] Council Regulation (EC) No. 2157/2001 of 8 October 2001 on the Statute for a European Company (SE), OJ L 294/1 as of 10 November 2001.

[52] Council Directive 2001/86/EC of 8 October 2001 supplementing the Statute for a European Company with regard to the Involvement of Employees, OJ L 294/22 as of 10 November 2001.

[53] See Art. 9 SE Regulation.

faster and more easily instead of being forced to create a complex network of subsidiaries governed by different national laws. Initially, not many enterprises took advantage of this new European company form. In the meantime, however, various German blue chip companies like, for example, Allianz, BASF and Porsche have changed their corporate form to that of a SE. This indicates that this new European company form has become more and more attractive.

5.2.3 Formation of the European Company

The SE is a company with a separate legal personality[54], its capital being divided into shares.[55] As with the German AG only the company's assets are liable for the debts of the SE.[56]

There are five ways of setting up a SE provided for in the SE Regulation:

- by merger of two or more existing public limited companies from at least two different EU Member States;[57]
- by the formation of a holding company promoted by public or private limited companies from at least two different EU Member States;[58]
- by the formation of a subsidiary of companies from at least two different EU Member States;[59]
- by a SE setting up another SE as a subsidiary;[60] and
- by transformation of a stock corporation which has, for at least two years, had a subsidiary in another Member State.[61]

The name of the European Company must have the letters 'SE' attached either as a prefix or a suffix.[62] It acquires its legal capacity for all legal forms upon registration[63], i.e. in the case of Germany, upon its registration in the commercial register.

5.2.4 Corporate Governance in the SE

The SE is free to choose its own management system.[64] On the one hand, it may adopt the two-tier system, as provided for under German law, consisting of a super-

[54] See Art. 1 para. 3 SE Regulation.

[55] See Art. 1 para. 2 sentence 1 SE Regulation.

[56] See Art. 1 para. 2 sentence 2 SE Regulation.

[57] See Art. 2 para. 1, 17 *et seq.* SE Regulation.

[58] See Art. 2 para. 2, 32 *et seq.* SE Regulation.

[59] See Art. 2 para. 3, 35 *et seq.* SE Regulation.

[60] See Art. 3 para. 2 SE Regulation.

[61] See Art. 3 para. 4, 37 *et seq.* SE Regulation.

[62] See Art. 11 para. 1 SE Regulation.

[63] See Art. 16 para. 1, 12 SE Regulation; notice the registration (as well as a deletion of such registration) shall be published both in the national gazette as well as in the Official Journal of the European Union, see Art. 13, 14 SE-Regulation.

[64] See Art. 38 lit. b SE Regulation.

visory board and a management board. On the other hand, the company may choose to adopt the Anglo-American one-tier system in which only a single administrative body exists—the executive board (*Verwaltungsrat*), which not only manages the company but also assumes a supervisory role. This administrative body may appoint one or more managing directors to deal with the day-to-day running of the business.

5.2.5 Employee Participation in the SE

Employee participation is regulated by the EU SE Directive and the German SE Participation Statute (SEBG). The question of employee participation can become a key aspect in the formation process of a SE if companies from different jurisdictions are involved. The main objective of the SEBG is to ensure that existing employment participation rights are not restricted when forming or changing into a SE. Such rights include information and consultation rights, as well as employment participation on the board of the SE if such participation rights existed before.[65]

The legal framework is based on the idea that the participation rights of the employees should be mutually negotiated between the employer and employees. This means that a special negotiating body must be formed with the task of negotiating an agreement regarding employees' involvement within the new company and setting it out in an agreement.[66]

In the event that the management of the companies develops plans to set up a SE, it is obliged to inform the employee representatives of the companies involved, the subsidiaries affected and the production units about their plans and to request them to set up a special negotiating body.[67] If no employee representative exists, then the employees must be informed directly.[68] It is the main duty of the special negotiating body to enter into a written agreement with the SE, or rather with the companies involved in the formation of the SE, regarding the employees' involvement in the SE. In doing so, the negotiation period is limited to six months which can, however, be extended to a year in total if the parties agree.[69] Both parties of the negotiating body can decide not to begin the negotiations, or also to break off negotiations. However, such a decision requires a two-thirds majority.[70]

In the event that an agreement is concluded between the management of the associated companies and the special negotiating body, the extent of employee participation is determined by such agreement. To a great extent the parties to the agreement are at liberty to make their own arrangements. However, if the parties cannot reach an agreement, special contingency rules (*Auffangregelungen*) take ef-

[65] See Sec. 1 para. 1 sentence 2 SEBG.

[66] See Art. 3 paras. 1 and 3 SE-Directive; Sec. 4 para. 1 SEBG.

[67] See Sec. 4 para. 2 sentence 1 SEBG.

[68] See Sec. 4 para. 2 sentence 2 SEBG.

[69] See Sec. 20 SEBG.

[70] See Sec. 16 para. 1 sentence 1 SEBG.

fect. These contain rules regard the establishment of a works council in a SE[71] and the board-level co-determination of employees.[72]

In the case of the establishment of a SE by way of transformation of a national stock corporation (such as an AG), the co-determination rules remain as they were prior to the transformation ('before as after').[73] In the case of all other methods of formation, the statutory rule offers more options: board-level co-determination by virtue of law takes place if a quorum of SE employees had up to now been subject to one form of co-determination.[74] This varies according to the method of formation (in the case of a SE formed by merger, a quorum of 25%[75], in the case of a SE formed by a holding company, a quorum of 50%[76]). However, if the quorum has not been reached, but the special negotiating body nevertheless passed a resolution for the use of co-determination by virtue of law, then board-level co-determination will also be implemented.[77] If none of the companies involved in the SE formation is subject to statutory board-level co-determination, then a board-level co-determination will also not take place in the SE.

In the case of a board-level co-determination by virtue of law, the employees of the SE, their subsidiaries and production units/plants or their representative body have the right to elect or appoint a certain number of the members of the supervisory board, or executive board respectively, or to recommend or reject their appointment.[78] The number of employee representatives on the supervisory board or executive board of the SE is proportionate to the highest number of employee representatives existing in the bodies of the companies involved at the time of formation of the SE (principle of protection of acquired rights).[79]

If German companies are subject to employee co-determination rules (e.g. under the Co-Determination Act, *Mitbestimmungsgesetz* or the One-Third Co-Determination Act, *Drittelbeteiligungsgesetz*)[80], the respective level of co-determination may well be transferred to the SE depending on the outcome of the above-described negotiation process.

5.2.6 Possible Use of the SE

The use of an SE can be particularly advantageous in the following cases:

[71] See Secs. 22 *et seq.* SEBG.

[72] See Secs. 34 *et seq.* SEBG.

[73] See Secs. 34 para. 1 no. 1, 35 para. 1 SEBG.

[74] See Sec. 35 para. 2 SEBG.

[75] See Sec. 34 para. 1 no. 2 lit. a SEBG.

[76] See Sec. 34 para. 1 no. 3 lit. a SEBG.

[77] See Sec. 34 para. 1 nos. 2 lit. b, 3 lit. b SEBG.

[78] See Sec. 35 para. 2 sentence 1 SEBG.

[79] See Sec. 35 para. 2 sentence 2 SEBG.

[80] For a detailed discussion of the German rules on employee participation see *supra*, Sect. 2.5.

5.2.6.1 Cross-Border Merger of Companies by Using SE

A cross-border merger of completely independent companies being combined with a company which has been set up specifically for this reason and which, possibly, has its registered office in a third Member State, does not at first glance seem to be a takeover by the one company of the other, but rather to be a 'merger of equals'. Therefore, psychological barriers are broken down between the management and employees promoting the development of an integrated corporate culture and European awareness among the employees (European Corporate Identity). Following the merger into a SE, the groups of shareholders can be merged completely so that any further restructuring activities cannot be obstructed by minority shareholders. Vis-à-vis clients and public authorities, a SE profits from a modern, European corporate image, as well as a uniform appearance in the capital, job and procurement markets.

5.2.6.2 Reorganization of the European Organizational Structure

The use of the SE legal form will enable those groups of companies already active in Europe to appear in all Member States using the same name and legal form and thus provide a completely uniform appearance. In the individual Member States, either legally independent subsidiaries, or dependent branches may be established. At the same time, the choice given between the one-tier and two-tier governance system offers the possibility of organizing all group companies in a uniform manner, for example in accordance with the Anglo-American board system. Management and control of the group companies are facilitated and the exchange of information between managing and supervising directors can be improved. In addition, small subsidiaries for which, in Germany, up to now virtually only the legal form of a GmbH was feasible, may now be organized in the form of a SE.

5.2.6.3 Change in the Corporate Governance Structure

Related to this issue, the transformation of an existing stock corporation (such as an AG) into a SE also makes the transition to the one-tier system of corporate governance easier. The SE can also be used to adapt the company's co-determination regulations. This option creates chances to reach a flexible, tailor-made compromise with the employees.

5.2.6.4 Cross-Border Transfer of Corporate Seat

Finally, the transformation of a national business vehicle into a SE can be considered when preparing for the transfer of the corporate seat to another EU Member State. In contrast to national companies which are, in Germany[81] (as in other Member

[81] In Germany, a transfer of the registered office to another jurisdiction would still be regarded as a ground for winding-up an AG; for the GmbH, however, the German legislature abandoned the corresponding provision in the course of the MoMiG, see Sect. 3.1.

States)[82], prohibited from moving their registered office to another member state, a SE can freely transfer its registered office from one Member State to another.[83]

5.3 The European Private Company (SPE)

5.3.1 The Commission Proposal on the Statute for a SPE

As the SE is a stock-corporation, requiring a comparatively high minimum statutory capital of EUR 120,000[84] it is suited mainly for large corporations, in particular as a holding company in an international group structure. However, small and medium-sized enterprises (SMEs), accounting for more than 99% of companies in the EU, will not be able to benefit from this company form.

In order to provide another pan-European business vehicle, the EU Commission, in 2008, submitted to the EU Council a proposal for a Council Regulation on the Statute for a European Private Company (*Societas Privata Europaea, SPE*).[85] This proposal aims at the introduction of a new European company form tailor-made for the specific need of SMEs intending to conduct cross-border business, allowing entrepreneurs to establish a SPE following the same simple and flexible company law provisions across all Member States. The proposal thereby intends to reduce compliance costs arising from the disparities between national rules, both on the formation and on the operation of companies.

In contrast to the corresponding statute for the SE, which sets out basic rules on the European level and relies on national company laws to fill in the gaps, the EU Commission's proposal for the SPE took a rather radical emphasis of contractual freedom. The proposal sets out only a basic set of rules regarding the general characteristics of the SPE, its formation, its capital, its internal organization and the transfer of the company's seat. For all other issues, however, the proposal relies on the shareholders to provide for the necessary rules themselves. To this end, the proposal contains an extensive list of subject matters, which shall be regulated by the shareholders in the articles of association, thus taking an approach perhaps best characterized as 'mandatory self-regulation'.

---

[82] For the UK see See *Gasque v. Commissioners of Inland Revenue [1940] 2 K.B. 80 (84)*: "It is not disputed that a company, formed under the Companies Act., has British nationality, though, unlike a natural person, it cannot change its nationality. So, too, I think such a company has a domicile—an English domicile if registered in England, and a Scottish domicile if registered in Scotland. The domicile of origin, or the domicile of birth, using with respect to a company a familiar metaphor, clings to it throughout its existence."; *Carl Zeiss Stiftung v. Rayner & Keeler Ltd. et al. (No. 3) [1970] 1 Ch. 506 (544):* "A corporation cannot, I think, of its own volition and apart from its proper law, abandon one domicile and adopt another, as a natural person can. Its primary domicile must be under the law under which it was incorporated."

[83] See Art. 8 SE Regulation.

[84] See Art. 4 para. 2 SE Regulation.

[85] COM (2008) 396/3.

5.3.2 Controversial Issues

Although the need for a European business vehicle for SMEs and group companies is generally acknowledged, the EU Commission's proposal has been heavily debated in the current legislative procedure. Though experts compliment the Commission for having avoided the peculiarities that have prevented the SE from becoming a more successful option for European entrepreneurs,[86] some Member States have raised objections. While as of the time of this writing, broad agreement has been reached on most parts, in particular three issues are still controversial, which—unsurprisingly—comprise (1) the seat of a SPE, (2) the amount of its statutory minimum capital and (3) the board-level participation of employees.

Regarding the seat of the SPE, the proposal of the EU Commission allows the SPE to have its registered office and its real seat in different Member States. While some Member States support this proposal, others are in favor of prohibiting such separation of the registered office (corporate seat) and the center of its administration (real seat). Still others prefer to leave this question to be decided entirely by national law.

With regard to the minimum statutory capital of the SPE, the EU Commission proposed to set the capital figure to (only) EUR 1. Some Member States have objected to this amount and preferred a higher minimum capital requirement. The Swedish Council Presidency, as well as the Hungarian Council Presidency proposed to allow Member States to set a higher minimum statutory capital requirement up to a maximum of EUR 8,000. However, so far no consensus has been reached.

The most difficult issue remaining in the legislative procedure seems to be that of employee participation. Due to different historical developments, traditions and legal arrangements for employee co-determination differ greatly among the Member States. While in some Member States (as e.g. in the UK) a mandatory co-determination on the company's board-level is unknown, other Member States (like Germany) have a longstanding tradition of such co-determination and, therefore, have expressed concerns about the possible loss of employees' rights acquired under national law if the SPE was used to circumvent national legislation on this matter.

5.4 The EU Cross-Border Mergers Directive and Its Implementation in Germany

5.4.1 Case Study

Case Study

B just read about some new developments on cross-border mergers within the EU and asks **C** to prepare a short memo on the questions:
What options are available to effect a cross-border merger?

[86] See e.g. Report of the Reflection Group on the Future of EU Company Law as of 5 April 2011, p. 30.

What are the necessary steps in a cross-border merger proceeding under the EU cross-border merger directive?

5.4.2 General Background

The EU Cross-Border Mergers Directive[87] was adopted on 20 September 2005 and was to be implemented into the national law of the Member States by the end of 2007.

The new legal framework aims to facilitate cross-border mergers of limited liability companies, which in the past were often quite burdensome and costly. The cross-border mergers directive aimed at abolishing typical risks and uncertainties regarding the legal framework for such transactions. This is especially relevant for small and medium-sized companies wishing to operate in more than one EU Member State, but not throughout the whole EU and not wanting to have to establish a European Company (SE).

5.4.3 Implementation in Germany

With the introduction of a specific statute on 25 April 2007 amending the Transformation Act (*Umwandlungsgesetz, UmwG*), Germany implemented the corporate guidelines of the EU Cross-Border Mergers Directive. The rules on employee participation in cross-border mergers were dealt with separately in specific legislation on employee participation in cross-border mergers (*Gesetz über die Mitbestimmung der Arbeitnehmer bei einer grenzüberschreitenden Verschmelzung*) which had already come into force on 29 December 2006. Tax issues relating to cross-border mergers were also regulated by specific legislation (*Gesetz über steuerliche Begleitmaßnahmen zur Einführung der Europäischen Gesellschaft und zur Änderung weiterer steuerlicher Maßnahmen, SEStEG*).

These new German rules have now created a reliable legal framework for so-called 'inbound' mergers of corporations, i.e. mergers of corporations from other EU Member States or a Member State of the European Economic Area (EEA), i.e. Norway, Iceland or Liechtenstein, into German corporations, as well as for so-called 'outbound' mergers of German corporations into corporations of other EU or EEA Member States. The new provisions on cross-border mergers apply to corporations formed in accordance with the law of an EU or EEA Member State and having their registered office, their central administration or their principal place of business within the EU or EEA. In Germany, they will apply to the German stock corporation (AG), the limited partnership by shares (KGaA), the German limited liability company (GmbH), as well as to the 'German' SE. However, these rules on cross-border mergers are only applicable to corporations, but not to partnerships. Furthermore,

[87] Directive 2005/56/EC of the European Parliament and of the Council of 26 October 2005 on Cross-Border Mergers of Limited Liability Companies, OJ L 310/1 as of 25 November 2005.

these rules only apply to mergers; other forms of cross-border reorganization (e.g. a cross-border de-merger or a spin-off) are not included. However, the ECJ's decision in the case of *SEVIC* (as outlined below), according to which cross-border mergers are protected by the Freedom of Establishment, are applicable also to partnerships, as well as to other forms of cross border reorganization.

5.4.4 Essential Steps in a Cross-Border Merger Proceeding

The essential steps to be taken and documents to be prepared in a cross-border merger proceeding are:

- *Common Draft Terms of Cross-Border Mergers:* The common draft terms of cross-border mergers form the basis of any cross-border merger. The minimum content of the common terms is mandatorily prescribed by the EU Cross-Border Mergers Directive.[88] The national German merger agreement (*Verschmelzungsplan*) requires such content as: the names and registered offices of the merging companies, the ratio applicable to the exchange of shares and the amount of any cash payments, the date from which the shares will entitle their holders to share in profits, the date from which the transactions of the merging companies will be treated for accounting purposes as being those of the company resulting from the cross-border merger, any special rights conferred upon shareholders, as well as the effect of the merger on the employees. Additionally, the common terms must also include the statutes of the company resulting from the cross-border merger, as well as information on the procedure for the employee participation and information on the valuation of the assets and liabilities being transferred to the company resulting from the merger;[89]
- *Merger Report of the Management:* The management of each of the merging companies shall draw up a merger report containing certain mandatory information, e.g. explaining the common terms of the merger, the ratio applicable for the exchange of shares and the amount of any cash payment.[90] In addition, the merger report shall also explain the implications of the cross-border merger for the creditors and employees of the merging companies.[91] The merger report shall be made available to the shareholders and works council (or to the employees if no works council exists) no later than one month prior to the general meeting of shareholders to be held to approve the common terms;[92]
- *Independent Expert Report:* The common terms of the cross-border merger need to be verified by independent experts.[93] The independent expert report must be

[88] See Art. 5 Cross-Border Mergers Directive.

[89] See Sec. 122c para. 2 UmwG.

[90] See Sec. 8 UmwG.

[91] See Sec. 122e sentence 1 UmwG.

[92] See Sec. 122e sentence 2 UmwG.

[93] See Secs. 122f sentence 1, Secs. 9–12 UmwG.

available no later than one month prior to the required[94] approval of the cross-border merger by the shareholders;[95]

- *Shareholder Approval:* If all the shares of the transferring company are held by the absorbing company, an approval by the shareholders of the transferring company is not necessary.[96] In all other cases, the general meeting of each of the merging companies must decide on the approval of the common terms in accordance with the relevant national laws. The shareholders may make their approval of the cross-border merger subject to the condition that the details of the employee participation have to be explicitly approved by them;[97]
- *Registration of the Cross-Border Merger:* The registration process is divided into several steps; the requirements for each merging company shall be reviewed separately under the respective applicable law. For example, if a German company is the transferring company, its management is responsible for filing the merger with the competent Commercial Register in Germany.[98] The Commercial Register will then examine whether the legal requirements regarding the merger have been fulfilled under German law and, if so, will issue a certificate to that effect to be submitted to the register of the absorbing or new company.[99] The absorbing (or new) company shall subsequently apply for registration of the merger with its (if applicable, foreign) register within a period of six months and upon presentation of said certificate. The effectiveness of the merger depends on the law applicable to the absorbing (or new) company; the register responsible for that company shall be obliged to notify the Commercial Register of the German transferring company of the merger taking effect, whereupon the commercial register of the German transferring company shall register the effectiveness;[100]
- *Employee Participation:* Provisions regarding employee participation rights in the case of a cross-border merger are set out in the Act on Employee Participation in the Case of a Cross-Border Merger (*Gesetz über die Mitbestimmung der Arbeitnehmer bei einer grenzüberschreitenden Verschmelzung, MgVG)*. The system of employee participation is similar to that which is implemented when establishing a SE by way of a merger. As a basic principle, the participation regime following a cross-border merger is governed by the legislation of the country in which the absorbing company has its registered office.[101] The MgVG provides for an agreement to be negotiated by employee representatives and representatives of the company ('negotiation solution'). For this purpose, a special negotiating body has to be formed which represents employees from all affected

[94] See Secs. 13, 122 g UmwG.

[95] See Sec. 122f sentence 2 UmwG.

[96] See Sec. 122g para. 2 UmwG.

[97] See Sec. 122g para. 1 UmwG.

[98] See Sec. 122k para. 2 UmwG.

[99] See Sec. 122k para. 2 UmwG.

[100] See Sec. 122k para. 4 UmwG.

[101] See Sec. 4 MgVG.

countries.[102] The management of the merging companies and the special negotiating body create an agreement on the participation of the employees.[103] If no agreement can be reached, a set of statutory contingency rules applies. In principle, these tie up the pre-merger proportion of employee representatives in the supervisory or administrative body of the companies which were merged. The number of employee representatives in the supervisory or administrative body of the company resulting from the merger is based on the highest proportion of employee representatives among the merged companies.[104]

5.4.5 The SEVIC Decision of the ECJ

In its *SEVIC* decision of 2005[105], the ECJ handed down another landmark decision expanding a company's options for cross-border restructuring and mobility under Art. 49, 54 TFEU. This decision remains particularly important for scenarios which are not covered by the Cross-Border Mergers Directive (such as a merger of partnerships). In *SEVIC*, the ECJ held that the refusal of the German courts to register a cross-border merger between a Luxembourg S.A. and the German SEVIC Systems AG constituted an unjustified restriction of the Freedom of Establishment. Restrictions could only be justified for overriding public interests (none of which was applicable), but a general refusal of such a merger (as under the German transformation laws) was not justified. Thus, as long as the EU Cross-Border Mergers Directive had not been implemented in all Member States, this ECJ judgment provided for an alternative option. Even after the implementation of the Cross-Border Mergers Directive in the Member States, the decision still is important, as it (1) applies to non-corporate business forms, such as partnerships and (2) allows cross-border restructuring measures other than mergers, e.g. de-mergers, divisions or spin-offs.[106]

5.5 International Joint Ventures—A Check List for Relevant Issues

5.5.1 Commercial Background for Establishing a Joint Venture

Joint ventures have become more and more important, especially in the cross-border activities of business organizations. The increasing internationalization of commerce and the trend towards globalization in many industries have contributed to this increasing popularity of joint venture agreements between business organiza-

[102] See Secs. 6 para. 1, 7 MgVG.

[103] See Sec. 22 MgVG.

[104] See Secs. 23 *et seq.* MgVG.

[105] ECJ, case C-411/03 *SEVIC* ECR [2005] I-10805.

[106] For a comprehensive analysis of the SEVIC judgement see Siems 2007, pp. 307 *et seq.*

tions from different jurisdictions. The term 'joint venture' is a commercial, rather than a legal, term and usually means a business project or venture undertaken between two commercial entities. As transactions and projects constantly increase in size and urgency, the resources of individual companies may quickly become exhausted, particularly where a number of foreign jurisdictions are involved. Thus, it makes more sense to enter into a joint venture with another company or companies. A joint venture can take many different legal forms, for example it can take the form of a partnership, a joint-venture company (also known as a 'JVC') or may simply be in the form of a contractual agreement between two companies wishing to work together on a common project (e.g. a large-scale building project). The name 'joint venture' implies a degree of equality in the relationship of the parties involved, i.e. each company may contribute different things—be it capital, know-how, personnel, local knowledge, contacts, brand name etc. However, whatever the advantages of a joint venture for the individual parties, there is also always an element of sacrifice involved in such a joint venture, for example a sacrifice of the control and flexibility which a company might otherwise have enjoyed if it had continued its business project on its own. So why form or undertake a joint venture?

Apart from the reasons already mentioned above (i.e. contribution of various resources etc.), a joint venture can be a very flexible and cost-effective way for companies to gain the benefit of each other's strengths, in particular where foreign jurisdictions are concerned. An example may be two companies, one established in a developed country (for example US or Europe) and another company established in a less-developed country (for example Africa or India). The US/European company can, for example, offer expertise, personnel, capital and goods or services, whereas the less-developed company may not be able to contribute much capital, but can instead provide critical knowledge of the market, contacts and knowledge of the regulatory environment. In such a case, a joint venture could be very successful. There are, of course, also other commercial reasons why parties wish to enter into joint ventures. Here are some of the most important reasons:

- *Cost Savings* can be achieved by sharing the costs of research and development or of large capital investments with a joint venture partner (particularly in many industries such as electronics, defense, pharmaceuticals, telecommunications etc. where such investment and research costs are phenomenal).
- *Risk Sharing.* As with cost sharing, it makes sense to share the burden of risk, particularly where significant financial risks are involved, with another party. For example, some projects of considerable size, such as power stations or infrastructure projects are often undertaken in the form of joint ventures.
- *Technology.* As technology is another rapidly changing medium for exchange of skills and information, technical skills and resources can be 'shared' more effectively between joint venture partners.
- *Expanding the Customer Base.* International joint ventures provide the most effective route for a joint venture partner to expand its customer base, simply by using a joint venture partner's strengths and already existent knowledge of a certain geographic market etc., or buying into an existing distribution or sales network through another joint venture partner.

- *Gaining Access to Emerging Markets.* In some cases, joint ventures may be the only realistic route for gaining entry to new emerging markets (for example in some eastern European and Asian countries) where access to local knowledge etc. is often a necessity.
- *New Technical Markets.* In some technological areas where constant rapid change itself produces new markets, effective entry into such markets can be facilitated by entering into a joint venture partnership with a company that already has existing knowledge and expertise in that area.
- *Surviving Global Competition.* Particularly on an international scale, the merger of similar businesses between several parties may be desirable in order to establish economies of scale and other advantages to meet international competition.
- *Better Financing Through Joint Venture.* By forming a joint venture with a financial partner, an acquisition may be more easily financed than would otherwise have been possible on a go-it-alone basis.
- *Stepping Stone for Acquisitions.* A joint venture may be a first step in an eventual disposal or acquisition of a business.
- *Catalyst for Change.* Sometimes there is a less obvious reason for setting up a joint venture other than the above-mentioned. Examples may be a wish to create change or to stimulate activity in a particular area of a company's business.

5.5.2 Outline of Key Issues for Establishing a Joint Venture

Now we will present a brief outline which focuses on the key issues to be taken into consideration when establishing a joint venture. Joint ventures are typically formed on the basis of ongoing business relationships and with the aim of governing a jointly owned business. Not surprisingly, no standard joint venture exists, but rather the legal framework will depend, *inter alia*, on the business objectives of the parties, their location and legal background and, finally, on the nature and the size of the business.

Since most jurisdictions do not provide for specific legal rules on joint ventures, the legal design of joint ventures will usually be left to the parties and their lawyers. The joint venture agreement often provides for the establishment of a specific legal entity, serving as the business vehicle. Here, finding the right balance between the law governing the agreement between the parties to the joint venture and the law applicable to the vehicle often poses a challenge.

A business lawyer advising on the structure of a joint venture would, in particular, ask the following questions:

- What type of joint venture vehicle should be established (usually a corporation such as a GmbH, but sometimes a partnership may be preferable e.g. for tax purposes)?
- Where should the joint venture company be located?
- What kind of human resources and assets (people, services, technology etc.) will have to be contributed by each party?

- In the case of a corporation (GmbH, AG) as a joint venture vehicle, how are the shares divided? Is a 50:50 split adequate?
- Minority protection: If a 50:50 split is not chosen, how is the party with a minority interest protected? (Participation in important decisions, veto right, protection against dilution of equity, distribution of profits, access to relevant information, 'exit' rights etc.)?
- Non-compete clauses: What is the scope of non-compete clauses with regard to competitors of the parties to the joint venture?
- What happens in the case of a termination of the joint venture?
- What happens in the case of an insolvency of the joint venture vehicle?

References

Cheffins BR (1997) Company law—theory, structure and operation. Oxford University Press, Oxford

Kieninger EM (2004) The legal framework of regulatory competition based on company mobility: EU and US compared. GLJ 6:741–770

Kjellgren A (2000) On the border of abuse—the jurisprudence of the European Court of Justice on Circumvention, Fraud and Other Misuses of Community Law. EBLR 11:179–194

Sandrock O (1979) Die Konkretisierung der Überlagerungstheorie. In: Sandrock O (ed) Festschrift für Günther Beitzke. de Gruyter, Berlin, pp 669–696

Schulz M (2006) European challenges for German corporate law: an analysis of the recent jurisprudence of the European Court of Justice on the freedom of establishment and its impact on German Company Law and Conflict of Laws. In: Miller RA, Zumbansen PC (eds) Annual of German & European law, vol. II/III 2004–2005. Berghahn Books, New York, pp 132–155

Schulz M, Sester P (2002) Höchstrichterliche Harmonisierung der Kollisionsregeln im europäischen Gesellschaftsrecht: Durchbruch der Gründungstheorie nach "Überseering". EWS 13(12):545–552

Schulz M, Wasmeier O (2010) Geschäftsleiterhaftung bei Auslandsgesellschaften—Entwicklung, Stand und Perspektiven. RIW 56(10):657–667

Sester P, Cárdenas JL (2005) The Extra-communitarian effects of centros, Überseering and Inspire Art with Regard to Fourth Generation Association Agreements. ECFR 2:398–412

Siems M (2007) SEVIC: Beyond cross-border mergers. EBOR 8:307–316

Sonnenberger HJ, Bauer F (2007) Proposal of the Deutscher Rat für Internationales Privatrecht for European and national legislation in the field of international company law. In: Sonnenberger HJ (ed) Vorschläge und Berichte zur Reform des europäischen und deutschen internationalen Gesellschaftsrechts. Siebeck, Tübingen, pp 65–122

Supplementary Materials

6

Abstract

The following chapter provides selected supplementary materials. Section 6.1 contains a convenience translation into English of selected relevant German statutes. Section 6.2 presents some exemplary corporate documents, in particular, a simple English version of a GmbH's articles of association and an English translation of typical rules of procedure for the management of a GmbH. Finally, Sect. 6.3 contains a selection of publications on German, international and comparative issues of business law which may prove useful for those readers who want to conduct further studies in this field.

Contents

6.1 Convenience Translations

6.1.1 Excerpts from the German Act on Limited Liability Companies (*GmbH-Gesetz*)

▶ NOTE: Translation into English is intended as a convenience translation for non-German speaking readers. While the authors have striven to ensure that the two texts are as similar as possible, translation accuracy cannot be guaranteed. In cases of discrepencies between the two texts, reference should be made to the official German text.

M. Schulz, O. Wasmeier, *The Law of Business Organizations*,
DOI 10.1007/978-3-642-17793-4_6, © Springer-Verlag Berlin Heidelberg 2012

Erster Abschnitt Errichtung der Gesellschaft	Part One Establishment of the Company
§ 1 *Zweck; Gründerzahl*	*§ 1* *Purpose, Number of Founders*
Gesellschaften mit beschränkter Haftung können nach Maßgabe der Bestimmungen dieses Gesetzes zu jedem gesetzlich zulässigen Zweck durch eine oder mehrere Personen errichtet werden.	Companies with limited liability can be established by one or more persons according to the provisions of this Law for any legally permissible purpose.
§ 2 *Form des Gesellschaftsvertrags*	*§ 2* *Form of the Articles of Association*
(1) Der Gesellschaftsvertrag bedarf notarieller Form. Er ist von sämtlichen Gesellschaftern zu unterzeichnen.	(1) The Articles of Association must be notarized. They must be signed by all shareholders.
(1a) Die Gesellschaft kann in einem vereinfachten Verfahren gegründet werden, wenn sie höchstens drei Gesellschafter und einen Geschäftsführer hat. Für die Gründung im vereinfachten Verfahren ist das in der Anlage bestimmte Musterprotokoll zu verwenden. Darüber hinaus dürfen keine vom Gesetz abweichenden Bestimmungen getroffen werden. Das Musterprotokoll gilt zugleich als Gesellschafterliste. Im Übrigen finden auf das Musterprotokoll die Vorschriften dieses Gesetzes über den Gesellschaftsvertrag entsprechende Anwendung.	(1a) The company can be established by way of a simplified formation procedure, provided the company has not more than three shareholders and one managing director. For this simplified formation procedure the standard form protocol (attached as an annex) has to be used with no deviations. from the statutory framework allowed. The standard form protocol will also be deemed as the list of shareholders. Apart from that, the regulations of this Act regarding the articles of association of the company will apply mutatis mutandis.
(2) Die Unterzeichnung durch Bevollmächtigte ist nur auf Grund einer notariell errichteten oder beglaubigten Vollmacht zulässig.	(2) Signing by authorized representatives requires a Power of Attorney recorded or certified by a Notary.
§ 3 *Inhalt des Gesellschaftsvertrags*	*§ 3* *Content of the Articles of Association*
(1) Der Gesellschaftsvertrag muss enthalten:	(1) The Articles of Association must contain:
1. die Firma und den Sitz der Gesellschaft,	1. the name and registered seat of the company,
2. den Gegenstand des Unternehmens,	2. the object of the company,
3. den Betrag des Stammkapitals,	3. the amount of the registered share capital,
4. die Zahl und die Nennbeträge der Geschäftsanteile, die jeder Gesellschafter gegen Einlage auf das Stammkapital (Stammeinlage) übernimmt.	4. the number and the amount of shares which each shareholder must contribute to the share capital (original contribution).
(2) Soll das Unternehmen auf eine gewisse Zeit beschränkt sein oder sollen den Gesellschaftern außer der Leistung von Kapitaleinlagen noch andere Verpflichtungen gegenüber der Gesellschaft auferlegt werden, so bedürfen auch diese Bestimmungen der Aufnahme in den Gesellschaftsvertrag.	(2) Should the enterprise be established for a limited period of time, or should other obligations towards the company be imposed on the shareholders other than the capital contribution payments, then these provisions must also be included in the Articles of Association.

§ 4 *Firma*	*§ 4* *Company Name*
Die Firma der Gesellschaft muss, auch wenn sie nach § 22 des Handelsgesetzbuchs oder nach anderen gesetzlichen Vorschriften fortgeführt wird, die Bezeichnung „Gesellschaft mit beschränkter Haftung" oder eine allgemein verständliche Abkürzung dieser Bezeichnung enthalten.	The name of the company must contain the term "limited liability company", or a generally understandable abbreviation of this designation, even if the existing company name is retained in accordance with Sec. 22 of the Commercial Code or in accordance with other statutory provisions.
§ 4a *Sitz der Gesellschaft*	*§ 4a* *Registered Office of the Company*
Sitz der Gesellschaft ist der Ort im Inland, den der Gesellschaftsvertrag bestimmt.	The registered office of the company is the domestic place designated in the Articles of Association.
§ 5 *Stammkapital; Geschäftsanteil*	*§ 5* *Registered Share Capital; Share*
(1) Das Stammkapital der Gesellschaft muss mindestens fünfundzwanzigtausend Euro betragen.	(1) The registered share capital of the company must amount to a minimum of twenty-five thousand Euros.
(2) Der Nennbetrag jedes Geschäftsanteils muss auf volle Euro lauten. Ein Gesellschafter kann bei Errichtung der Gesellschaft mehrere Geschäftsanteile übernehmen.	(2) The amount of each share capital contribution has to be denominated in full Euro. Upon registration, a shareholder may take over several shares.
(3) Die Höhe der Nennbeträge der einzelnen Geschäftsanteile kann verschieden bestimmt werden. Die Summe der Nennbeträge aller Geschäftsanteile muss mit dem Stammkapital übereinstimmen.	(3) The amount of each share capital contribution can be determined differently. The sum of the share capital contributions must equal the registered share capital.
(4) Sollen Sacheinlagen geleistet werden, so müssen der Gegenstand der Sacheinlage und der Nennbetrag des Geschäftsanteils, auf den sich die Sacheinlage bezieht, im Gesellschaftsvertrag festgesetzt werden. Die Gesellschafter haben in einem Sachgründungsbericht die für die Angemessenheit der Leistungen für Sacheinlagen wesentlichen Umstände darzulegen und beim Übergang eines Unternehmens auf die Gesellschaft die Jahresergebnisse der beiden letzten Geschäftsjahre anzugeben.	(4) Where contributions are to be made in kind, the items comprising the contribution in kind and the amount of the share capital contribution they are to cover must be stated in the Articles of Association. The shareholders shall, in a report on formation using contributions in kind, set out the major considerations supporting the appropriateness of the valuation of the non-cash contributions and, where a business is transferred to the company, the results of the last two fiscal years must be stated.
§ 5a *Unternehmergesellschaft*	*§ 5a* *Entrepreneurial Company*
(1) Eine Gesellschaft, die mit einem Stammkapital gegründet wird, das den Betrag des Mindeststammkapitals nach § 5 Abs. 1 unterschreitet, muss in der Firma abweichend von § 4 die Bezeichnung „Unternehmergesellschaft (haftungsbeschränkt)" oder „UG (haftungsbeschränkt)" führen.	(1) A company which is established with a registered share capital below the amount prescribed in Sec. 5 para. 1 is required to use the firm name "Entrepreneurial Company (with limited liability) or "UG" (with limited liability), in deviation from Sec. 4.

(2) Abweichend von § 7 Abs. 2 darf die Anmeldung erst erfolgen, wenn das Stammkapital in voller Höhe eingezahlt ist. Sacheinlagen sind ausgeschlossen.	(2) In deviation from Sec. 7 para. 2 the Entrepreneurial Company may only file for the application of its registration if the share capital has been fully paid up. Contributions in kind are not permitted.
(3) In der Bilanz des nach den §§ 242, 264 des Handelsgesetzbuchs aufzustellenden Jahresabschlusses ist eine gesetzliche Rücklage zu bilden, in die ein Viertel des um einen Verlustvortrag aus dem Vorjahr geminderten 2Jahresüberschusses einzustellen ist. Die Rücklage darf nur verwandt werden	(3) In the balance sheet of the annual account (to be prepared according to Secs. 242, 264 of the German Commercial Code) the UG is required to include a statutory reserve amounting to a quarter of the annual surplus minus the accumulated deficit of the preceding year. This reserve may only be used for
1. für Zwecke des § 57c;	1. the purposes set out in Sec. 57c;
2. zum Ausgleich eines Jahresfehlbetrags, soweit er nicht durch einen Gewinnvortrag aus dem Vorjahr gedeckt ist;	2. offsetting an annual loss to the extent it is not covered by a profit from the preceding year;
3. zum Ausgleich eines Verlustvortrags aus dem Vorjahr, soweit er nicht durch einen Jahresüberschuss gedeckt ist.	3. offsetting a loss carried forward, insofar as it is not covered by the annual profits.
(4) Abweichend von § 49 Abs. 3 muss die Versammlung der Gesellschafter bei drohender Zahlungsunfähigkeit unverzüglich einberufen werden.	(4) In deviation from Sec. 49 para. 3 the shareholders' meeting has to be called in case of the UG's imminent inability to pay its debts.
(5) Erhöht die Gesellschaft ihr Stammkapital so, dass es den Betrag des Mindeststammkapitals nach § 5 Abs. 1 erreicht oder übersteigt, finden die Absätze 1 bis 4 keine Anwendung mehr; die Firma nach Absatz 1 darf beibehalten werden.	(5) If the company increases its registered share capital to the extent that it reaches or exceeds the amount of the minimum statutory capital pursuant to Sec. 5 para. 1, para. 1–4 do not apply; and the company name according to para. 1 may be retained.
§ 6 *Geschäftsführer*	*§ 6* *Managing Director*
(1) Die Gesellschaft muss einen oder mehrere Geschäftsführer haben.	(1) The company must have one or more managing directors.
(2) Geschäftsführer kann nur eine natürliche, unbeschränkt geschäftsfähige Person sein. Geschäftsführer kann nicht sein, wer	(2) Only a natural person with unrestricted legal capacity may serve as managing director. A person cannot be a managing director, who
1. als Betreuter bei der Besorgung seiner Vermögensangelegenheiten ganz oder teilweise einem Einwilligungsvorbehalt (§ 1903 des Bürgerlichen Gesetzbuchs) unterliegt,	1. as a person under guardianship, with respect to the managing of his financial affairs, is partially or totally subject to a consent requirement pursuant to Sec. 1903 of the German Civil Code,
2. aufgrund eines gerichtlichen Urteils oder einer vollziehbaren Entscheidung einer Verwaltungsbehörde einen Beruf, einen Berufszweig, ein Gewerbe oder einen Gewerbezweig nicht ausüben darf, sofern der Unternehmensgegenstand ganz oder teilweise mit dem Gegenstand des Verbots übereinstimmt,	2. by judgment of a court or an enforceable decision of an administrative agency, is not allowed to practice a certain profession or trade or a branch thereof, to the extent that the business object wholly or partially corresponds with the prohibition,

3. wegen einer oder mehrerer vorsätzlich begangener Straftaten	3. has been convicted of one or more of the following premeditated criminal offences:
a) des Unterlassens der Stellung des Antrags auf Eröffnung des Insolvenzverfahrens (Insolvenzverschleppung),	a) omission to file for insolvency proceedings (delay in filing a petition for insolvency),
b) nach den §§ 283 bis 283d des Strafgesetzbuches (Insolvenzstraftaten),	b) pursuant to Sec. 283–283d of the German Penal Code (crimes relating to insolvency of the company),
c) der falschen Angaben nach § 82 dieses Gesetzes oder § 399 des Aktiengesetzes,	c) false statements pursuant to Sec. 82 of the German Act on Limited Liability Companies or pursuant to Sec. 399 of the German Stock Corporation Act,
d) der unrichtigen Darstellung nach § 400 des Aktiengesetzes, § 331 des Handelsgesetzbuchs, § 313 des Umwandlungsgesetzes oder § 17 des Publizitätsgesetzes oder	d) incorrect statements pursuant to Sec. 400 of the German Stock Corporation Act, Sec. 331 of the German Commercial Code, Sec. 313 of the German Transformation Act or Sec. 17 of the German Publicity Act, or
e) nach den §§ 263 bis 264a oder den §§ 265b bis 266a des Strafgesetzbuches zu einer Freiheitsstrafe von mindestens einem Jahr	e) pursuant to Sec. 263–264a or Secs. 265b-266a of the German Penal Code to imprisonment of at least one year
verurteilt worden ist; dieser Ausschluss gilt für die Dauer von fünf Jahren seit der Rechtskraft des Urteils, wobei die Zeit nicht eingerechnet wird, in welcher der Täter auf behördliche Anordnung in einer Anstalt verwahrt worden ist. Satz 2 Nr. 3 gilt entsprechend bei einer Verurteilung im Ausland wegen einer Tat, die mit den Satz 2 Nr. 3 genannten Taten vergleichbar ist.	This disqualification applies for a period of five years after the sentence became final, such period shall not include any time during which the convicted person was confined to an institution by official order. Sentence 2 no. 3 applies mutatis mutandis for a conviction abroad for a crime comparable to those listed in Sentence 2 no. 3.
(3) Zu Geschäftsführern können Gesellschafter oder andere Personen bestellt werden. Die Bestellung erfolgt entweder im Gesellschaftsvertrag oder nach Maßgabe der Bestimmungen des dritten Abschnitts.	(3) Shareholders or other persons can be appointed as managing directors. The appointment is effected either through the Articles of Association or in accordance with the provisions of Part Three herein.
(4) Ist im Gesellschaftsvertrag bestimmt, dass sämtliche Gesellschafter zur Geschäftsführung berechtigt sein sollen, so gelten nur die der Gesellschaft bei Festsetzung dieser Bestimmung angehörenden Personen als die bestellten Geschäftsführer.	(4) If the Articles of Association provide that all shareholders are authorized to manage the company, only such persons who are shareholders of the company when this provision is adopted shall be deemed to be the appointed managing directors.
(5) Gesellschafter, die vorsätzlich oder grob fahrlässig einer Person, die nicht Geschäftsführer sein kann, die Führung der Geschäfte überlassen, haften der Gesellschaft solidarisch für den Schaden, der dadurch entsteht, dass diese Person die ihr gegenüber der Gesellschaft bestehenden Obliegenheiten verletzt.	(5) Shareholders who intentionally, or by grossly negligent behaviour, leave the management of the company up to a person who cannot be a managing director, are jointly liable to the company for the damage resulting from the fact that such person breaches his obligations towards the company.

§ 7 *Anmeldung der Gesellschaft*	*§ 7* *Application for the Entry of the Company*
(1) Die Gesellschaft ist bei dem Gericht, in dessen Bezirk sie ihren Sitz hat, zur Eintragung in das Handelsregister anzumelden.	(1) The company must be registered with the commercial register of the court in whose district the company has its registered office.
(2) Die Anmeldung darf erst erfolgen, wenn auf jeden Geschäftsanteil, soweit nicht Sacheinlagen vereinbart sind, ein Viertel des Nennbetrages eingezahlt ist. Insgesamt muss auf das Stammkapital mindestens soviel eingezahlt sein, dass der Gesamtbetrag der eingezahlten Geldeinlagen zuzüglich des Gesamtnennbetrags der Geschäftsanteile, für die Sacheinlagen zu leisten sind, die Hälfte des Mindeststammkapitals gemäß § 5 Abs. 1 erreicht.	(2) The application may not be made until at least one quarter of every share has been paid in, unless contributions in kind have been agreed upon. The total amount of the cash contribution paid, plus the total amount of contributions in kind, must equal at least one half of the required minimum share capital pursuant to Sec. 5 para. 1.
(3) Die Sacheinlagen sind vor der Anmeldung der Gesellschaft zur Eintragung in das Handelsregister so an die Gesellschaft zu bewirken, daß sie endgültig zur freien Verfügung der Geschäftsführer stehen.	(3) Prior to the application of the company for registration with the commercial register, contributions in kind must be provided to the company in a way that they are finally at the free disposal of the managing directors.
§ 8 *Inhalt der Anmeldung*	*§ 8* *Content of the Application*
(1) Der Anmeldung müssen beigefügt sein:	(1) The following must be enclosed in the application:
1. der Gesellschaftsvertrag und im Fall des § 2 Abs. 2 die Vollmachten der Vertreter, welche den Gesellschaftsvertrag unterzeichnet haben, oder eine beglaubigte Abschrift dieser Urkunden,	1. the articles of association and, in the case of Sec. 2 para. 2, the powers of attorney of the authorized representatives who have signed the articles of association, or a certified copy of these documents,
2. die Legitimation der Geschäftsführer, sofern dieselben nicht im Gesellschaftsvertrag bestellt sind,	2. the evidence of appointment of the managing directors, if they are not appointed in the articles of association,
3. eine von den Anmeldenden unterschriebene Liste der Gesellschafter, aus welcher Name, Vorname, Geburtsdatum und Wohnort der letzteren sowie die Nennbeträge und die laufenden Nummern der von einem jeden derselben übernommenen Geschäftsanteile ersichtlich sind,	3. a list of shareholders, signed by the applicants, indicating each shareholders' surname, first name, date of birth and place of residence, as well as the nominal amounts and numbers of the shares subscribed by them,
4. im Fall des § 5 Abs. 4 die Verträge, die den Festsetzungen zugrunde liegen oder zu ihrer Ausführung geschlossen worden sind, und der Sachgründungsbericht,	4. in the case of Sec. 5 para. 4, the contracts which form the basis for the stipulation, or which were concluded for the purpose of their implementation, and the report on formation through contributions in kind,

5. wenn Sacheinlagen vereinbart sind, Unterlagen darüber, dass der Wert der Sacheinlagen den Nennbetrag der dafür übernommenen Geschäftsanteile erreicht,	5. if contributions in kind have been stipulated, documents evidencing that the value of the contributions in kind reaches the nominal amount of the subscribed shares,
(2) In der Anmeldung ist die Versicherung abzugeben, dass die in § 7 Abs. 2 und 3 bezeichneten Leistungen auf die Geschäftsanteile bewirkt sind und dass der Gegenstand der Leistungen sich endgültig in der freien Verfügung der Geschäftsführer befindet. Das Gericht kann bei erheblichen Zweifeln an der Richtigkeit der Versicherung Nachweise (unter anderem Einzahlungsbelege) verlangen.	(2) The application must contain the assurance that the contributions described in Sec. 7 paras. 2 and 3 in respect of the shares, have been made and that the subject-matter of the payments are finally at the free disposal of the managing directors. In the case of serious doubt, the court may request further proof of evidence (inter alia pay-in slips).
(3) In der Anmeldung haben die Geschäftsführer zu versichern, dass keine Umstände vorliegen, die ihrer Bestellung nach § 6 Abs. 2 Satz 2 Nr. 2 und 3 sowie Satz 3 entgegenstehen, und dass sie über ihre unbeschränkte Auskunftspflicht gegenüber dem Gericht belehrt worden sind. Die Belehrung nach § 53 Abs. 2 des Bundeszentralregistergesetzes kann schriftlich vorgenommen werden; sie kann auch durch einen Notar oder einen im Ausland bestellten Notar, durch einen Vertreter eines vergleichbaren rechtsberatenden Berufs oder einen Konsularbeamten erfolgen.	(3) In the application, the managing directors must confirm that no circumstances exist which, pursuant to Sec. 6 para. 2 sentence 2 nos. 2 and 3, as well as sentence 3, would prevent their appointment, and that they have been advised of their unrestricted duty to provide information to the court. The notification under Sec. 53 para. 2 of the Central Register may be performed in written form, it may also be performed by a notary, or by a notary appointed in a foreign country, or by a representative of a similar legal profession, or by a consular official.
(4) In der Anmeldung sind ferner anzugeben,	(4) The application shall also include:
1. eine inländische Geschäftsanschrift,	1. a domestic business address,
2. Art und Umfang der Vertretungsbefugnis der Geschäftsführer	2. the nature and scope of the power of representation of the managing directors
(5) Für die Einreichung von Unterlagen nach diesem Gesetz gilt § 12 Abs. 2 des Handelsgesetzbuchs entsprechend.	(5) For the submission of documents under this Act, Sec. 12 para. 2 of the Commercial Code will apply mutatis mutandis.
§ 9c *Ablehnung der Eintragung*	*§ 9c* *Refusal of Registration*
(1) Ist die Gesellschaft nicht ordnungsgemäß errichtet und angemeldet, so hat das Gericht die Eintragung abzulehnen. Dies gilt auch, wenn Sacheinlagen nicht unwesentlich überbewertet worden sind.	(1) Where the company has not been duly established or has not been properly filed for registration, the court must refuse to register the company. This also applies where contributions in kind have been overrated to an extent which is not insignificant.
(2) Wegen einer mangelhaften, fehlenden oder nichtigen Bestimmung des Gesellschaftsvertrages darf das Gericht die Eintragung nach Absatz 1 nur ablehnen, soweit diese Bestimmung, ihr Fehlen oder ihre Nichtigkeit	(2) The court may refuse registration pursuant to para. 1 because of an insufficient, missing or void provision of the articles of association only insofar as such provision, its absence or its invalidity

1. Tatsachen oder Rechtsverhältnisse betrifft, die nach § 3 Abs. 1 oder auf Grund anderer zwingender gesetzlicher Vorschriften in dem Gesellschaftsvertrag bestimmt sein müssen oder die in das Handelsregister einzutragen oder von dem Gericht bekannt zu machen sind,	1. relates to facts or legal relationships which, pursuant to Sec. 3 para. 1 or due to other mandatory statutory provisions, have to be specified in the articles of association, or which have to be registered in the commercial register or have to be announced by the court;
2. Vorschriften verletzt, die ausschließlich oder überwiegend zum Schutze der Gläubiger der Gesellschaft oder sonst im öffentlichen Interesse gegeben sind, oder	2. breaches provisions which are enacted exclusively or predominantly for the protection of the creditors of the company or are otherwise in the public interest, or
3. die Nichtigkeit des Gesellschaftsvertrages zur Folge hat.	3. would lead to the invalidity of the articles of association.
§ 10 *Inhalt der Eintragung*	*§ 10* *Content of the Entry*
(1) Bei der Eintragung in das Handelsregister sind die Firma und der Sitz der Gesellschaft, eine inländische Geschäftsanschrift, der Gegenstand des Unternehmens, die Höhe des Stammkapitals, der Tag des Abschlusses des Gesellschaftsvertrags und die Personen der Geschäftsführer anzugeben. Ferner ist einzutragen, welche Vertretungsbefugnis die Geschäftsführer haben.	(1) The entry in the commercial register must indicate the name and registered office of the company, a domestic business address, the object of the company, the amount of registered share capital, the date on which the articles of association were concluded, as well as the identities of the managing directors. In addition, the scope of the power of representation of the managing directors must also be registered.
(2) Enthält der Gesellschaftsvertrag eine Bestimmung über die Zeitdauer der Gesellschaft oder über das genehmigte Kapital, so sind auch diese Bestimmungen einzutragen. Wenn eine Person, die für Willenserklärungen und Zustellungen an die Gesellschaft empfangsberechtigt ist, mit einer inländischen Anschrift zur Eintragung in das Handelsregister angemeldet wird, sind auch diese Angaben einzutragen; Dritten gegenüber gilt die Empfangsberechtigung als fortbestehend, bis sie im Handelsregister gelöscht und die Löschung bekannt gemacht worden ist, es sei denn, dass die fehlende Empfangsberechtigung dem Dritten bekannt war.	(2) If the articles of association contain a provision on the duration of the company or the authorized capital, such provisions must also be registered. If a person, authorized to receive legal declarations and notifications addressed to the company, applies for registration in the commercial register, this information must also be registered. Vis-à-vis third parties, the authority to receive legal declarations and notifications for the company is deemed to continue until this authority is deleted in the commercial register and such deletion has been published, unless the third party knows about the lack of authority to receive legal declarations and notifications for the company.
§ 11 *Rechtszustand vor der Eintragung*	*§ 11* *Legal Situation prior to Registration*
(1) Vor der Eintragung in das Handelsregister des Sitzes der Gesellschaft besteht die Gesellschaft mit beschränkter Haftung als solche nicht.	(1) Prior to the entry of the company's seat in the commercial register, the limited liability company does not exist.
(2) Ist vor der Eintragung im Namen der Gesellschaft gehandelt worden, so haften die Handelnden persönlich und solidarisch.	(2) Any persons acting in the name of the company prior to registration are personally and jointly liable.

§ 12 *Bekanntmachungen der Gesellschaft*	*§ 12* *Notices of the Company*
Bestimmt das Gesetz oder der Gesellschaftsvertrag, dass von der Gesellschaft etwas bekannt zu machen ist, so erfolgt die Bekanntmachung im elektronischen Bundesanzeiger (Gesellschaftsblatt). Daneben kann der Gesellschaftsvertrag andere öffentliche Blätter oder elektronische Informationsmedien als Gesellschaftsblätter bezeichnen. Sieht der Gesellschaftsvertrag vor, dass Bekanntmachungen im Bundesanzeiger erfolgen, so ist die Bekanntmachung im elektronischen Bundesanzeiger ausreichend.	In case of notification requirements under law or by the articles of association, notices shall be published in the electronic Federal Gazette (notice of the company). The articles of association may indicate other journals or electronic media as the notices of the company. If the articles of association provide that notices have to be published in the Federal Gazette, then a publication in the electronic Federal Gazette will suffice.

Zweiter Abschnitt Rechtsverhältnisse der Gesellschaft und der Gesellschafter	Part Two Legal Relationships of the Company and the Shareholders
§ 13 *Juristische Person; Handelsgesellschaft*	*§ 13* *Juristic Person; Commercial Company*
(1) Die Gesellschaft mit beschränkter Haftung als solche hat selbständig ihre Rechte und Pflichten; sie kann Eigentum und andere dingliche Rechte an Grundstücken erwerben, vor Gericht klagen und verklagt werden.	(1) The limited liability company as such has rights and duties of its own, it can acquire property and other rights in real estate and can sue and be sued in court.
(2) Für die Verbindlichkeiten der Gesellschaft haftet den Gläubigern derselben nur das Gesellschaftsvermögen.	(2) Only the assets of the company are available to satisfy the liabilities of the company to its creditors.
(3) Die Gesellschaft gilt als Handelsgesellschaft im Sinne des Handelsgesetzbuchs.	(3) The company is deemed to be a commercial company in the sense of the Commercial Code.
§ 15 *Übertragung von Geschäftsanteilen*	*§ 15* *Transfer of Shares*
(1) Die Geschäftsanteile sind veräußerlich und vererblich.	(1) The shares are both transferable and inheritable.
(2) Erwirbt ein Gesellschafter zu seinem ursprünglichen Geschäftsanteil weitere Geschäftsanteile, so behalten dieselben ihre Selbständigkeit.	(2) If a shareholder acquires shares additional to his original share, these retain their independence.
(3) Zur Abtretung von Geschäftsanteilen durch Gesellschafter bedarf es eines in notarieller Form geschlossenen Vertrags.	(3) A transfer of shares by shareholders requires a notarized contract.
(4) Der notariellen Form bedarf auch eine Vereinbarung, durch welche die Verpflichtung eines Gesellschafters zur Abtretung eines Geschäftsanteils begründet wird. Eine ohne diese Form getroffene Vereinbarung wird jedoch durch den nach Maßgabe des vorigen Absatzes geschlossenen Abtretungsvertrag gültig.	(4) A notarized contract is also required where a shareholder commits himself to transfer a share. An agreement entered into without following this formal requirement will, however, become valid based on a share transfer agreement concluded in accordance with the previous paragraph.

(5) Durch den Gesellschaftsvertrag kann die Abtretung der Geschäftsanteile an weitere Voraussetzungen geknüpft, insbesondere von der Genehmigung der Gesellschaft abhängig gemacht werden.	(5) The articles of association may include additional requirements to be met for the transfer of shares, in particular, an approval requirement by the company.
§ 16 *Rechtsstellung bei Wechsel der Gesellschafter oder Veränderung des Umfangs ihrer Beteiligung; Erwerb vom Nichtberechtigten*	*§ 16* *Legal Position in the case of a Change of Shareholders or Change of the Extent of their Shareholding; Bona Fide Acquisition*
(1) Im Verhältnis zur Gesellschaft gilt im Fall einer Veränderung in den Personen der Gesellschafter oder des Umfangs ihrer Beteiligung als Inhaber eines Geschäftsanteils nur, wer als solcher in der im Handelsregister aufgenommenen Gesellschafterliste (§ 40) eingetragen ist. Eine vom Erwerber in Bezug auf das Gesellschaftsverhältnis vorgenommene Rechtshandlung gilt als von Anfang an wirksam, wenn die Liste unverzüglich nach Vornahme der Rechtshandlung in das Handelsregister aufgenommen wird.	(1) In the case of changes regarding the shareholders or the extent of their participation, only the person who is registered in the list of shareholders (§ 40) entered in the commercial register, is deemed to be the holder of the share vis-à-vis the company. Legal acts regarding the company performed by the purchaser are immediately deemed to be valid, provided that the list of shareholders has been entered into the commercial register, without undue delay, subsequent to the execution of the legal act.
(2) Für Einlageverpflichtungen, die in dem Zeitpunkt rückständig sind, ab dem der Erwerber gemäß Absatz 1 Satz 1 im Verhältnis zur Gesellschaft als Inhaber des Geschäftsanteils gilt, haftet der Erwerber neben dem Veräußerer.	(2) The purchaser is jointly liable with the seller for share capital contributions which are outstanding at the time when the purchaser is deemed to be the owner of the share vis-à-vis the company, according to para. 1 sentence 1.
(3) Der Erwerber kann einen Geschäftsanteil oder ein Recht daran durch Rechtsgeschäft wirksam vom Nichtberechtigten erwerben, wenn der Veräußerer als Inhaber des Geschäftsanteils in der im Handelsregister aufgenommenen Gesellschafterliste eingetragen ist. Dies gilt nicht, wenn die Liste zum Zeitpunkt des Erwerbs hinsichtlich des Geschäftsanteils weniger als drei Jahre unrichtig und die Unrichtigkeit dem Berechtigten nicht zuzurechnen ist. Ein gutgläubiger Erwerb ist ferner nicht möglich, wenn dem Erwerber die mangelnde Berechtigung bekannt oder infolge grober Fahrlässigkeit unbekannt ist oder der Liste ein Widerspruch zugeordnet ist. Die Zuordnung eines Widerspruchs erfolgt aufgrund einer einstweiligen Verfügung oder aufgrund einer Bewilligung desjenigen, gegen dessen Berechtigung sich der Widerspruch richtet. Eine Gefährdung des Rechts des Widersprechenden muss nicht glaubhaft gemacht werden.	(3) The purchaser may legally acquire a share, or a right in a share, from a non-entitled owner by way of a legal transaction, provided that the seller is on the list of shareholders entered into the commercial register. This does not apply if, at the time of the acquisition of the respective shares, the list of shareholders was incorrect for a period of less than three years, and such deficiency is not attributable to the actual owner. A bona fide acquisition is also not possible if the purchaser knows, or, but for his grossly negligent behavior, should have known about the lack of authority of the seller, or if an objection is entered in the list of shareholders. The allocation of an objection is entered based on a temporary injunction or based on the consent of the person against whose entitlement the objection is directed. The objecting party does not have to show the potential of adverse effects against their rights.

§ 30 *Kapitalerhaltung*	§ 30 *Preservation of Share Capital*
(1) Das zur Erhaltung des Stammkapitals erforderliche Vermögen der Gesellschaft darf an die Gesellschafter nicht ausgezahlt werden. Satz 1 gilt nicht bei Leistungen, die bei Bestehen eines Beherrschungs- oder Gewinnabführungsvertrags (§ 291 des Aktiengesetzes) erfolgen oder durch einen vollwertigen Gegenleistungs- oder Rückgewähranspruch gegen den Gesellschafter gedeckt sind. Satz 1 ist zudem nicht anzuwenden auf die Rückgewähr eines Gesellschafterdarlehens und Leistungen auf Forderungen aus Rechtshandlungen, die einem Gesellschafterdarlehen wirtschaftlich entsprechen.	(1) The assets of the company required to maintain the registered share capital must not be repaid to the shareholders. Sentence 1 shall not apply to payments which are made under an existing domination or profit transfer agreement (Sec. 291 Stock Corporation Act), or which are covered by a fully valuable claim for repayment against the shareholders. Sentence 1 shall also apply neither to the repayment of a shareholder loan or to payments on claims resulting from transactions which economically can be compared to a shareholder loan.
(2) Eingezahlte Nachschüsse können, soweit sie nicht zur Deckung eines Verlustes am Stammkapital erforderlich sind, an die Gesellschafter zurückgezahlt werden. Die Zurückzahlung darf nicht vor Ablauf von drei Monaten erfolgen, nachdem der Rückzahlungsbeschluß nach § 12 bekanntgemacht ist. Im Fall des § 28 Abs. 2 ist die Zurückzahlung von Nachschüssen vor der Volleinzahlung des Stammkapitals unzulässig. Zurückgezahlte Nachschüsse gelten als nicht eingezogen.	(2) Additional contribution payments may be repaid to the shareholders if they are not required to cover a loss of the registered share capital. Such repayments must not be made before the expiration of three months after a shareholder resolution on the repayment was announced pursuant to Sec. 12. In case of Sec. 28 para. 2, the repayment of additional contribution payments is prohibited until the registered share capital has been fully paid in. Repaid additional contribution payments are deemed to have not been paid.
§ 31 *Erstattung verbotener Rückzahlungen*	§ 31 *Refunding of Prohibited Repayments*
(1) Zahlungen, welche den Vorschriften des § 30 zuwider geleistet sind, müssen der Gesellschaft erstattet werden.	(1) Payments made in breach of the provisions of Sec. 30 must be repaid to the company.
(2) War der Empfänger in gutem Glauben, so kann die Erstattung nur insoweit verlangt werden, als sie zur Befriedigung der Gesellschaftsgläubiger erforderlich ist.	(2) If the recipient acted in good faith, a refund may only be claimed to the extent necessary to satisfy the company's creditors.
(3) Ist die Erstattung von dem Empfänger nicht zu erlangen, so haften für den zu erstattenden Betrag, soweit er zur Befriedigung der Gesellschaftsgläubiger erforderlich ist, die übrigen Gesellschafter nach Verhältnis ihrer Geschäftsanteile. Beiträge, welche von einzelnen Gesellschaftern nicht zu erlangen sind, werden nach dem bezeichneten Verhältnis auf die übrigen verteilt.	(3) Where a refund cannot be obtained from the recipient, the other shareholders are liable in relation to their shares for the amount to be refunded, to the extent required for the satisfaction of the company's creditors. Amounts that cannot be obtained from individual shareholders shall be allocated to the other shareholders in relation to their shares.
(4) Zahlungen, welche auf Grund der vorstehenden Bestimmungen zu leisten sind, können den Verpflichteten nicht erlassen werden.	(4) The persons obligated to make payments on the basis of the above provisions cannot be released from the required payments.

(5) Die Ansprüche der Gesellschaft verjähren in den Fällen des Absatzes 1 in zehn Jahren sowie in den Fällen des Absatzes 3 in fünf Jahren. Die Verjährung beginnt mit dem Ablauf des Tages, an welchem die Zahlung, deren Erstattung beansprucht wird, geleistet ist. In den Fällen des Absatzes 1 findet § 19 Abs. 6 Satz 2 entsprechende Anwendung.	(5) The claims of the company are time-barred after ten years in the case of para. 1 and after five years in the cases of para. 3. The period of limitations commences with the end of the day on which the payment, for which a refund was claimed, is made. In the cases of para. 1, Sec. 19 para. 6 sentence 2 shall apply mutatis mutandis.
(6) Für die in den Fällen des Absatzes 3 geleistete Erstattung einer Zahlung sind den Gesellschaftern die Geschäftsführer, welchen in betreff der geleisteten Zahlung ein Verschulden zur Last fällt, solidarisch zum Ersatz verpflichtet. Die Bestimmungen in § 43 Abs. 1 und 4 finden entsprechende Anwendung.	(6) The managing directors who culpably caused a payment are jointly and severally liable to the shareholders for the refund of a payment pursuant to para. 3. The provisions of Sec. 43 paras. 1 and 4 will apply mutatis mutandis.

Dritter Abschnitt Vertretung und Geschäftsführung	Part Three Representation and Management
§ 35 *Vertretung der Gesellschaft*	*§ 35* *Representation of the Company*
(1) Die Gesellschaft wird durch die Geschäftsführer gerichtlich und außergerichtlich vertreten. Hat eine Gesellschaft keinen Geschäftsführer (Führungslosigkeit), wird die Gesellschaft für den Fall, dass ihr gegenüber Willenserklärungen abgegeben oder Schriftstücke zugestellt werden, durch die Gesellschafter vertreten	(1) The company is represented by the managing directors in and out of court. Where a company has no managing director (lack of management), the company is represented by its shareholders with regard to legal declarations or letters addressed to the company
(2) Sind mehrere Geschäftsführer bestellt, sind sie alle nur gemeinschaftlich zur Vertretung der Gesellschaft befugt, es sei denn, dass der Gesellschaftsvertrag etwas anderes bestimmt. Ist der Gesellschaft gegenüber eine Willenserklärung abzugeben, genügt die Abgabe gegenüber einem Vertreter der Gesellschaft nach Absatz 1. An die Vertreter der Gesellschaft nach Abs. 1 können unter der im Handelsregister eingetragenen Geschäftsanschrift Willenserklärungen abgegeben und Schriftstücke für die Gesellschaft zugestellt werden. Unabhängig hiervon können die Abgabe und die Zustellung auch unter der eingetragenen Anschrift der empfangsberechtigten Person nach § 10 Abs. 2 Satz 2 erfolgen.	(2) If several managing directors are appointed, they may only jointly represent the company unless otherwise stipulated in the articles of association. In the case of legal declarations addressed to the company, they can be delivered to only one representative of the company according to para. 1. Legal declarations and documents can be delivered to the representatives of the company pursuant to para. 1 under the business address registered in the commercial register. Regardless of this, delivery may also be effected under the registered address of a person who is authorized to receive declarations and notifications addressed to the company in accordance with Sec. 10 para. 2 sentence 2.

(3) Befinden sich alle Geschäftsanteile der Gesellschaft in der Hand eines Gesellschafters oder daneben in der Hand der Gesellschaft und ist er zugleich deren alleiniger Geschäftsführer, so ist auf seine Rechtsgeschäfte mit der Gesellschaft § 181 des Bürgerlichen Gesetzbuchs anzuwenden. Rechtsgeschäfte zwischen ihm und der von ihm vertretenen Gesellschaft sind, auch wenn er nicht alleiniger Geschäftsführer ist, unverzüglich nach ihrer Vornahme in eine Niederschrift aufzunehmen.	(3) If all the shares of the company are held by one shareholder or by one shareholder and the company, and if such shareholder simultaneously is its only managing director, then Sec. 181 of the German Civil Code shall be applied to his legal transactions with the company. Legal transactions between him and the company represented by him must be recorded without delay after their performance, even if he is not the only managing director.
§ 37 *Beschränkung der Vertretungsbefugnis*	*§ 37* *Restriction of Representative Authority*
(1) Die Geschäftsführer sind der Gesellschaft gegenüber verpflichtet, die Beschränkungen einzuhalten, welche für den Umfang ihrer Befugnis, die Gesellschaft zu vertreten, durch den Gesellschaftsvertrag oder, soweit dieser nicht ein anderes bestimmt, durch die Beschlüsse der Gesellschafter festgesetzt sind.	(1) The managing directors are obligated towards the company to adhere to the restrictions on the scope of their authority to represent the company imposed by the articles of association or, unless the articles of association provide otherwise, the resolutions of the shareholders.
(2) Gegen dritte Personen hat eine Beschränkung der Befugnis der Geschäftsführer, die Gesellschaft zu vertreten, keine rechtliche Wirkung. Dies gilt insbesondere für den Fall, dass die Vertretung sich nur auf gewisse Geschäfte oder Arten von Geschäften erstrecken oder nur unter gewissen Umständen oder für eine gewisse Zeit oder an einzelnen Orten stattfinden soll, oder dass die Zustimmung der Gesellschafter oder eines Organs der Gesellschaft für einzelne Geschäfte erfordert ist.	(2)Restrictions on the right of the managing directors to represent the company have no legal effect with respect to third parties. This applies, in particular, to cases where the representation only extends to certain transactions or types of transactions or is supposed to take place only under certain circumstances or for a certain time or at particular places, or where the consent of the shareholders, or of an executive body of the company, is required for individual transactions.
§ 38 *Widerruf der Bestellung*	*§ 38* *Revocation of the Appointment*
(1) Die Bestellung der Geschäftsführer ist zu jeder Zeit widerruflich, unbeschadet der Entschädigungsansprüche aus bestehenden Verträgen.	(1) The appointment of the managing directors may be revoked at any time notwithstanding any claims for damages resulting from existing contracts.
(2) Im Gesellschaftsvertrag kann die Zulässigkeit des Widerrufs auf den Fall beschränkt werden, dass wichtige Gründe denselben notwendig machen. Als solche Gründe sind insbesondere grobe Pflichtverletzung oder Unfähigkeit zur ordnungsmäßigen Geschäftsführung anzusehen.	(2) The articles of association may restrict the right of revocation where good cause deems it necessary. Such reasons would include, specifically, a gross breach of duty and incompetent management.

§ 39 *Anmeldung der Geschäftsführer*	*§ 39* *Application for Registration of the Managing Directors*
(1) Jede Änderung in den Personen der Geschäftsführer sowie die Beendigung der Vertretungsbefugnis eines Geschäftsführers ist zur Eintragung in das Handelsregister anzumelden.	(1) An application shall be made for every change regarding the persons acting as managing directors, as well as the termination of a managing director's power of representation, to be registered in the commercial register.
(2) Der Anmeldung sind die Urkunden über die Bestellung der Geschäftsführer oder über die Beendigung der Vertretungsbefugnis in Urschrift oder öffentlich beglaubigter Abschrift beizufügen.	(2) The documents regarding the appointment of the managing directors, or the termination of the power of representation, must be attached to the application in the original or in a certified copy.
(3) Die neuen Geschäftsführer haben in der Anmeldung zu versichern, dass keine Umstände vorliegen, die ihrer Bestellung nach § 6 Abs. 2 Satz 2 Nr. 2 und 3 sowie Satz 3 entgegenstehen und dass sie über ihre unbeschränkte Auskunftspflicht gegenüber dem Gericht belehrt worden sind. § 8 Abs. 3 Satz 2 ist anzuwenden.	(3) The new managing directors must affirm in the application that no circumstances exist which would prevent their appointment pursuant to Sec. 6 para. 2 sentences 2 no. 2 and 3 and sentence 3, and that they have been advised of their unrestricted duty to provide information to the court. Sec. 8 para. 3 sentence 2 is applicable.
§ 40 *Liste der Gesellschafter*	*§ 40* *List of Shareholders*
(1) Die Geschäftsführer haben unverzüglich nach Wirksamwerden jeder Veränderung in den Personen der Gesellschafter oder des Umfangs ihrer Beteiligung eine von ihnen unterschriebene Liste der Gesellschafter zum Handelsregister einzureichen, aus welcher Name, Vorname, Geburtsdatum und Wohnort der letzteren sowie die Nennbeträge und die laufenden Nummern der von einem jeden derselben übernommenen Geschäftsanteile zu entnehmen sind. Die Änderung der Liste durch die Geschäftsführer erfolgt auf Mitteilung und Nachweis.	(1) Upon effect of each change in the identity of the shareholders or the size of their shareholding, the managing directors shall, without undue delay, submit to the commercial register a list of the shareholders, signed by the managing directors, providing the surname, first name, date of birth and place of residence of the shareholders, as well as, the nominal amounts and the serial numbers of their share capital contributions. The list of shareholders will be amended upon notification and proof of change.

(2) Hat ein Notar an Veränderungen nach Absatz 1 Satz 1 mitgewirkt, so hat er unverzüglich nach deren Wirksamwerden ohne Rücksicht auf etwaige später eintretende Unwirksamkeitsgründe die Liste anstelle der Geschäftsführer zu unterschreiben, zum Handelsregister einzureichen und eine Abschrift der geänderten Liste an die Gesellschaft zu übermitteln. Die Liste muss mit der Bescheinigung des Notars versehen sein, dass die geänderten Eintragungen den Veränderungen entsprechen, an denen er mitgewirkt hat, und die übrigen Eintragungen mit dem Inhalt der zuletzt im Handelsregister aufgenommenen Liste übereinstimmen.	(2) If a notary has participated in the amendments according to para. 1 sentence 1, he must sign the list of shareholders without undue delay instead of the managing directors, regardless of future potential grounds for invalidity; he must then submit the list to the commercial register and send a copy of the amended list to the company. The list must be accompanied by a notification from the notary to the effect that the newly filed registrations correspond with those amendments with which the notary assisted and that the other registrations correspond with the contents of the last list of shareholders which was entered into the commercial register.
(3) Geschäftsführer, welche die ihnen nach Absatz 1 obliegende Pflicht verletzen, haften den Gläubigern der Gesellschaft für den daraus entstandenen Schaden als Gesamtschuldner.	(3) Managing directors who breach their duties pursuant to para. 1 are jointly and severally liable to the creditors of the company for the resulting damages.
§ 41 *Buchführung*	*§ 41* *Accounting*
Die Geschäftsführer sind verpflichtet, für die ordnungsmäßige Buchführung der Gesellschaft zu sorgen.	The managing directors are obligated to ensure that the company keeps proper accounting.
§ 42 *Bilanz*	*§ 42* *Balance Sheet*
(1) In der Bilanz des nach den §§ 242, 264 des Handelsgesetzbuchs aufzustellenden Jahresabschlusses ist das Stammkapital als gezeichnetes Kapital auszuweisen.	(1) In the balance sheet to be drafted as part of the annual accounts prepared in accordance with Secs. 242 and 264 of the Commercial Code, the registered share capital shall be shown as subscribed capital.
(2) Das Recht der Gesellschaft zur Einziehung von Nachschüssen der Gesellschafter ist in der Bilanz insoweit zu aktivieren, als die Einziehung bereits beschlossen ist und den Gesellschaftern ein Recht, durch Verweisung auf den Geschäftsanteil sich von der Zahlung der Nachschüsse zu befreien, nicht zusteht. Der nachzuschießende Betrag ist auf der Aktivseite unter den Forderungen gesondert unter der Bezeichnung „Eingeforderte Nachschüsse" auszuweisen, soweit mit der Zahlung gerechnet werden kann. Ein dem Aktivposten entsprechender Betrag ist auf der Passivseite in dem Posten „Kapitalrücklage" gesondert auszuweisen.	(2) The right of the company to call additional contribution payments of the shareholders shall be shown as an asset in the balance sheet, insofar as such has already been resolved by the shareholders, and, the shareholders are not entitled to be released from their obligation to make additional contribution payments. The additional contribution payments to be paid have to be shown on the assets side of the balance sheet among the receivables, under the heading "Additional Contribution Payments Called ", insofar as their payment can be expected. An amount corresponding to such asset shall be shown separately on the liabilities side of the balance sheet under the heading "Capital Reserve".

(3) Ausleihungen, Forderungen und Verbindlichkeiten gegenüber Gesellschaftern sind in der Regel als solche jeweils gesondert auszuweisen oder im Anhang anzugeben; werden sie unter anderen Posten ausgewiesen, so muss diese Eigenschaft vermerkt werden.	(3) As a general rule, loans, receivables and liabilities against shareholders shall be shown as such, in each case separately, or shall be indicated in the annex. If they are shown under other headings, this fact must be indicated.
§ 42a *Vorlage des Jahresabschlusses und des Lageberichts*	*§ 42a* *Submission of Annual Accounts and Management Report*
(1) Die Geschäftsführer haben den Jahresabschluss und den Lagebericht unverzüglich nach der Aufstellung den Gesellschaftern zum Zwecke der Feststellung des Jahresabschlusses vorzulegen. Ist der Jahresabschluss durch einen Abschlussprüfer zu prüfen, so haben die Geschäftsführer ihn zusammen mit dem Lagebericht und dem Prüfungsbericht des Abschlussprüfers unverzüglich nach Eingang des Prüfungsberichts vorzulegen. Hat die Gesellschaft einen Aufsichtsrat, so ist dessen Bericht über das Ergebnis seiner Prüfung ebenfalls unverzüglich vorzulegen.	(1) The managing directors must submit the annual accounts and the management report to the shareholders for their approval without undue delay after their preparation. If the annual accounts have to be audited, the managing directors must submit the annual accounts, the management report and the report of the auditor, without undue delay, upon receipt of the report of the auditor account. If the company has a supervisory board, its report on the results of its findings also has to be submitted without undue delay.
(2) Die Gesellschafter haben spätestens bis zum Ablauf der ersten acht Monate oder, wenn es sich um eine kleine Gesellschaft handelt (§ 267 Abs. 1 des Handelsgesetzbuchs), bis zum Ablauf der ersten elf Monate des Geschäftsjahrs über die Feststellung des Jahresabschlusses und über die Ergebnisverwendung zu beschließen. Der Gesellschaftsvertrag kann die Frist nicht verlängern. Auf den Jahresabschluß sind bei der Feststellung die für seine Aufstellung geltenden Vorschriften anzuwenden.	(2) The shareholders have to resolve upon the approval of the annual accounts, and the appropriation of profits, at the latest by the expiration of the first eight months of the fiscal year or, in the case of a small company (Sec. 267 para. 1 of the Commercial Code), by the expiration of the first eleven months. The articles of association may not extend this time period. The provisions that govern the preparation of the annual accounts shall also apply to its approval.
(3) Hat ein Abschlußprüfer den Jahresabschluß geprüft, so hat er auf Verlangen eines Gesellschafters an den Verhandlungen über die Feststellung des Jahresabschlusses teilzunehmen.	(3) If an auditor has examined the annual accounts, upon the request of a shareholder, he must participate in the discussions on the approval of the annual accounts.
(4) Ist die Gesellschaft zur Aufstellung eines Konzernabschlusses und eines Konzernlageberichts verpflichtet, so sind die Absätze 1 bis 3 entsprechend anzuwenden. Das Gleiche gilt hinsichtlich eines Einzelabschlusses nach § 325 Abs. 2a des Handelsgesetzbuchs, wenn die Gesellschafter die Offenlegung eines solchen beschlossen haben.	(4) If the company has to prepare consolidated annual accounts and a group management report, paras. 1 to 3 apply mutatis mutandis. The same shall apply to the individual annual accounts pursuant to Sec. 325 para. 2a of the Commercial Code, if the shareholders have resolved upon the publication of such statements.

§ 43 *Haftung der Geschäftsführer*	*§ 43* *Liability of the Managing Directors*
(1) Die Geschäftsführer haben in den Angelegenheiten der Gesellschaft die Sorgfalt eines ordentlichen Geschäftsmannes anzuwenden.	(1) The managing directors must exercise the due care of a prudent businessman when managing the affairs of the company.
(2) Geschäftsführer, welche ihre Obliegenheiten verletzen, haften der Gesellschaft solidarisch für den entstandenen Schaden.	(2) Managing directors who violate their duties are jointly and severally liable to the company for the resulting damages.
(3) Insbesondere sind sie zum Ersatz verpflichtet, wenn den Bestimmungen des § 30 zuwider Zahlungen aus dem zur Erhaltung des Stammkapitals erforderlichen Vermögen der Gesellschaft gemacht oder den Bestimmungen des § 33 zuwider eigene Geschäftsanteile der Gesellschaft erworben worden sind. Auf den Ersatzanspruch finden die Bestimmungen in § 9b Abs. 1 entsprechende Anwendung. Soweit der Ersatz zur Befriedigung der Gläubiger der Gesellschaft erforderlich ist, wird die Verpflichtung der Geschäftsführer dadurch nicht aufgehoben, dass dieselben in Befolgung eines Beschlusses der Gesellschafter gehandelt haben.	(3) In particular, they are liable to pay compensation if, contrary to the provisions of Sec. 30, payments are made from the assets of the company or if, in contravention of the provisions of Sec. 33, the company acquires its own shares. The provisions of Sec. 9b para. 1 will apply mutatis mutandis to the claim for compensation. To the extent that compensation is required to satisfy the company's creditors, the managing directors will not be relieved of their duty due to the fact that they acted in accordance with a shareholders' resolution.
(4) Die Ansprüche auf Grund der vorstehenden Bestimmungen verjähren in fünf Jahren.	(4) Claims based on the aforementioned provisions become time-barred after a period of five years.
§ 45 *Rechte der Gesellschafter*	*§ 45* *Rights of the Shareholders*
(1) Die Rechte, welche den Gesellschaftern in den Angelegenheiten der Gesellschaft, insbesondere in bezug auf die Führung der Geschäfte zustehen, sowie die Ausübung derselben bestimmen sich, soweit nicht gesetzliche Vorschriften entgegenstehen, nach dem Gesellschaftsvertrag.	(1) The rights of the shareholders in relation to the affairs of the company, specifically regarding the management of the business and how these rights are to be exercised, are governed by the articles of association, unless the statutory provisions provide otherwise.
(2) In Ermangelung besonderer Bestimmungen des Gesellschaftsvertrags finden die Vorschriften der §§ 46 bis 51 Anwendung.	(2) In the absence of special regulations in the articles of association, the provisions of Secs. 46–51 apply.
§ 46 *Aufgabenkreis der Gesellschafter*	*§ 46* *Area of Responsibilities of the Shareholders*
Der Bestimmung der Gesellschafter unterliegen:	The shareholders shall decide on the following:
1. die Feststellung des Jahresabschlusses und die Verwendung des Ergebnisses;	1. the approval of the annual accounts and the use of profits;
1a. die Entscheidung über die Offenlegung eines Einzelabschlusses nach internationalen Rechnungslegungsstandards (§ 325 Abs. 2a des Handelsgesetzbuches) und über die Billigung des von den Geschäftsführern aufgestellten Abschlusses;	1a. the decision on the publication of a single account according to international accounting standards (Sec. 325 Abs. 2a of the Commercial Code), and on the approval of the account prepared by the managing directors;

1b. die Billigung eines von den Geschäftsführern aufgestellten Konzernabschlusses;	1b. the approval of the consolidated account prepared by the managing directors;
2. die Einforderung der Einlagen;	2. the calling in of share capital contributions;
3. die Rückzahlung von Nachschüssen;	3. the repayment of additional contribution payments;
4. die Teilung, die Zusammenlegung sowie die Einziehung von Geschäftsanteilen;	4. the splitting, consolidation and redemption of shares;
5. die Bestellung und die Abberufung von Geschäftsführern sowie die Entlastung derselben;	5. the appointment and removal of managing directors, as well as the formal approval of their conduct of the business;
6. die Maßregeln zur Prüfung und Überwachung der Geschäftsführung;	6. the measures for examining and supervising the management of the company;
7. die Bestellung von Prokuristen und von Handlungsbevollmächtigten zum gesamten Geschäftsbetrieb;	7. the appointment of holders of general signing powers (Prokurists) and of authorized signatories with powers extending to the whole business;
8. die Geltendmachung von Ersatzansprüchen, welche der Gesellschaft aus der Gründung oder Geschäftsführung gegen Geschäftsführer oder Gesellschafter zustehen, sowie die Vertretung der Gesellschaft in Prozessen, welche sie gegen die Geschäftsführer zu führen hat.	8. the assertion of compensation claims against the managing directors or shareholders, to which the company is entitled regarding the way in which the company was formed or managed, and representing the company in lawsuits against the managing directors.
§ 47 *Abstimmung*	*§ 47* *Voting*
(1) Die von den Gesellschaftern in den Angelegenheiten der Gesellschaft zu treffenden Bestimmungen erfolgen durch Beschlussfassung nach der Mehrheit der abgegebenen Stimmen.	(1) The decisions to be made by the shareholders in matters of the company are effected by means of a resolution passed by a majority of the votes cast.
(2) Jeder Euro eines Geschäftsanteils gewährt eine Stimme.	(2) Every Euro of a share carries one vote.
(3) Vollmachten bedürfen zu ihrer Gültigkeit der Textform.	(3) Powers of attorney must be in writing in order to be valid.
(4) Ein Gesellschafter, welcher durch die Beschlussfassung entlastet oder von einer Verbindlichkeit befreit werden soll, hat hierbei kein Stimmrecht und darf ein solches auch nicht für andere ausüben. Dasselbe gilt von einer Beschlussfassung, welche die Vornahme eines Rechtsgeschäfts oder die Einleitung oder Erledigung eines Rechtsstreits gegenüber einem Gesellschafter betrifft.	(4) A shareholder may not vote or exercise voting rights on behalf of others where a resolution is to be passed to formally approve his conduct of business or release him from a liability. The same applies to a resolution relating to the conclusion of a legal transaction or the initiation or termination of a lawsuit against a shareholder.

§ 48 *Gesellschafterversammlung*	*§ 48* *Shareholders' Meeting*
(1) Die Beschlüsse der Gesellschafter werden in Versammlungen gefasst.	(1) Shareholders' resolutions are adopted at assemblies.
(2) Der Abhaltung einer Versammlung bedarf es nicht, wenn sämtliche Gesellschafter in Textform mit der zu treffenden Bestimmung oder mit der schriftlichen Abgabe der Stimmen sich einverstanden erklären.	(2) A meeting need not be held if all of the shareholders declare in writing their agreement of the decision being taken, or to the casting of votes by written ballot.
(3) Befinden sich alle Geschäftsanteile der Gesellschaft in der Hand eines Gesellschafters oder daneben in der Hand der Gesellschaft, so hat er unverzüglich nach der Beschlussfassung eine Niederschrift aufzunehmen und zu unterschreiben.	(3) If all of the shares of the company are held by one shareholder, or by one shareholder and the company, such shareholder shall prepare and sign minutes immediately after the adoption of the resolution.
§ 49 *Einberufung der Versammlung*	*§ 49* *Convening of the Meeting*
(1) Die Versammlung der Gesellschafter wird durch die Geschäftsführer berufen.	(1) The shareholders' meeting is convened by the managing directors.
(2) Sie ist außer den ausdrücklich bestimmten Fällen zu berufen, wenn es im Interesse der Gesellschaft erforderlich erscheint.	(2) In addition to the cases expressly provided for, it is to be convened when it appears necessary in the interest of the company.
(3) Insbesondere muss die Versammlung unverzüglich berufen werden, wenn aus der Jahresbilanz oder aus einer im Laufe des Geschäftsjahres aufgestellten Bilanz sich ergibt, dass die Hälfte des Stammkapitals verloren ist.	(3) A shareholder's meeting shall, in particular, be convened without delay if it is apparent from the annual financial statements, or from a balance sheet prepared in the course of the fiscal year, that half of the registered share capital has been lost.
§ 50 *Minderheitsrechte*	*§ 50* *Minority Rights*
(1) Gesellschafter, deren Geschäftsanteile zusammen mindestens dem zehnten Teil des Stammkapitals entsprechen, sind berechtigt, unter Angabe des Zwecks und der Gründe die Berufung der Versammlung zu verlangen.	(1) Shareholders, whose combined shares amount to at least one tenth of the share capital, are, upon stating the purpose and reasons, entitled to request that a shareholders' meeting be convened.
(2) In gleicher Weise haben die Gesellschafter das Recht zu verlangen, dass Gegenstände zur Beschlussfassung der Versammlung angekündigt werden.	(2) Similarly, shareholders are entitled to demand that matters be resolved at the meeting be announced.
(3) Wird dem Verlangen nicht entsprochen oder sind Personen, an welche dasselbe zu richten wäre, nicht vorhanden, so können die in Absatz 1 bezeichneten Gesellschafter unter Mitteilung des Sachverhältnisses die Berufung oder Ankündigung selbst bewirken. Die Versammlung beschließt, ob die entstandenen Kosten von der Gesellschaft zu tragen sind.	(3) If this request is not complied with or if persons to whom this request should be addressed are not available, the shareholders specified in para. 1 may themselves convene the meeting or make the announcement, having first communicated the relevant facts. The meeting decides whether the costs incurred must be borne by the company.

§ 51a *Auskunfts- und Einsichtsrecht*	*§ 51a* *Right to Information and Inspection*
(1) Die Geschäftsführer haben jedem Gesellschafter auf Verlangen unverzüglich Auskunft über die Angelegenheiten der Gesellschaft zu geben und die Einsicht der Bücher und Schriften zu gestatten.	(1) Immediately, upon request, the managing directors shall inform each shareholder about the affairs of the company, and shall allow such shareholders inspection of the books and records.
(2) Die Geschäftsführer dürfen die Auskunft und die Einsicht verweigern, wenn zu besorgen ist, dass der Gesellschafter sie zu gesellschaftsfremden Zwecken verwenden und dadurch der Gesellschaft oder einem verbundenen Unternehmen einen nicht unerheblichen Nachteil zufügen wird. Die Verweigerung bedarf eines Beschlusses der Gesellschafter.	(2) The managing directors may refuse to provide information and allow such inspection, if there is reason to fear that the shareholder will use it for purposes unrelated to the company and thereby, cause harm to the company or an affiliated enterprise which is not insignificant. Such refusal requires a shareholders' resolution.
(3) Von diesen Vorschriften kann im Gesellschaftsvertrag nicht abgewichen werden.	(3) The articles of association may not deviate from these provisions.
§ 52 *Aufsichtsrat*	*§ 52* *Supervisory Board*
(1) Ist nach dem Gesellschaftsvertrag ein Aufsichtsrat zu bestellen, so sind § 90 Abs. 3, 4, 5 Satz 1 und 2, § 95 Satz 1, § 100 Abs. 1 und 2 Nr. 2 und Abs. 5, § 101 Abs. 1 Satz 1, § 103 Abs. 1 Satz 1 und 2, §§ 105, 107 Abs. 4, 110 bis 114, 116 des Aktiengesetzes in Verbindung mit § 93 Abs. 1 und 2 Satz 1 und 2 des Aktiengesetzes, § 124 Abs. 3 Satz 2, §§ 170, 171 des Aktiengesetzes entsprechend anzuwenden, soweit nicht im Gesellschaftsvertrag ein anderes bestimmt ist.	(1) If the articles of association provide that a supervisory board has to be appointed, Sec. 90 paras. 3, 4, 5 sentences 1 and 2, Sec. 95 sentence 1, Sec. 100 paras. 1 and 2 no. 2 and para. 5, Sec. 101 para. 1 sentence 1, Sec. 103 para. 1 sentences 1 and 2, Secs. 105, 107 para. 4, Secs. 110–114, Sec. 116 of the Stock Corporation Act in conjunction with Sec. 93 paras. 1 and 2 sentences 1 and 2 of the Stock Corporation Act, Sec. 124 para. 3 sentence 2 and Secs. 170 and 171 of the Stock Corporation Act apply mutatis mutandis unless otherwise provided for in the articles of association.

Vierter Abschnitt Abänderung des Gesellschaftsvertrages	Part Four Amendments to the Articles of Association
§ 53 *Form der Satzungsänderung*	*§ 53* *Form of the Amendments to the Articles of Association*
(1) Eine Abänderung des Gesellschaftsvertrags kann nur durch Beschluss der Gesellschafter erfolgen.	(1) The articles of association may only be amended by a shareholders' resolution.
(2) Der Beschluss muss notariell beurkundet werden, derselbe bedarf einer Mehrheit von drei Vierteln der abgegebenen Stimmen. Der Gesellschaftsvertrag kann noch andere Erfordernisse aufstellen.	(2) The resolution must be notarized and requires a majority of three fourths of the votes cast. The articles of association may also stipulate additional requirements.
(3) Eine Vermehrung der den Gesellschaftern nach dem Gesellschaftsvertrag obliegenden Leistungen kann nur mit Zustimmung sämtlicher beteiligter Gesellschafter beschlossen werden.	(3) An increase in the payments required to be made by the shareholders under the articles of association can only be made with the consent of all of the shareholders involved.

§ 54 *Anmeldung und Eintragung der Satzungsänderung*	*§ 54* *Application and Registration of Amendments to the Articles of Association*
(1) Die Abänderung des Gesellschaftsvertrags ist zur Eintragung in das Handelsregister anzumelden. Der Anmeldung ist der vollständige Wortlaut des Gesellschaftsvertrags beizufügen; er muss mit der Bescheinigung eines Notars versehen sein, dass die geänderten Bestimmungen des Gesellschaftsvertrags mit dem Beschluss über die Änderung des Gesellschaftsvertrags und die unveränderten Bestimmungen mit dem zuletzt zum Handelsregister eingereichten vollständigen Wortlaut des Gesellschaftsvertrags übereinstimmen.	(1) An application for any amendment to the articles of association must be registered with the commercial register. The complete text of the articles of association shall be attached to the application; it must contain a notary's certificate confirming that the amended provisions of the articles of association correspond with the resolution regarding the amendment to the articles of association, and that the unchanged provisions comply with the complete text of the articles of association as last submitted to the commercial register.
(2) Bei der Eintragung genügt, sofern nicht die Abänderung die in § 10 bezeichneten Angaben betrifft, die Bezugnahme auf die bei dem Gericht eingereichten Dokumente über die Abänderung.	(2) For the registration it is sufficient to refer to the documents submitted to the court regarding the amendment, provided the amendment does not concern the matters referred to in Sec. 10.
(3) Die Abänderung hat keine rechtliche Wirkung, bevor sie in das Handelsregister des Sitzes der Gesellschaft eingetragen ist.	(3) The amendment has no legal effect until it is registered in the commercial register of the registered office of the company.
§ 60 *Auflösungsgründe*	*§ 60* *Reasons for dissolution*
(1) Die Gesellschaft mit beschränkter Haftung wird aufgelöst:	(1) A limited liability company is dissolved:
1. durch Ablauf der im Gesellschaftsvertrag bestimmten Zeit;	1. by expiration of the time period of its existence stipulated in the articles of association;
2. durch Beschluß der Gesellschafter; derselbe bedarf, sofern im Gesellschaftsvertrag nicht ein anderes bestimmt ist, einer Mehrheit von drei Vierteilen der abgegebenen Stimmen;	2. by a resolution of the shareholders; this requires a majority of three fourths of the votes cast, unless otherwise stipulated in the articles of association
3. durch gerichtliches Urteil oder durch Entscheidung des Verwaltungsgerichts oder der Verwaltungsbehörde in den Fällen der §§ 61 und 62;	3. by a court decision or by decree of the administrative court or of the administrative authorities in cases under Sec. 61 and 62;
4. durch die Eröffnung des Insolvenzverfahrens; wird das Verfahren auf Antrag des Schuldners eingestellt oder nach der Bestätigung eines Insolvenzplans, der den Fortbestand der Gesellschaft vorsieht, aufgehoben, so können die Gesellschafter die Fortsetzung der Gesellschaft beschließen;	4. by the institution of insolvency proceedings; if the proceedings are closed upon request of the debtor or repealed after confirmation of an insolvency plan providing for the continuation of the company, the shareholders can resolve the continuation of the company;
5. mit der Rechtskraft des Beschlusses, durch den die Eröffnung des Insolvenzverfahrens mangels Masse abgelehnt worden ist;	5. upon a final decision rejecting the opening of insolvency proceedings for lack of assets;

6. mit der Rechtskraft einer Verfügung des Registergerichts, durch welche nach § 399 des Gesetzes über das Verfahren in Familiensachen und in den Angelegenheiten der freiwilligen Gerichtsbarkeit ein Mangel des Gesellschaftsvertrags festgestellt worden ist;	6. upon a final decision of the registered court by which pursuant to Sec. 399 of the Act on Procedure of Familiy Matters and Matters of Non-Contentious Jurisdiction, a defect in the articles of association has been determined;
7. durch die Löschung der Gesellschaft wegen Vermögenslosigkeit nach § 394 des Gesetzes über das Verfahren in Familiensachen und in den Angelegenheiten der freiwilligen Gerichtsbarkeit.	7. by the cancellation of the company due to lack of assets pursuant to Sec. 394 of the Act on Procedure of Familiy Matters and Matters of Non-Contentious Jurisdiction.
(2) Im Gesellschaftsvertrag können weitere Auflösungsgründe festgesetzt werden.	(2) The articles of association may provide for further reasons for dissolution.
§ 64 *Haftung für Zahlungen nach Zahlungsunfähigkeit oder Überschuldung*	*§ 64* *Liability for Payments after Illiquidity or Over-indebtedness*
Die Geschäftsführer sind der Gesellschaft zum Ersatz von Zahlungen verpflichtet, die nach Eintritt der Zahlungsunfähigkeit der Gesellschaft oder nach Feststellung ihrer Überschuldung geleistet werden. Dies gilt nicht von Zahlungen, die auch nach diesem Zeitpunkt mit der Sorgfalt eines ordentlichen Geschäftsmanns vereinbar sind. Die gleiche Verpflichtung trifft die Geschäftsführer für Zahlungen an Gesellschafter, soweit diese zur Zahlungsunfähigkeit der Gesellschaft führen mussten, es sei denn, dies war auch bei Beachtung der in Satz 2 bezeichneten Sorgfalt nicht erkennbar. Auf den Ersatzanspruch finden die Bestimmungen in § 43 Abs. 3 und 4 entsprechende Anwendung.	The managing directors are liable to compensate the company for payments made after the company has become insolvent, or after its over-indebtedness has been ascertained. This does not apply to payments which are compatible with the due care of a prudent businessman. The managing directors shall have the same obligation for payments to shareholders to the extent that such payments resulted in the illiquidity of the company, unless this was not foreseeable even when applying the due care referred to in sentence 2. The provisions of Sec. 43 paras. 3 and 4 shall apply accordingly to the claim for compensation.
§ 65 *Anmeldung und Eintragung der Auflösung*	*§ 65* *Application and Registration of the Dissolution*
(1) Die Auflösung der Gesellschaft ist zur Eintragung in das Handelsregister anzumelden. Dies gilt nicht in den Fällen der Eröffnung oder der Ablehnung der Eröffnung des Insolvenzverfahrens und der gerichtlichen Feststellung eines Mangels des Gesellschaftsvertrags. In diesen Fällen hat das Gericht die Auflösung und ihren Grund von Amts wegen einzutragen. Im Falle der Löschung der Gesellschaft (§ 60 Abs. 1 Nr. 7) entfällt die Eintragung der Auflösung.	(1) The dissolution of the company shall be filed for registration in the commercial register. This shall not apply in the case of the institution or the denial of the institution of insolvency proceedings, or in the case of a judicial decision on a defect in the articles of association. In such cases, the court shall register the dissolution and its reasons ex officio. In the case of the cancellation of the company (Sec. 60 para. 1 no. 7), a registration of the dissolution is not required.
(2) Die Auflösung ist von den Liquidatoren in den Gesellschaftsblättern bekanntzumachen. Durch die Bekanntmachung sind zugleich die Gläubiger der Gesellschaft aufzufordern, sich bei derselben zu melden.	(2) The dissolution must be published by the liquidators in the company's gazettes. The publication shall simultaneously call upon the creditors of the company to report to the company.

6.1.2 Excerpts from the German Stock Corporation Act (*AktG*)

§ 76 *Leitung der Aktiengesellschaft*	*§ 76* *Management of the Stock Corporation*
(1) Der Vorstand hat unter eigener Verantwortung die Gesellschaft zu leiten.	(1) The management board shall manage the company under its own responsibility.
(2) Der Vorstand kann aus einer oder mehreren Personen bestehen. Bei Gesellschaften mit einem Grundkapital von mehr als drei Millionen Euro hat er aus mindestens zwei Personen zu bestehen, es sei denn, die Satzung bestimmt, dass er aus einer Person besteht. Die Vorschriften über die Bestellung eines Arbeitsdirektors bleiben unberührt.	(2) The management board may comprise of one or more persons. In case of companies with a registered share capital of more than three million Euros, it shall comprise of at least two persons, unless the articles of association stipulate that it shall comprise of one person. The provisions concerning the appointment of a labor director shall remain unaffected.
(3) Mitglied des Vorstands kann nur eine natürliche, unbeschränkt geschäftsfähige Person sein. Mitglied des Vorstands kann nicht sein, wer	(3) Only a natural person with unrestricted legal capacity may be a member of the management board. A person cannot be a member of the management board, who
1. als Betreuter bei der Besorgung seiner Vermögensangelegenheiten ganz oder teilweise einem Einwilligungsvorbehalt (§ 1903 des Bürgerlichen Gesetzbuchs) unterliegt,	1. is a person under guardianship, with respect to the managing of his financial affairs, is partially or totally subject to a consent requirement pursuant to Sec. 1903 of the Civil Code,
2. aufgrund eines gerichtlichen Urteils oder einer vollziehbaren Entscheidung einer Verwaltungs-behörde einen Beruf, einen Berufszweig, ein Gewerbe oder einen Gewerbezweig nicht ausüben darf, sofern der Unternehmensgegenstand ganz oder teilweise mit dem Gegenstand des Verbots übereinstimmt,	2. by judgment of a court or an enforceable decision of an administrative agency, is not allowed to practice a certain profession or trade or a branch thereof, to the extent that the business object wholly or partially corresponds with the prohibition,
3. wegen einer oder mehrerer vorsätzlich begangener Straftaten	3. has been convicted of one or more of the following premeditated criminal offences:
a) des Unterlassens der Stellung des Antrages auf Eröffnung des Insolvenzverfahrens (Insolvenzverschleppung),	a) omission to file for insolvency proceedings (delay in filing a petition for insolvency),
b) nach den §§ 283 bis § 283 d des Strafgesetzbuches (Insolvenzstraftaten),	b) pursuant to Secs. 283–283d of the German Penal Code (crimes relating to insolvency of the company),
c) der falschen Angaben nach § 399 dieses Gesetzes oder § 82 des Gesetzes betreffend die Gesellschaften mit beschränkter Haftung,	c) false statements pursuant to Sec. 399 of this Act or pursuant to Sec. 82 of the German Act on Limited Liability Companies,
d) der unrichtigen Darstellung nach § 400 dieses Gesetzes, § 331 des Handelsgesetzbuches, § 313 des Umwandlungsgesetzes oder § 17 des Publizitätsgesetzes,	d) incorrect statements pursuant to Sec. 400 of this Act, Sec. 331 of the German Commercial Code, Sec. 313 of the German Act on Corporate Restructuring or Sec. 17 of the German Publicity Act, or

e) nach den §§ 263 bis 264a oder den §§ 265b bis 266a des Strafgesetzbuches zu einer Freiheitsstrafe von mindestens einem Jahr verurteilt worden ist; dieser Ausschluss gilt für die Dauer von fünf Jahren seit der Rechtskraft des Urteils, wobei die Zeit nicht eingerechnet wird, in welcher der Täter auf behördliche Anordnung in einer Anstalt verwahrt worden ist. Satz 2 Nr. 3 gilt entsprechend bei einer Verurteilung im Ausland wegen einer Tat, die mit den in Satz 2 Nr. 3 genannten Taten vergleichbar ist.	e) pursuant to Secs. 263–264a or Secs. 265b-266a of the German Penal Code to imprisonment of at least one year. This disqualification applies for a period of five years after the sentence became final, such period shall not include any time during which the convicted person was confined to an institution by an official order. Sentence 2 no. 3 shall apply accordingly in the case of a conviction in a foreign country for an offense comparable to the offenses mentioned in sentence 2 no. 3 above.
§ 93 *Sorgfaltspflicht und Verantwortlichkeit der Vorstandsmitglieder*	*§ 93* *Duty of Care and Liability of Members of the Management Board*
(1) Die Vorstandsmitglieder haben bei ihrer Geschäftsführung die Sorgfalt eines ordentlichen und gewissenhaften Geschäftsleiters anzuwenden. Eine Pflichtverletzung liegt nicht vor, wenn das Vorstandsmitglied bei einer unternehmerischen Entscheidung vernünftigerweise annehmen durfte, auf der Grundlage angemessener Information zum Wohle der Gesellschaft zu handeln. Über vertrauliche Angaben und Geheimnisse der Gesellschaft, namentlich Betriebs- oder Geschäftsgeheimnisse, die den Vorstandsmitgliedern durch ihre Tätigkeit im Vorstand bekanntgeworden sind, haben sie Stillschweigen zu bewahren. Die Pflicht des Satzes 3 gilt nicht gegenüber einer nach § 342b des Handelsgesetzbuchs anerkannten Prüfstelle im Rahmen einer von dieser durchgeführten Prüfung.	(1) The members of the management board shall exercise the due care of a prudent and conscientious businessman when managing the company. There is no breach of duty if the member of the management board, when making an entrepreneurial decision, could reasonably assume he was acting on the basis of appropriate information and for the benefit of the company. The members of the management board shall not disclose confidential information and secrets of the company, in particular trade or business secrets which have become known to them as a result of their activities on the management board. The duty set out in sentence 3 shall not apply to an auditing office recognized pursuant to Sec. 342b of the Commercial Code in the context of an audit carried out by it.
(2) Vorstandsmitglieder, die ihre Pflichten verletzen, sind der Gesellschaft zum Ersatz des daraus entstehenden Schadens als Gesamtschuldner verpflichtet. Ist streitig, ob sie die Sorgfalt eines ordentlichen und gewissenhaften Geschäftsleiters angewandt haben, so trifft sie die Beweislast. Schließt die Gesellschaft eine Versicherung zur Absicherung eines Vorstandsmitglieds gegen Risiken aus dessen beruflicher Tätigkeit für die Gesellschaft ab, ist ein Selbstbehalt von mindestens 10 Prozent des Schadens bis mindestens zur Höhe des Eineinhalbfachen der festen jährlichen Vergütung des Vorstandsmitglieds vorzusehen.	(2) Members of the management board who breach their duties shall be jointly and severally liable to the company for any resulting damage. They shall bear the burden of proof where there is a dispute as to whether or not they exercised the due care of a prudent and conscientious businessman. If the company takes out insurance covering a member of the management board against risks arising from their professional activity for the company, a participation of at least ten percent of the damages, up to the level of at least one-and-a-half times the fixed annual remuneration of the member of the management board, shall be provided for.

§ 161 *Erklärung zum Corporate Governance Kodex*	*§ 161* *Statement regarding the Corporate Governance Code*
(1) Vorstand und Aufsichtsrat der börsennotierten Gesellschaft erklären jährlich, dass den vom Bundesministerium der Justiz im amtlichen Teil des elektronischen Bundesanzeigers bekannt gemachten Empfehlungen der „Regierungskommission Deutscher Corporate Governance Kodex" entsprochen wurde und wird oder welche Empfehlungen nicht angewendet wurden oder werden und warum nicht. Gleiches gilt für Vorstand und Aufsichtsrat einer Gesellschaft, die ausschließlich andere Wertpapiere als Aktien zum Handel an einem organisierten Markt im Sinn des § 2 Abs. 5 des Wertpapierhandelsgesetzes ausgegeben hat und deren ausgegebene Aktien auf eigene Veranlassung über ein multilaterales Handelssystem im Sinn des § 2 Abs. 3 Satz 1 Nr. 8 des Wertpapierhandelsgesetzes gehandelt werden.	(1) The management board and the supervisory board of publicly listed companies shall state annually that the recommendations of the "Government Commission's German Corporate Governance Codes", published by the Federal Ministry of Justice in the official part of the electronic Federal Gazette, have been and are being adhered to or which recommendations were not or are not being adhered to and for what reasons. The same shall apply to the management board and to the supervisory board of a company which exclusively issued securities other than shares for trading in an organized market within the meaning of Sec. 2 para. 5 of the Securities Trading Act, and whose issued shares are traded at its own instigation on a multi-lateral trading system within the meaning of Sec. 2 para. 3 sentence 1 no. 8 of the Securities Trading Act.
(2) Die Erklärung ist auf der Internetseite der Gesellschaft dauerhaft öffentlich zugänglich zu machen.	(2) The statement shall be made permanently available to the public on the homepage of the company.
§ 327a *Übertragung von Aktien gegen Barabfindung*	*§ 327a* *Transfer of Shares against Cash Compensation*
(1) Die Hauptversammlung einer Aktiengesellschaft oder einer Kommanditgesellschaft oder einer Kommanditgesellschaft auf Aktien kann auf Verlangen eines Aktionärs, dem Aktien der Gesellschaft in Höhe von 95 vom Hundert des Grundkapitals gehören (Hauptaktionär), die Übertragung der Aktien der übrigen Aktionäre (Minderheitsaktionäre) auf den Hauptaktionär gegen Gewährung einer angemessenen Barabfindung beschließen. § 285 Abs. 2 Satz 1 findet keine Anwendung.	(1) Upon the request of a stockholder holding shares in the company which account for 95% of the registered share capital (principal stockholder), the general stockholders' meeting of a stock corporation or a partnership limited by shares can resolve on the transfer of the shares held by the other stockholders (minority stockholders) to the principal stockholder in return for adequate cash compensation. Sec. 285 para. 2 sentence 1 shall not apply.
(2) Für die Feststellung, ob dem Hauptaktionär 95 vom Hundert der Aktien gehören, gilt § 16 Abs. 2 und 4.	(2) Sec. 16 paras. 2 and 4 shall apply when determining whether the principal stockholder holds 95% of the shares.
§ 327b *Barabfindung*	*§ 327b* *Cash Compensation*
(1) Der Hauptaktionär legt die Höhe der Barabfindung fest; sie muss die Verhältnisse der Gesellschaft im Zeitpunkt der Beschlussfassung ihrer Hauptversammlung berücksichtigen. Der Vorstand hat dem Hauptaktionär alle dafür notwendigen Unterlagen zur Verfügung zu stellen und Auskünfte zu erteilen.	(1) The principal stockholder shall specify the amount of cash compensation; such compensation shall take into account the company's situation at the time that the resolution was adopted. The management board shall provide the principal stockholder with all of the documents and information necessary for this purpose.

(2) Die Barabfindung ist von der Bekanntmachung der Eintragung des Übertragungsbeschlusses in das Handelsregister an mit jährlich 5 Prozentpunkten über dem jeweiligen Basiszinssatz nach § 247 des Bürgerlichen Gesetzbuchs zu verzinsen; die Geltendmachung eines weiteren Schadens ist nicht ausgeschlossen.	(2) Annual interest of 5 percentage points above the relevant basic risk-free rate of interest, as stated in Sec. 247 of the Civil Code, shall be due on the cash compensation with effect from the date on which the registration in the commercial register of the resolution on the transfer of shares is announced, and claims for further damages shall not be precluded.
(3) Vor Einberufung der Hauptversammlung hat der Hauptaktionär dem Vorstand die Erklärung eines im Geltungsbereichs dieses Gesetzes zum Geschäftsbetrieb befugten Kreditinstitut zu übermitteln, durch die das Kreditinstitut die Gewährleistung für die Erfüllung der Verpflichtung des Hauptaktionärs übernimmt, den Minderheitsaktionären nach Eintragung des Übertragungsbeschlusses unverzüglich die festgelegte Barabfindung für die übergegangenen Aktien zu zahlen.	(3) Before the stockholders' meeting is convened, the principal stockholder shall submit to the management board a declaration from a credit institution, authorized to operate in the area of application of this Act, warranting performance of the principal stockholder's obligation to pay the minority stockholder the agreed cash compensation for the transferred shares promptly once the resolution on the transfer of such shares has been registered.
§ 327c *Vorbereitung der Hauptversammlung*	*§ 327c* *Preparation of the Stockholders' Meeting*
(1) Die Bekanntmachung der Übertragung als Gegenstand der Tagesordnung hat folgende Angaben zu enthalten:	(1) The publication that the transfer is an item on the agenda must contain the following information:
1. Firma und Sitz des Hauptaktionärs, bei natürlichen Personen Name und Adresse;	1. name and registered seat of the principal stockholder and, in case of natural persons, the name and address;
2. die vom Hauptaktionär festgelegte Barabfindung	2. the cash compensation specified by the principal stockholder
(2) Der Hauptaktionär hat der Hauptversammlung einen schriftlichen Bericht zu erstatten, in dem die Voraussetzungen für die Übertragung dargelegt und die Angemessenheit der Barabfindung erläutert und begründet werden. Die Angemessenheit der Barabfindung ist durch einen oder mehrere sachverständige Prüfer zu prüfen. Diese werden auf Antrag des Hauptaktionärs vom Gericht ausgewählt und bestellt. § 293a Abs. 2 und 3, § 293c Abs. 1 Satz 3 bis 5, Abs. 2 sowie die §§ 293d und 293e sind sinngemäß anzuwenden.	(2) The principal stockholder shall render a written report which sets out the requirements for the transfer and describes and justifies the adequateness of the cash compensation to the stockholders' meeting. The adequateness of the cash compensation shall be examined by one or more expert auditors. Such auditors shall be selected and appointed by the court, upon the request of the principal stockholder. Sec. 293a para. 2 and 3, Sec. 293c para. 1 sentences 3–5, para. 2 and Sec. 293d and 293e will apply respectively.
(3) Von der Einberufung der Hauptversammlung an sind in dem Geschäftsraum der Gesellschaft zur Einsicht der Aktionäre auszulegen:	(3) The following shall be available for inspection by the stockholders in the offices of the company, as of the date that the stockholders' meeting is to be called:
1. der Entwurf des Übertragungsbeschlusses;	1. the draft resolution on the transfer of shares;

2. die Jahresabschlüsse und Lageberichte für die letzten drei Geschäftsjahre;	2. the annual accounts and management reports for the previous three fiscal years;
3. der nach Absatz 2 Satz 1 erstattete Bericht des Hauptaktionärs;	3. the principal stockholder's report pursuant to para. 2 sentence 1;
4. der nach Absatz 2 Satz 2 bis 4 erstattete Prüfungsbericht.	4. the audit report pursuant to para. 2 sentences 2–4.
(4) Auf Verlangen ist jedem Aktionär unverzüglich und kostenlos eine Abschrift der in Absatz 3 bezeichneten Unterlagen zu erteilen.	(4) Upon request, each stockholder shall be provided with a copy of the documents listed in para. 3 immediately and free of charge.
(5) Die Verpflichtungen nach den Absätzen 3 und 4 entfallen, wenn die in Absatz 3 bezeichneten Unterlagen für denselben Zeitraum über die Internetseite der Gesellschaft zugänglich sind.	(5) The obligations pursuant to paras. 3 and 4 do not apply if the documents described in para. 3 are available during the same period of time on the website of the company.
§ 327d *Durchführung der Hauptversammlung*	*§ 327d* *Procedure of the Stockholders' Meeting*
In der Hauptversammlung sind die in § 327c Abs. 3 bezeichneten Unterlagen auszulegen. Der Vorstand kann dem Hauptaktionär Gelegenheit geben, den Entwurf des Übertragungsbeschlusses und die Bemessung der Höhe der Barabfindung zu Beginn der Verhandlung mündlich zu erläutern.	The documents designated in Sec. 327c para. 3 shall be laid out during the stockholders' meeting. The management board may give the principal stockholder the opportunity to comment on the draft resolution regarding the transfer and the assessment of the amount of the cash compensation at the beginning of the proceedings.

6.1.3 Excerpts from the German Commercial Code (*HGB*)

§ 124 *[Rechtliche Selbständigkeit; Zwangsvollstreckung in Gesellschaftsvermögen]*	*§ 124* *Legal Personality; Enforcement against Assets of the Partnership*
(1) Die offene Handelsgesellschaft kann unter ihrer Firma Rechte erwerben und Verbindlichkeiten eingehen, Eigentum und andere dingliche Rechte an Grundstücken erwerben, vor Gericht klagen und verklagt werden.	(1) The general commercial partnership can, in its own name, acquire rights, enter into obligations, acquire property and other rights in real estate, as well as sue and be sued in court.
(2) Zur Zwangsvollstreckung in das Gesellschaftsvermögen ist ein gegen die Gesellschaft gerichteter vollstreckbarer Schuldtitel erforderlich.	(2) An enforcement against the assets of the partnership requires a legally enforceable debt against the partnership.
§ 128 *[Persönliche Haftung der Gesellschafter]*	*§ 128* *Personal Liability of the Partners*
Die Gesellschafter haften für die Verbindlichkeiten der Gesellschaft den Gläubigern als Gesamtschuldner persönlich. Eine entgegenstehende Vereinbarung ist Dritten gegenüber unwirksam.	The partners are jointly and severally liable to satisfy the creditors for the liabilities of the partnership. Any opposing agreement is void vis-á-vis third parties.

§ 238 *Buchführungspflicht*	*§ 238* *Legal Obligation to Keep Books*
(1) Jeder Kaufmann ist verpflichtet, Bücher zu führen und in diesen seine Handelsgeschäfte und die Lage seines Vermögens nach den Grundsätzen ordnungsmäßiger Buchführung ersichtlich zu machen. Die Buchführung muss so beschaffen sein, dass sie einem sachverständigen Dritten innerhalb angemessener Zeit einen Überblick über die Geschäftsvorfälle und über die Lage des Unternehmens vermitteln kann. Die Geschäftsvorfälle müssen sich in ihrer Entstehung und Abwicklung verfolgen lassen.	(1) Every businessman is obliged to keep accounts and records and to disclose in these documents his business transactions and his financial status according to the standards of proper accounting. The accounting must be performed in a way that a third party expert can get an overview of the business transactions and the position of the enterprise within reasonable time,. The business transactions must be traceable from their development until their settlement.
§ 325 *Offenlegung*	*§ 325* *Disclosure/Publication*
(1) Die gesetzlichen Vertreter von Kapitalgesellschaften haben für diese den Jahresabschluss beim Betreiber des elektronischen Bundesanzeigers elektronisch einzureichen. Er ist unverzüglich nach seiner Vorlage an die Gesellschafter, jedoch spätestens vor Ablauf des zwölften Monats des dem Abschlussstichtag nachfolgenden Geschäftsjahrs, mit dem Bestätigungsvermerk oder dem Vermerk über dessen Versagung einzureichen. Gleichzeitig sind der Lagebericht, der Bericht des Aufsichtsrats, die nach § 161 des Aktiengesetzes vorgeschriebene Erklärung und, soweit sich dies aus dem eingereichten Jahresabschluss nicht ergibt, der Vorschlag für die Verwendung des Ergebnisses und der Beschluss über seine Verwendung unter Angabe des Jahresüberschusses oder Jahresfehlbetrags elektronisch einzureichen. Angaben über die Ergebnisverwendung brauchen von Gesellschaften mit beschränkter Haftung nicht gemacht zu werden, wenn sich anhand dieser Angaben die Gewinnanteile von natürlichen Personen feststellen lassen, die Gesellschafter sind. Werden zur Wahrung der Frist nach Satz 2 oder Absatz 4 Satz 1 der Jahresabschluss und der Lagebericht ohne die anderen Unterlagen eingereicht, sind der Bericht und der Vorschlag nach ihrem Vorliegen, die Beschlüsse nach der Beschlussfassung und der Vermerk nach der Erteilung unverzüglich einzureichen. Wird der Jahresabschluss bei nachträglicher Prüfung oder Feststellung geändert, ist auch die Änderung nach Satz 1 einzureichen. Die Rechnungslegungsunterlagen sind in einer Form einzureichen, die ihre Bekanntmachung nach Absatz 2 ermöglicht.	(1) The legal representatives of corporations must file the annual account online with the operator of the electronic Federal Gazette. The annual account has to be filed without undue delay after its submission to the shareholders, but at the latest prior to the end of the twelfth month following the end of the fiscal year. It has to be filed together with the certification of the annual account or notification of its refusal. In addition, the management report, the report of the supervisory board, the statement pursuant to Sec. 161 of the Stock Corporation Act, and to the extent that the proposal for the use of the results and the resolution as to its use are not apparent from the filed annual accounts, the proposal for the use of the profits and the resolution as to their use, specifying the annual surplus or annual deficit, shall also be filed electronically. Limited liability companies need not disclose the use of the profits, if such disclosures would reveal the profit shares of natural persons who are shareholders. If, in order to meet the time limit set in sentence 2 or para. 4 sentence 1, the annual account and the management report are filed without the other records, then the report and proposal shall be filed without undue delay after their availability, the resolutions after their adoption and the notation after its issuance. If the annual account is changed, after subsequent audits or determinations, then that change shall also be filed pursuant to sentence 1. The accounting documents have to be submitted in such a way that a publication described in para. 2 above is possible.

Further Translations

- For translations of other German statutes and ordinances, e.g. the German Civil Code (*BGB*), the German Judicature Act (*GVG*), the German Insolvency Act (*InsO*) see the website of the German Federal Ministry of Justice (*Bundesministerium der Justiz*), available at: http://www.gesetze-im-internet.de/Teilliste_translations.html.
- For translations of rules and regulations pertaining to capital markets and securities trading see the website of the German Federal Financial Supervisory Authority (*Bundesanstalt für Finanzdienstleistungsaufsicht*) available at: http://www.bafin.de.

6.2 Examples of Corporate Documents

6.2.1 Articles of Association of a *GmbH*

Articles of Association of [company name] GmbH

§ 1 Company Name, Seat

1.1 The name of the company is [company name] GmbH.

1.2 The seat of the company is in [•].

§ 2 Purpose of the Company

2.1 The purpose of the company is the acquisition, administration and/or disposal of interests in other businesses for the company's own account.

2.2 The company may conduct all business which may directly or indirectly serve its purpose. It may establish branch offices, within and outside of Germany, and may participate in other companies with the same or a similar purpose.

§ 3 Financial Year The financial year of the company shall be the calendar year.

§ 4 Share Capital

4.1 The share capital of the company amounts to € 25,000 (in words: twenty-five thousand Euros).

4.2 The share capital of the company is divided into two shares with the serial number 1 in the nominal amount of € 15,000 and the serial number 2 in the nominal amount of € 10,000.

4.3 The share capital of the company is subscribed as follows:
[•] GmbH with its registered seat in [•], registered in the commercial register at [•] under number HRB [•] has subscribed for both shares against a cash contribution in the nominal amount of each share.

4.4 The contribution in respect of such share shall be paid up in full upon formation of the company.

§ 5 Management and Representation

5.1 The company shall have one or several managing directors. If only one managing director has been appointed, he shall represent the company alone. If two or more managing directors have been appointed, the company shall be represented by two managing directors acting jointly or by one managing director acting together with a *Prokurist*. By a shareholders' resolution one or several managing directors may be authorised to represent the company alone and/or may be released from the restrictions set out under Sec. 181 of the German Civil Code.

5.2 The managing directors are obliged to adhere to the instructions of the shareholders and, in particular, to comply with the provisions set out in the rules of procedure. They are further obliged to obtain the prior approval of the shareholders for any business transactions as designated by the shareholders.

§ 6 Supervisory Board

6.1 The shareholders may resolve to establish a Supervisory Board.

6.2 The provisions of Sec. 52 para. 1 of the German Code on Limited Liability Companies (*GmbHG*), and the sections of the German Stock Corporation Code (*AktG*) referred to therein, shall apply to the Supervisory Board only if and to the extent that the shareholders have reached a resolution with a majority of three quarters of the votes cast.

6.3 The Supervisory Board shall supervise the management. By shareholders' resolution passed with a majority of three quarters of the votes cast, the shareholders may convey additional tasks and areas of competence upon the Supervisory Board, in particular with respect to the appointment and dismissal of managing directors, entering into, amending and terminating employment contracts with managing directors, authorising managing directors to represent the company alone, passing rules of procedure for the management and providing instructions to the management.

6.4 The shareholders may, at any time and with simple majority of the votes cast, resolve that those provisions of German Stock Corporation Law, declared applicable by shareholders' resolution in accordance with § 6.2 above, shall no longer be applicable.

§ 7 Shareholders' Resolution

7.1 Shareholders' resolutions shall generally be adopted at shareholders' meetings. Shareholders' resolutions may, however, also be passed verbally (i.e. by telephone), or in writing (i.e. by letter or by telefax), without convening and holding a shareholders' meeting, provided that all shareholders give their consent and approval.

7.2 The shareholders' meeting has a quorum if more than 50% of the share capital is represented.

7.3 Shareholders' resolutions shall be passed with a simple majority of the votes cast, unless otherwise provided for in these Articles or under mandatory law.

§ 8 Annual Accounts

8.1 The annual accounts and status reports shall be prepared by the managing directors within the prescribed statutory period and, in the case that an audit is required by statute or by shareholder resolution, the annual accounts and status reports shall be submitted for the audit. The managing directors shall submit the annual accounts, status report and audit report, if any, to the shareholders following completion and without delay.

8.2 The profit shown in the accounts adopted by the shareholders' meeting shall be distributed to the shareholders in accordance with their shareholding, unless the shareholders resolve to transfer them into the reserves or carry them forward to the next financial year.

§ 9 Transfer of Shares

9.1 The transfer of shares, or parts thereof, requires the approval of the shareholders' meeting in order to be effective. No approval shall be required for the transfer of shares to another shareholder already holding shares in the company.

9.2 In addition to the approval of the shareholders' meeting, the transfer of parts of shares shall also require the approval of the company.

§ 10 Publications

10.1 Notices and official publications of the company shall be made only through the electronic Federal Gazette (*elektronischer Bundesanzeiger*).

§ 11 Severability

11.1 If any provisions of these Articles are or become invalid, the validity of the other provisions shall not be affected. The invalid provision shall be replaced by a provision which comes as close as possible to the business purpose of the invalid provision.

6.2.2 Rules of Procedure for the Management Board of a *GmbH*

Rules of Procedure for the Management Board of [company name] **GmbH** The shareholders' meeting of [company name] GmbH has introduced the following rules of procedure for the management board of [company name] GmbH:

§ 1 Authority of the Management Board

1.1 The rights and duties of the management board result from statutory law, the articles of association, shareholders' resolutions, the service agreements of the managing directors and the regulations set out in these rules of procedure.

1.2 The management board shall exercise the due care of a prudent businessman when managing the company.

1.3 The business of the company shall be performed jointly, and with joint responsibility, by the members of the management board. Each managing director is, in the interest of the company, obligated to cooperate with the other managing directors.

1.4 The responsibilities of the managing directors can be regulated by a schedule of responsibilities. This schedule of responsibilities shall be set up by the management board and requires the approval of the shareholders' meeting.

1.5 The members of the management board shall keep each other informed about all important business matters.

§ 2 Resolution by the Shareholders' Meeting

2.1 The management board shall report to the shareholders' meeting regarding the plans for the upcoming year, in accordance with the time schedule set out by the shareholders' meeting. They shall, in particular, report on the financial, investment and personnel planning as well as on the objectives of the company.

2.2 The management board shall report to the shareholders' meeting with respect to the ongoing business. Important business matters, which are not included in the annual forecast, shall be presented in written form for resolution by the shareholders. The shareholders' meeting shall also resolve upon the details of the reporting system to be followed by the management board.

2.3 The following matters shall require the approval of the shareholders' meeting:

- Determination of, and any amendments to, the basic business policy of the company.
- Determination of, and any amendments to, the annual budget, and measures which deviate by more than EUR [•], to the disadvantage of the company, from the budget.
- Any legal acts, which are likely to have an influence on companies belonging to the [company name] group (i.e. companies which are affiliated with such group within the meaning of Secs. 15 *et seq* German Stock Corporation Act (AktG)).
- Taking up or granting of loans which are not provided for in the budget.
- Granting of any other loan, surety or other liabilities to the extent that each individual amount exceeds EUR [•].
- Acquisition, divestiture or encumbrance of shares in other companies.
- Execution or termination of lease agreements not provided for in the budget.
- Execution, amendment or termination of service agreements with employees with a gross remuneration of more than EUR [•] per annum.
- Granting of, or amendment to, profit participations, or granting of, or amendments to, pensions.
- Employment or termination of employment of *Prokurists,* with the exception of any individual power of attorney given for individual legal acts.
- Change of auditors, tax advisors or legal counsels active on behalf of the company.
- Execution, amendment or termination of agreements with companies which are affiliated with a shareholder, managing director or a relative of such persons, or with persons who are relatives of a shareholder or managing director.
- Acquisition or encumbrance of real estate and similar rights.
- Execution, amendment or termination of enterprise contracts.
- Matters outside the ordinary course of business.

§ 3 Amendments to these Rules of Procedure Amendments to these rules of procedure shall be made by the shareholders' meeting.

§ 4 Commencement of these Rules of Procedure These rules of procedure for the management board of [company name] GmbH shall enter into force with immediate effect.

Selected Literature on German, International and Comparative Issues of Business Law

Beinert, Dieter/Burmeister, Frank/Tries, Hermann-Josef, Mergers & Acquisitions in Germany, München 2009.

Cahn, Andreas/Donald, David C., Comparative Company Law: Text and Cases on the Laws Governing Corporations in Germany, the UK and the USA, Cambridge 2010.

Denny, Mark, Corporate Acquisitions and Mergers: Germany, in: *Begg, Peter F. C.* (*Editor-in-Chief*), Corporate Acquisitions and Mergers, Alphen aan den Rijn, 2010.

Dornseifer, Frank (*Ed.*) Corporate Business Forms in Europe, Bern 2005.

Foster, Nigel/Sule, Satish, German Legal System and Laws, 4th edition, Oxford 2010.

Hewitt, Ian, Hewitt on Joint Ventures, 5th edition, London 2011.

Kraakman, Reinier/Davies, Paul/Hansmann, Henry/Hertig, Gerard/Hopt, Klaus/Kanda, Hideki/Rock, Edward, The Anatomy of Corporate Law, A Comparative and Functional Approach, 2nd edition Oxford 2009.

Mäntysaari, Petri, Comparative Corporate Governance, Shareholders as a Rule-maker, Berlin 2005.

Meister, Burkhard W./Heidenhain, Martin H./Rosengarten, Joachim, The German Limited Liabilitiy Company, 7th revised edition, München 2010.

Müller, Klaus J., The GmbH—A Guide to the German Limited Liability Company, 2nd edition, München 2009.

DuPlessis, Jean J./Großfeld, Bernhard/Luttermann, Claus/Saenger, Ingo/Sandrock, Otto, German Corporate Governance in International and European Context, Berlin 2007.

Reimann, Mathias/Zekoll, Joachim, Introduction to German Law, München 2005.

Robbers, Gerhard, An Introduction to German Law, 4th edition, Baden-Baden 2006.

Seibert, Ulrich, Close Corporation—Reforming Private Company Law: European and International Perspectives, 8 European Business Organization Law Review (EBOR), 83 (2007).

Stummel, Dieter, Standardvertragsmuster zum Handels- und Gesellschaftsrecht Deutsch-Englisch, 4th edition, München 2009.

Wendler, Michael/Tremml, Bernd/Buecker, Bernhard (*Eds.*), Key Aspects of German Business Law, 4th Edition, Berlin 2008.

Wirth, Gerhard/Arnold, Michael/Morshäuser, Ralf/Greene, Mark, Corporate Law in Germany, 2nd revised edition, Munich 2010.

Index

M. Schulz, O. Wasmeier, *The Law of Business Organizations*,
DOI 10.1007/978-3-642-17793-4, © Springer-Verlag Berlin Heidelberg 2012

MIX
Papier aus verantwortungsvollen Quellen
Paper from responsible sources
FSC® C105338

If you have any concerns about our products,
you can contact us on
ProductSafety@springernature.com

In case Publisher is established outside the EU,
the EU authorized representative is:
Springer Nature Customer Service Center GmbH
Europaplatz 3, 69115 Heidelberg, Germany

Printed by Libri Plureos GmbH
in Hamburg, Germany